King and Chaos

TURNING POINT
ELECTIONS

General Editors: Gerald Baier and R. Kenneth Carty

Since Confederation, Canadians have gone to the polls over forty times in general elections. Sometimes the ruling party was re-elected, other times the government changed hands, but, more often than not, the country would carry on as if little had happened. However, some elections were different. They stirred up underlying divisions, generated debates, gave rise to influential personalities, and energized and reshaped the electorate – ultimately changing the direction the country would follow. Those elections were "turning points." The volumes in this series tell the stories of these turning point elections, focusing on the players, the issues at stake, the campaigns, and the often surprising outcomes that would fundamentally reshape Canadian politics and society. For a list of other titles in the series, see the UBC Press website, ubcpress.ca/turning-point -elections.

King and Chaos

The 1935 Canadian General Election

DAVID MACKENZIE

UBCPress · Vancouver · Toronto

32 31 30 29 28 27 26 25 24 23   5 4 3 2 1

Printed in Canada on FSC-certified ancient-forest-free paper
(100% post-consumer recycled) that is processed chlorine- and acid-free.

Library and Archives Canada Cataloguing in Publication

Title: King and chaos : the 1935 Canadian general election /
David MacKenzie.
Names: MacKenzie, David Clark, author.
Series: Turning point elections.
Description: Series statement: Turning point elections |
Includes bibliographical references and index.
Identifiers: Canadiana (print) 20230144020 | Canadiana (ebook) 20230144071 |
ISBN 9780774868808 (softcover) | ISBN 9780774868815 (PDF) |
ISBN 9780774868822 (EPUB)
Subjects: LCSH: Canada. Parliament—Elections, 1935. |
LCSH: Depressions—1929—Influence. | LCSH: Political parties—Canada. |
LCSH: Political campaigns—Canada. | CSH: Canada—Politics and
government—1930-1935.
Classification: LCC FC577 .M33 2023 | DDC 971.062/3—dc23

Canada Council Conseil des arts
for the Arts du Canada

BRITISH COLUMBIA
ARTS COUNCIL

BRITISH
COLUMBIA

UBC Press gratefully acknowledges the financial support for our publishing
program of the Government of Canada, the Canada Council for the Arts,
and the British Columbia Arts Council.

This book has been published with the help of a grant from the Canadian
Federation for the Humanities and Social Sciences, through the Awards to
Scholarly Publications Program, using funds provided by the Social Sciences
and Humanities Research Council of Canada.

UBC Press
The University of British Columbia
2029 West Mall
Vancouver, BC V6T 1Z2
www.ubcpress.ca

Contents

Foreword
Turning Point Elections
and the Case of the 1935 Election

Gerald Baier and R. Kenneth Carty

FREE, COMPETITIVE ELECTIONS are the lifeblood of modern democracies. Nowhere has this been more apparent than in Canada, a country cobbled together by bargaining politicians who then continually remade it over a century and a half by their electoral ambitions, victories, and losses. In a continually changing country, the political parties that emerged to manage this electoral competition also found themselves continually changing as they attempted to reflect and shape the country they sought to govern. The stories of these politicians, these parties, and these elections are a critical part of the twists and turns that have produced Canada.

Canadians have now gone to the polls in forty-four national general elections. The rules, participants, personalities, and issues have varied over time, but the central quest has always been the same – to win the right to govern a complex and dynamic country. About twice as often as not, the electorate has stuck with whom they know and favoured incumbents with the governing mantle. Only about a third of the time have the government's opponents, promising something new or different, been elevated to power. But whatever the outcome over all forty-four elections, the contest for the top prize has ultimately been between the Liberal and Conservative

Parties. While other challengers have come and gone, and some have even endured, the persistence of the Liberal/Conservative dichotomy has defined the effective bounds of Canada's democratic politics.

More than one hundred years ago, a visiting French observer, André Siegfried, argued that Canadian elections were essentially meaningless because the two core parties were little more than unprincipled reflections of one another, preoccupied only with their continued existence. To the extent this was true, it reflected Canadian politicians' determination to build "big-tent" political parties able to appeal to the wide range of discordant regions and interests, religious and language groups, and parochial claims that dominated the country's political life and public conversations. If the Liberal Party dominated national electoral politics over the twentieth century, to become labelled as the country's "natural governing party," it was because its tent was larger and rooted in an overwhelming mastery of Quebec constituencies. And so a long list of Liberal leaders – Wilfrid Laurier, Mackenzie King, Louis St. Laurent, Pierre Trudeau, Jean Chrétien – kept leading their party back to office election after election. In a country being continually transformed on almost every conceivable dimension, electoral outcomes were remarkably stoic in comparison.

Occasionally, though, conditions allowed for rather abrupt disruptions of this seeming political tranquility. There were exceptions to the familiar story of incumbents cruising to victory. In part, those occasions reflected the workings of a first-past-the-post electoral system that was capable of generating both stability and volatility. The difference between hanging on to power or being roundly booted from grace could be a change of just a few percentage points in a party's support, or a strong showing by one or more third parties bleeding off a portion of the vote of one of the big-tent parties. So some elections were different, thrusting new and exciting personalities to the fore, generating principled debates on fundamental issues, electrifying and engaging the electorate, and reshaping the parties and the dynamics of party competition, all with lasting consequences for the direction the country would follow. These elections stand out as turning points.

The stories of the turning point elections are more than simply accounts of compelling figures, dramatic campaigns, and new political alignments. They also reveal how the pressures of demographic, socio-economic, and regional change were challenging the status quo; how the elections broke the political moulds of previous contests; and how the turn played out in the politics, policies, and governments of succeeding decades. In each of the turning point elections, we see how the evolving political landscape allowed politicians to crystallize, and often personify, the issues of a distinctive agenda and create a campaign that mobilized and reshaped the complex coalitions of supporters that constituted the nation's political parties. Each turning point constituted the starting point for a new and different cycle in the contest between the two great big-tent parties that have dominated the struggle for power and office and defined the nature and evolution of Canadian democracy.

THE EARLY TWENTIETH CENTURY had its share of global shocks that redefined borders, economies, social relations, and everyday lives, not to mention the activities and role of governments. Two world wars, the Great Depression, and the Cold War politics of the nuclear age all redefined the place of the state in domestic and international politics, alongside fundamental societal and economic change. Canada was no stranger to these shocks; as in many other countries, they collectively altered the Canadian state and Canadian politics.

The Great Depression and efforts to ameliorate its most negative effects are really the genesis of Canada's modern welfare state. The changes brought about by the Depression endure to this day in the responsibilities of Canada's federal government, its relationship with the provinces, the forms of government organization and spending, and the kinds of visions that still regularly get tested and debated in federal elections. An election in the midst of this crisis was bound to be a turning point for Canadian politics.

David MacKenzie guides us through a depression-ravaged country looking for answers from politicians and governments for the widespread dislocation and disruption caused by unprecedented global economic conditions. The Conservative government of R.B. Bennett spent the years prior to the election trying to conceive of the proper role of government in ameliorating the worst consequences of this economic catastrophe. Voters ultimately had the chance to weigh in and chose a dramatic change in government to seek a new approach to government intervention and provision of social goods.

As MacKenzie illustrates, the 1935 election was not just a clash of ideas; it was also a tremendous clash of personalities. The leaders of the two most competitive parties are among the most compelling characters in the history of Canadian politics. MacKenzie vividly recounts the different styles and manner of these titanic figures.

Liberal leader William Lyon Mackenzie King, the eventual winner of the election, was by the time of the 1935 election a wily veteran of Canadian political life, preparing for his second act on the national stage. Prime minister for most of the 1920s, he was slow to respond at the start of the Depression and saw his Liberals removed from power. The colourful King would leave a generational mark on the country and his political party before he was finished.

Bennett was an equally compelling character. He had no one to blame but himself if his government's response to the first years of the Depression seemed inadequate to Canadian voters. Bennett dominated his cabinet and party. He was distrusting of others and imperious in style. His dominance of the party left it inadequately prepared organizationally and financially for the 1935 election. Few of his cabinet colleagues chose to seek re-election, and there were no provincial Conservative governments to organize campaigns and support, as there had been in 1930 when he was elected prime minister. Most critically, his governing style and policy hesitation splintered the Conservative Party. His minister of trade and commerce, H.H. Stevens, left the Conservatives to form the Reconstruction Party. The party campaigned on a more economic interventionist role for government than Bennett was willing to commit to, and it ran the third-highest number of candidates in the 1935 election.

The Reconstruction Party was not the only new party to emerge ahead of the election. The Co-operative Commonwealth Federation and Social Credit Party were more successful at electing parliamentarians than the Reconstruction Party, and they also maintained a much longer presence in national affairs. These parties represented renewed regional discontent, and their modest success came from support concentrated in the West, primarily in Alberta for Social Credit, and in Manitoba, Saskatchewan, and British Columbia for the CCF.

These factors of economic context, personalities, and realignment of the party system combined to make the 1935 election one of the country's major turning points. The rise of new electoral communications through radio, an increase in the diversity of candidates, and new audiences for electoral appeals made the election, and this detailed account, even more captivating.

Preface

THE WRITING OF HISTORIES of Canadian federal elections has increased in recent years, and for good reason. Elections tell us a lot about the country and its peoples, about the issues that were considered important, about the causes that motivated people into action, and about the things that united Canadians, as well as those that divided them. In addition, more can be learned from an analysis of the various other aspects of an election campaign, from the number of parties, their platforms, and their candidates, to the size of the turnout, who could vote and who could not, and the regional distribution of the vote. Federal elections provide the closest thing to a snapshot of the country at any given moment.

In a simpler way, elections are also memorable and remarkable moments in history, with people of diverse backgrounds and prominence debating important matters of public interest. Hundreds of thousands participate, some just by voting, others more actively, in the press; on the radio, television, and Internet; on the campaign trail – criticizing opponents and cajoling voters, assembling and managing teams of friends and allies, participating in rallies and other public events, and raising campaign funds. All these groups are brought together in pursuit of the same goal – victory at the polls. Character and circumstance are jammed tightly together in a brief moment in time.

There are also a handful of elections that stand out from the others as particularly important, when the issues debated are, if not unique, then exceptional in their importance to the future of the country. Such important elections come in different shapes and sizes and can range from the re-election of an existing government to a complete changing of the guard, a generational shift symbolized by the creation of a new government. They may reflect what is about to happen by heralding a new direction in Canadian public policy or what has already happened by publicly confirming dramatic social and political changes that have already occurred. Either way, examining these elections is important for our understanding of Canadian history.

For these reasons, I was particularly pleased to have been asked early in 2020 by the series editors and UBC Press to contribute a volume on the 1935 federal election to this new series on "turning point" elections. Not only is the series itself a good thing in making an important contribution to the study of Canadian history, but also, as someone who has studied Canadian electoral history for many years, I was aware of two things: one, that 1935 easily fit into the premise of a series on turning point elections and, two, that up to that point, very little had been written specifically about it.

The 1930s, and the interwar period more generally, must be one of the most studied eras in Canadian history. The devastation of the Depression; the social, political, cultural, and technological upheaval both at home and abroad; and the slow descent into war have attracted historians for decades. Virtually all the known archival sources are open and relatively accessible; bookshelves are filled with memoirs and biographies of important politicians, journalists, academics, business leaders, informed observers, and critics, along with academic studies on politics, economics, society, media, race and gender, in both French and English, and from West to East. It is a little surprising to find in all this historical scholarship so little attention paid to the one moment in the middle of the decade when the Canadian voting public expressed its judgment on the major issues of the day.

The election of 1935 was a turning point. It represented the ending of the old National Policy established by the Conservative government in the 1870s, with its focus on tariffs, railways, and immigration. That year signalled the advent of a new era and a turn to the new priorities of a modern industrial society. Unemployment and social welfare, economic planning, federal-provincial relations, regional disparities and growing resentment, and constitutional change crowded out the older debates over reciprocity, freight rates, and fidelity to the Empire. It also was the first election for a group of new political parties, born in the Depression, that would permanently alter the Canadian political landscape. Equally significant, this election revealed another major and enduring development – the growing power and importance, as well as the discontent, of Western Canada in national affairs. Canadian federal politics were different after 1935.

WRITING CAN BE A rather solitary experience, until the time comes to turn a manuscript into a book. Then you must rely on the help of dedicated and skilled people to transform your text into the final product that sits on bookstore shelves. This is certainly the case with this book, and I must acknowledge the whole team of professionals at UBC Press for their work on this project.

First, I must thank series editors Gerald Baier and Ken Carty for inviting me to contribute to this new series. Special thanks to senior editor Randy Schmidt for shepherding the project from start to finish, and for his perceptive comments, guidance, and general encouragement throughout. What follows would not have been possible without his support. Particular thanks to production editor Katrina Petrik, for overseeing the months-long production process.

For their work on my behalf, I would also like to thank Brit Schottelius and Carmen Tiampo at UBC Press, as well as copy editor Francis Chow, proofreader Kristy Lynn Hankewitz, and indexer Judy Dunlop. Finally, I would like to acknowledge the input of the two anonymous reviewers, who offered some very wise and concrete suggestions to help improve the book.

My thanks to everyone – your contributions are most appreciated. Any errors that remain are mine.

King and Chaos

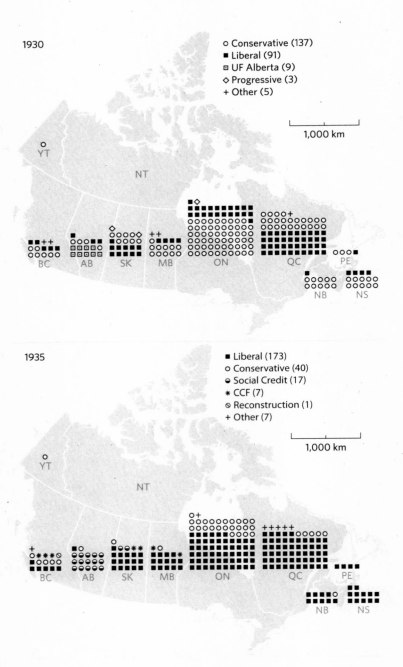

1930

- o Conservative (137)
- ■ Liberal (91)
- ▣ UF Alberta (9)
- ◇ Progressive (3)
- + Other (5)

1,000 km

1935

- ■ Liberal (173)
- o Conservative (40)
- ◕ Social Credit (17)
- ✳ CCF (7)
- ◈ Reconstruction (1)
- + Other (7)

1,000 km

Introduction

It became an intensely political decade, a decade of political
radicalism, of new concepts of the economic role of government, and of the creation of new political parties and new
political institutions to apply these concepts in practice.

– H. Blair Neatby[1]

THE ONE GREAT ISSUE that pervaded the 1935 Canadian federal
election – and made it a pivotal moment in Canadian history – was
the Great Depression. Canadians, for the most part, could agree on
the problem – the economic devastation was apparent for all to
see – but there was much less certainty about what to do about it.
The Depression affected people differently, and how they understood
it and responded to it depended on who they were, where they lived,
and what they did. The Depression meant different things to different people, but it also provided the context for the one moment
in 1935 when Canadian voters had the opportunity to express their
choice on which government was best able to meet the economic
crisis. The 1935 vote was the electoral expression of Canada's response to the Great Depression.

All the issues in the campaign were in some way the product of the Depression. The Canadian economy was more dependent on international trade compared with most other industrial nations, and it was easily affected by changes in the international scene and by growing restrictions on international trade. By the end of the 1920s, Canadian farmers were producing more wheat and other foodstuffs than they could sell. Several important industries were doing likewise: the newsprint industry had overexpanded and prices were already on the way down; the market for cars was not expanding and automobile manufacturers were making more than could be sold. Overproduction, falling prices, and the contraction in world trade led to serious deflation.

Canada was largely dragged into the Depression by the collapse of world trade, and it had to wait for the revival of world trade to come out of it. Closely connected to the American economy, the Canadian economy had little hope for recovery until the US economy revived. Nor was the Depression a continuous event; there was a series of slumps and recoveries across the decade. Rock bottom was hit in the first quarter of 1933, followed by a slow, uneven recovery that continued beyond the 1935 election. Pre-Depression economic levels were not attained before the outbreak of the Second World War in 1939.

Everything fell in the Depression, it seemed, except unemployment, mortgage debt, interest payments, and rain. Canada was a major exporter of grains and other foodstuffs, fish, livestock, newsprint, lumber, and minerals, and the collapse of overseas markets and international prices resulted in an unprecedented economic catastrophe. Canada's total exports dropped by nearly half between 1929 and 1933. Businesses closed, factories cut back production again and again, and the two major railways – which made up much of the backbone of the Canadian economy – slashed their workforces. Across the country, jobs were lost by the thousands as unemployment soared to record levels.

The hardest hit were those who worked in resource industries. In the 1930s, close to 35 percent of the workforce worked outdoors in primary production industries, including agriculture and construction. Most of these occupations were badly paid and often seasonal, and they were reliant on export markets for survival, which meant they were at the mercy of international forces.[2] At the same time, immigration policy continued to focus on attracting unskilled workers for the staple industries, which only helped to keep wages low and fill the ranks of the unemployed during bad economic times. Union members had a little more protection than the average worker, but there was relatively little that unions could do to save jobs or maintain prices; indeed, in the early Depression years, union membership began shrinking to some of the lowest levels since the First World War.

In the cities, hundreds of thousands of men and women were thrown out of work. Prices dropped, as did wages, and industries – from manufacturing to construction – withered, while the demands on governments at all levels for relief surged. By 1933, per capita income had dropped from 1929 levels by anywhere from 39 percent in New Brunswick to 71 percent in Saskatchewan.[3] For those who kept their jobs or lived on fixed incomes, conditions were not so bad; some even found themselves better off, as the prices of goods fell rapidly. Those who lost their jobs or worked seasonally or in more precarious circumstances were less fortunate. Those who fell through the cracks were left to the churches and local charities and hostels.

Unemployment rates never dropped below 10 percent in the 1930s. By mid-1933, close to 30 percent of the Canadian workforce was out of work; things had improved only marginally by election day in 1935. In 1939, the unemployment rate still lingered above 15 percent. And those numbers do not always tell the whole story, as tens of thousands more worked part-time jobs, or made do with seasonal work, or were underemployed. Nor did the numbers always include

Unemployment remained high throughout the Depression and life could be hard for those out of work. Many Canadians suffered in silence; others took to the streets. Pictured here are members of the Single Men's Unemployed Association marching to Bathurst Street United Church in Toronto (no date). | *Toronto Star,* Library and Archives Canada, C-029397

the women and men who were forced into retirement once they lost their jobs. And many of those who lived on farms could still be counted as employed even if they were starving.

For the unemployed, it was a very bad time. There was scarcely any social security net, and governments appeared to lack the capacity or the will to deal with the problem. There was a general sense that unemployment was the individual's fault, that one was lazy or incompetent. Governments at various levels acted on the premise that relief was to be turned to only as a last resort, and put up regulations and red tape to ensure that only the "worthy" received it. For municipalities, this usually meant that the needy had to prove residence in the local community. And relief was not given automatically or evenly across the country. Need had to be demonstrated, meaning that destitution was practically a prerequisite for relief. Single mothers might be turned away and told to seek support from their families. In British Columbia, Asian Canadians might be lucky to receive relief at half the rate provided for whites. In Central Canada and the Maritimes, Black Canadians were often denied relief outright.

Women's pay was already 40 to 60 percent lower than men's, and the Depression only limited their choices further. It was not unusual to hear working women being blamed for the high unemployment because a working woman took a job away from a man. Moreover, women were often the first to be let go from their jobs, based on the dubious logic that a man would have a family to support, while a woman would have a family to support *her*. The federal government specifically refused to hire married women, leading to a drop in the number of women in the federal civil service. Barred from other occupations and with their choices narrowing, working women increasingly came to dominate a few occupations, including waitressing and sales, domestic service, and teaching, nursing, and secretarial work.

As a result, unemployment became something of a political football in the 1935 election, serving as both a backdrop and a central issue in the campaign, as politicians of all stripes debated what caused it, who was responsible for it, and what was to be done about it. To many Canadians, the two leading federal politicians – Conservative prime minister R.B. Bennett and Liberal leader William Lyon Mackenzie King – appeared out of touch and indifferent. They dominated Canadian federal politics in the 1930s and were the major contenders in the 1935 election campaign, but neither seemed to have the answers. More than ever, thousands of Canadians were asking whether the traditional parties had any solution to unemployment at all, and they became increasingly willing to look elsewhere for new ideas. This search for answers to the problem of unemployment in the Great Depression was a key feature of the 1935 federal election.

Relief, Reaction, and Regionalism

Despite the rules and obstacles, well over 10 percent of the Canadian population was on relief at some point during the Depression. What they received was little more than subsistence-level support, most often in the form of vouchers that could be cashed in for food at a local store or turned over to landlords to pay the rent. Those caught working while on relief were cut off. For tens of thousands of Canadians, it was either relief or starvation. Living with the stigma and shame of having to line up at soup kitchens for a meal was just one more indignity to be endured.

Families felt the humiliation of seeking relief. Thousands of young unemployed men who could not prove residency were left to drift from town to town in search of work. On the one hand, it was believed that they *should* have been able to find a job, and they were therefore often denied relief; on the other, large groups of able-bodied men congregating at the edge of towns became a social problem. The spectre of social unrest and even revolution emerged in Canadian cities. Governments became concerned. The proposed solution was to get them out of the cities, where they might spark unrest, and to give them work. But it had to be work that no one else was doing, as there was no sense in replacing one set of workers with another.

To that end, in 1932 the Bennett government established work camps, run by the Department of National Defence, to house unemployed men. Young men were taken off the streets and shipped out to remote areas where they couldn't cause trouble. The camps, primarily in British Columbia, across the prairies, and in Northern Ontario, offered work clearing bush, building roads, and laying air strips. No one was forced into the camps or prevented from leaving, but existing economic conditions and the remoteness of the camps ensured that most men had little choice but to stay, especially during the winter months. The men were not paid wages but were given an allowance of twenty cents a day plus room and board. It kept them alive but offered little more than hard work, harsh rules, and boredom, and there was little in the way of recreation or outside contact. The project expanded quickly, and by the time the work camps were closed in 1936, 237 had been built and they had housed approximately 170,000 men for varying lengths of time.

Not surprisingly, there was a political dimension to the camps. They were occasionally places of unrest, where the men would protest against the working and living conditions and pay. Some tried to organize, but most efforts were quickly suppressed by the government, until July 1935, when a large group went on strike and launched a cross-country trek to bring their demands to the federal government. The trekkers were stopped in Regina, and a serious riot erupted when the authorities tried to disperse them. It came at the worst time for the Bennett government as the riot coincided with the start of the election campaign. Bennett had nothing to fear from the strikers electorally, as the men in the camps were denied the vote (getting the vote was one of their strike demands),[4] but the entire affair gave the opposition parties more ammunition against the government during the election campaign.

The Depression affected the various regions of Canada differently, and these regional variations were underscored during the 1935 election campaign. Hard times had already hit the Maritimes in the 1920s, and the region continued to face serious economic troubles in the wake of the Maritime Rights Movement and the stopgap measures offered by the King Liberals in Ottawa. The slump of the

Government relief camps offered little more than hard work, harsh rules, and boredom. Occasionally, they were also places of unrest. Here men from work camps engage in road construction at Kimberley-Wasa, BC, in May 1934. | Department of National Defence, Library and Archives Canada, PA-036089

1930s only made things worse, as the out-migration of people was curtailed and many Maritimers, unable to access government relief in Central Canada and the West, returned home.

In Quebec, the Depression and industrialization were shaking the roots of traditional French Canadian society. Thousands of farmers went bankrupt and local communities and parishes fell deeply in debt because of the rising relief burden. The provincial government stepped in to help (itself falling deeper into debt), but the problem of rural depopulation persisted. In Montreal, unemployment was the issue as thousands of families slipped below the poverty line and survived on inadequate diets. Whereas Maritimers blamed Central Canada and Westerners blamed the East, French Canadians blamed Ottawa and domination by the English.

Ontario fared best, but that was little consolation to the unemployed in the cities or those working in the hardest-hit resource industries, such as pulp and paper and agriculture. On the other hand, the industries protected by the National Policy tariff were largely centred in southern Ontario (and to the east in Montreal), and there was also a greater concentration of government, retail, and white-collar work, which was less affected by the downswing. People there likely saw their incomes drop, but at least they were able to keep their jobs.

It was the West – and the prairies in particular – that was hardest hit by the slump and that experienced the greatest upheaval during the 1935 election. The Canadian system just wasn't working for the people of Western Canada. The trauma suffered during the First World War – from the demands placed on Western wheat producers to the ethnic divisions unleashed by the 1917 election – was followed in the 1920s by slow economic recovery, labour unrest, and political frustration. By the end of the decade, Canadian farmers were already facing tough international competition, and when the price of grain fell, an agricultural crisis ensued.

Making things much worse, in the 1930s the West experienced some of the coldest winters on record and suffered from plagues of grasshoppers, gophers, and various plant diseases. And there was relentless drought, which led to widespread crop failures year after year, as farms turned to dust and literally blew away. On some days, there was so much dust it could be dark at mid-day. In his memoir of the 1930s, popular historian James Gray remembers how the heat and high winds made Saskatchewan and Manitoba perpetually overcast:

The soil blowing across the roads and railway tracks was caught and held in the Russian thistle until it drifted to the tops of fences and snow-fences, and all that could be seen was the tops of the posts. In southern Alberta, the C.P.R. used snowploughs to clear the tracks of soil drifts ten feet high. From Calgary to Winnipeg there was almost nothing but dust, in a bowl that extended clear down to Texas.[5]

Acreage production dropped and net farm incomes plunged to record low levels. In the late 1920s, income from the sale of farm products averaged over $500 million per year; by the early 1930s, it had plummeted to $180 million.[6] Thanks to the years of drought, cold winters, dust storms, and plagues, Canadian production fell, but international competition remained stiff and kept the price of wheat low. Incomes fell dramatically, but mortgage payments did not, and the burden of fixed interest payments on debt remained. Money was scarce; in some cases, people reverted to bartering for food and goods. Thousands of farming families were destitute and found it impossible to carry on. Some sold their farms; others were forced out when the banks foreclosed. Thousands moved to the cities, some American settlers returned to the United States, and others moved northward in search of a wetter climate. The barren, abandoned farm of the dust bowl became the enduring symbol of the Depression in Western Canada, an era that historian Gerald Friesen described as "an identifiable period that affected the psychology of individual citizens, the fate of entire communities, and the image of the region."[7]

Provincial governments were forced to step in with relief, and when they teetered on the brink of bankruptcy, the federal government had to act. The first to go were the wheat pools, which had been successful in marketing prairie wheat in the 1920s. They collapsed in 1931, and Ottawa intervened to take over some of their marketing operations. In 1935, just weeks before the election, the new arrangement was made more permanent when the Bennett government created the Canadian Wheat Board. More direct support came from the Prairie Farm Rehabilitation Administration, created by Ottawa earlier in 1935 to funnel federal money for education programs, for land reclamation and water conservation, and for help on a variety of other projects.

One outcome of the Depression was that the Western provinces became more dependent on the federal government for support, a situation that only embittered federal-provincial relations. This heightened sense of regional grievance led to the creation of two new political parties just in time to contest the 1935 election – the Co-operative Commonwealth Federation and the Social Credit Party – and it sparked a political realignment, the ramifications of which are still felt today.

Unemployment and relief, federal-provincial relations, and regional grievances would all be at the heart of the 1935 election campaign and in a way never seen before in Canadian politics. The crisis of the Depression was a crisis of capitalism itself, and Canadians turned in multiple directions – from socialism to populism to evangelicalism – in search of answers. The old ways came under siege, and the policies of both traditional political parties (and the political debates reaching back to Confederation) were challenged. New parties appeared, each offering its own explanations and solutions. The Depression changed the political face of Canada, and it made the 1935 election a turning point in Canadian history.

Politics in the Great Depression

The Great Depression set the stage for the 1935 federal election. The scale and duration of the crisis made it impossible to explain away the unemployment, poverty, and destitution as a momentary blip in an economic cycle or as the result of people's laziness and unwillingness to work. More and more Canadians began questioning the underlying structure of the economy and the role of the state in Canadian society, looking at old problems in new and different ways. There were growing calls for government intervention in the economy through deficit spending, economic regulation and management, and social welfare. Others questioned whether either of the two leading parties and their leaders – Bennett and King – were up to the task.

The economic crisis also exposed a serious weakness in the Canadian constitution and in federalism itself, as the federal, provincial, and municipal governments debated over who bore the responsibility for the unemployed and destitute, while several provinces, especially in the West, faced bankruptcy and default. Canadians increasingly looked to government, particularly the federal government, as the institution best able to act to end the Depression, or at least alleviate the worst of its effects.

It was a very political decade and the Depression inevitably impacted politics. Canadians often blamed the Conservative government in Ottawa for the economic crisis, pointing, in particular, to Prime Minister Bennett, who had promised decisive action but failed to deliver. The federal Conservatives had long been the party of high tariffs, fiscal prudence, support for the Empire, and generally keeping out of the way of business. The crisis of the 1930s challenged these positions. First to go was reliance on the National Policy tariff, which had been used by Conservative leaders from Sir John A. Macdonald to Sir Robert Borden not only as the major source of federal revenue but also to foster and promote the growth of industry in Canada. Governments now had expanded sources of revenue, and the damage of Depression-era protectionism was evident. Trade would always remain important, but the Conservative focus now shifted to freer trade and more open markets.

Other changes followed in the months before the election, as the Conservative Party confronted the new realities of Depression-era Canada. The crisis in the country played out within the party and produced more division than anything else, with some members calling for dramatic action and active government while others stuck to the old ways of balanced budgets and retrenchment. Prime Minister Bennett appeared cold, distant, and uncaring, apparently unable to sympathize with the unemployed or destitute. He was equally unable to stem the tide of unrest in his own party as the followers of H.H. Stevens, Bennett's colleague and former cabinet minister, split with the party altogether just weeks before the election and formed the rival Reconstruction Party. Stevens's defection was particularly damaging to the Conservatives' prospects for victory in 1935, and it set off years of internal debate as the party remodelled itself to meet the challenges of modern Canadian society.

If there was any uncertainty for the federal Liberals and their leader, Mackenzie King, as they prepared for the 1935 election campaign, it was about the West. Traditional prairie Liberalism supported banking and electoral reform, and the maintenance of the Canadian National Railway and opposition to its amalgamation with the privately owned Canadian Pacific Railway. Above all, Western farmers needed markets for their goods, and this meant support for the lowering of import tariffs in return for the opening up of foreign markets, especially in the Empire and the United States. John Dafoe, the veteran editor of the *Winnipeg Free Press*, was the mouthpiece for this brand of Western Liberalism, dating back to before the First World War, and he remained a vociferous opponent of high-tariff Conservatism.

The idea of focusing on tariff reform as a way out of the Depression may have appealed to Dafoe and King in Ottawa, but for a growing number of Westerners in the mid-1930s the language of Liberalism now spoke of social reform, government services and welfare, and innovative fiscal policies. The Depression heightened awareness of the need for change in Canadian politics and added to the desire to improve the lives of all Canadians, not just those who might benefit from tariff reform. State intervention in the economy was the way of the future. Liberals could no longer satisfy Western demands, or placate Western alienation, by tinkering with the old policies of reciprocity, railways, and freight rates. Dafoe and King were becoming out of touch with the times, and the prairies were moving in another direction, away from the Liberal Party. The process was already underway, but it was highlighted in the 1935 election. As the West turned to more radical third parties and a stronger sense of regional identity emerged, the Liberals could no longer count on Western votes merely by offering an alternative to the Conservatives with lower tariffs and better freight rates.[8]

The traditional parties were dominated by the east and looked out for eastern interests, and they offered few solutions to the problems facing the West. Inevitably, new parties moved into this political void to stand in stark opposition to eastern Toryism, traditional prairie Liberalism, and "stand-patism." The 1935 election also signalled the end of the era of the National Policy – the policy of railway construction, tariff protection, and Western settlement. Canadians were now faced with the problems of regionalism and those arising from modern urban industrial society, and they were increasingly looking for action on unemployment, welfare, and economic regulation. In the election of 1930, the traditional political parties resisted change and stuck to the old policies. In 1935, that was no longer possible.

1

Depression Politics

The man-in-the-street, on whom the burdens of the depression have fallen more heavily than upon the industrialist and the financier, seems to have blamed the Government for his distress, and to have felt that the tariff, and an inadequate control of "big business," were the causes of his sufferings.

– "Capitalism under Fire," *The Round Table* (March 1935)[1]

MORE THAN ANYTHING ELSE, the election of 1935 was a referendum on one man: Conservative prime minister Richard Bedford Bennett. Born in New Brunswick in 1870 and trained as a lawyer, Bennett moved west to Calgary near the turn of the century, lured by a job invitation from Conservative senator James Lougheed. Thanks to hard work and a booming economy, he made a name for himself first in law, then in business, and finally in politics as a member of the Alberta Legislative Assembly before winning the federal riding for Calgary in 1911. He was already something of an outlier, being one of the few winning Conservative politicians in what was then largely Liberal territory. He served in various capacities in Sir Robert Borden's cabinet during the First World War, and in the 1920s served in both of Arthur Meighen's short-lived governments. When Meighen resigned the leadership in 1927, Bennett was the logical successor as Conservative leader: he knew the country from east to west; he was successful in business; he had cabinet experience; he displayed the leadership qualities of maturity, sobriety, and intelligence; and he had personal financial resources that he was willing to bring to the aid of his party.

He was without doubt intelligent, as well as hard-working, ambitious, self-confident, temperamental, proud, sensitive to criticism, bombastic, stubborn, and a man who almost always dressed formally. He was a well-groomed, teetotalling bachelor who developed a healthy appetite and lived a rather solitary life. He reportedly bought only one car in his lifetime, damaged it on the first day by driving into a tree, and never drove a car again. He never owned a home until after he had retired to England, choosing instead to live in rooming houses and hotels. His residence of choice while prime minister was a suite of rooms in Ottawa's Château Laurier. A story circulated that at the height of the Depression, Bennett asked to change rooms, moving to the front of the building because he disliked having to look out over the unemployed transient men lingering in the park outside his rear-facing windows.[2]

He could be autocratic, if not dictatorial, and was often accused of running a one-man show as prime minister. His fingerprints could be found over all of his government's important legislation, and few decisions were made without his approval. The standard Bennett joke had the prime minister relaxing at his favourite club (or walking alone on a street, or sitting at a conference table), talking to himself. A stranger sees him and asks what he is saying. The reply: "He's holding a cabinet meeting." He could justifiably claim most of the credit when things went well, but he was also an easy target when things went wrong.

Capable of acts of great generosity, concern, and empathy, Bennett was equally prone to being rude, dismissive, petty, paternalistic, and condescending. He also became involved in petty feuds and held great grudges, often against former friends and colleagues, and he was easily roused to indignation, to the point that it ruined several friendships over the course of his life. As long-time Conservative colleague Charles Cahan once said of Bennett, "the sun never sets on the day on which the Prime Minister hasn't insulted some good and loyal Conservative."[3] In 1917, while anticipating a Senate appointment from Prime Minister Borden – an appointment that he believed he had earned – Bennett launched into a bitter attack on his own party in the House of Commons. The Senate appointment evaporated. "His vanity," Borden wrote of Bennett, "makes him quite unbalanced."[4] In 1935, just weeks before calling the election, Bennett became embroiled in a public spat in the House of Commons with one of his own ministers over the number of ex-servicemen hired to work in government-owned canals. The two men glared at each other across the desk of the minister of justice. It may have been just a tempest in a teacup, the Toronto *Globe* editorialized, "but so many teacups are sizzling here in Ottawa these days."[5] Having a thin skin is never an asset in politics, and in Bennett's case it made him less able to inspire loyalty among his colleagues, as he alienated many of his erstwhile supporters, colleagues, Conservative journalists, and voters.

Bennett was perhaps a better leader than politician. Inclined to give orders rather than take them, and quick to anger when orders went unobeyed, he inspired fear more than loyalty in his colleagues. This made him the centre of the action when he held power but left him few friends when that power inevitably slipped away. His energy, intelligence, and quickness of mind helped when it came to strategy, ideas, and decisive action; his brusqueness and arrogance always made it more difficult to motivate people to actually get things done. His ambition, self-confidence, and penchant for keeping things to himself made him the essential leader, but they also almost guaranteed the failure of his government. Liberal Charles "Chubby" Power, no friend of the Conservative leader, called Bennett a "man of deep integrity and great patriotism," but added that there was "no question that Bennett *was* the Conservative Party."[6] In the view of journalist Grattan O'Leary, he was a "man of moods who seldom caught the ear of the House. As an orator he was powerful rather than persuasive." More to the point, as a politician, Bennett "was a combination of Billy Graham and Jack the Ripper."[7]

As prime minister, Bennett was blamed for the Depression. From Bennett buggies to Bennett blankets (newspapers used as blankets), his name became synonymous with hard times and deprivation. He assumed office claiming to have the answers, but failed to deliver on his promises and, as a wealthy man, appeared out of touch and unsympathetic to the average Canadian. He relied on traditional policies of balancing the budget and tariff protection, but now he faced the problems of a modern industrial society, ranging from social and labour issues to civil rights. Despite his fiscal conservativism, he was not ideologically opposed to government action or intervention in the economy, but those views were almost always lost or submerged beneath the more common caricature of Bennett the wealthy, uncaring, austere plutocrat.

The 1930 Election

Ironically, Bennett became prime minister because he was seen as the leader more in tune with the times, more sympathetic to the emerging problems of the Depression, and as the one politician who promised genuine action to meet the growing economic crisis. In 1930, as international prices fell and domestic unemployment spread, Liberal prime minister Mackenzie King rejected calls for the federal government to help the provinces with relief and support for the unemployed. He was particularly unwilling to release federal

cash when it came to the five provincial Conservative governments in British Columbia, Saskatchewan, New Brunswick, Nova
Scotia, and Ontario; they would only waste the money, he claimed.
King was pilloried for ignoring the poor; opposition MPs even
pulled out old copies of King's largely unread book *Industry and
Humanity* to throw his own words – which seemed to support
government action – back at him. Angered by the opposition
taunts, King, in a rare lapse of political judgment, denounced the
Tory provincial governments and vowed never to give them a cent
for relief. In the ensuing uproar, filled with heckling and cries of
"Shame!" King exploded: "I would not give them a five-cent piece."
This statement crystallized for a lot of Canadians what they could
expect from a future Liberal government, and it came to define the
Liberal election campaign.

In 1930, Bennett promised jobs over relief, and as opposition
leader he was able to set out a clear plan of action without the fear
of actually having to do anything. Across the aisle, the Liberal
government had provided neither jobs nor relief, and it was held
accountable for this failure. Extra campaign support on the ground
was provided by the five Conservative provincial governments, and
Bennett even made a real comeback in Quebec, home to one of only
two Liberal provincial governments (the other was that of Prince
Edward Island). Although the government of Louis-Alexandre
Taschereau maintained its disdain for the Conservatives, there was
support for Bennett in the Quebec business community and in the
rural areas outside of Montreal, where his conservative message
appealed even as memories of the Great War and conscription had
begun to fade.

The biggest issue in 1930, beyond King's insensitivity to the unemployed, was the tariff. It was an age of protectionism and
"beggar-thy-neighbour" policies that only exacerbated the effects
of the Depression as nation followed nation in raising protective
tariffs. Canada was affected perhaps more than most states, given

its dependence on international trade, but Bennett hastened the downward spiral of trade by not only joining but also promising to outdo the others by "blasting his way into foreign markets." After the 1930 election, Canada was to join an international trade dispute that ultimately did little to alleviate the effects of the Depression, but it was a memorable slogan used to good effect during the campaign. The Liberals had no response to Bennett's bold promise and were clearly on the defensive. They ran on their record – which was part of the problem – and claimed to have furthered Canadian autonomy internationally. Against this, Bennett was self-assured and a successful man of business (and he used his own money to finance the campaign and support the Conservative Party); he claimed to have the answers to the pressing domestic questions that had stumped the Liberals.

In the first of Canada's two Depression-era federal elections, the Conservatives were the clear winners. The popular vote was fairly close but Bennett won 137 seats. The West split fairly evenly between the two major parties despite its long history of supporting freer trade, while the Tories held the edge in the Maritimes and won an impressive 25 seats in Quebec. But the election was won in Ontario, where the Conservatives won 59 seats to the Liberals' 22. The Liberals were reduced to 91 seats, of which 39 (plus 1 Independent Liberal, Henri Bourassa) were in Quebec. This enhanced the role of French Canadians in the party but left Mackenzie King to defend his party against accusations that it was dominated by Quebec, French Canadians, and priests. Independent labour candidates had relatively little success, but in the West wins by J.S. Woodsworth and A.A. Heaps in Winnipeg and Angus MacInnis in Vancouver would have important repercussions over the next five years. The election also witnessed the end of the Western-based Progressives, a third party that had risen quickly in the aftermath of the Great War, emerged as a political force and the voice of the West in Ottawa, and faded just as swiftly by the end of the 1920s.[8] The two-party system was re-established in 1930 – but not for very long.

The Bennett Government

Bennett had four years – five at most – to do something about the economic crisis. It was an enormous task for any government, and failure to produce results would be punished severely on the next election day. The first task was to assemble a team with the breadth and experience to do the job. Besides being prime minister, Bennett ensured his dominance of the government by keeping the external affairs and finance portfolios for himself. To this one-man show he added the following: Hugh Guthrie (justice), a former Liberal who had deserted Wilfrid Laurier for Borden's Union Government in 1917; Anglo Montreal businessman Charles Cahan (secretary of state); H.H. Stevens (trade and commerce), his old friend and colleague from Vancouver; Robert Manion (railways), another former Ontario Liberal who joined the Unionists in 1917; and E.N. Rhodes (fisheries), a former premier of Nova Scotia. From Quebec, he chose three French Canadians: Arthur Sauvé (postmaster general), Arthur Duranleau (minister of marine), and Maurice Dupré (solicitor general). This cabinet remained largely unchanged until 1935, although Rhodes was shifted to finance when the burden became too great for Bennett.

Shorn of the rhetoric of change and dynamic action, Bennett's plan for the Depression was essentially to get the federal financial house in order, balance the budget, use the tariff to help revive trade, and limit relief expenditures as much as possible. He spent a good deal of his time over the next four years in pursuit of international solutions to the Depression, and was out of the country for much of that time. Soon after his election, he left for England to attend the 1930 Imperial Conference, and his attachment to Britain only grew over the years. He played an important role in the confirmation and ratification of the 1931 Statute of Westminster, which recognized

Prime Minister R.B. Bennett and his cabinet, March 13, 1931. The occasion is the making of a long-distance telephone call to Sir George Perley (Bennett's minister without portfolio) in South America. |
National Film Board of Canada, C-009076

the constitutional equality of the British Dominions and considerably broadened Canadian international autonomy. As promised, he boosted tariffs on imports of manufactured goods to the highest levels ever, largely in retaliation for the US Smoot-Hawley Tariff Act. His plan was to raise Canadian tariffs first and then negotiate mutual reductions with key trading partners in Washington and London. To that end, he chaired the 1932 Imperial Economic Conference in Ottawa in an effort to bring about bilateral trade agreements between the various members of the Commonwealth.[9] The following year, he ventured to Washington to initiate trade discussions with the new Democratic president, Franklin D. Roosevelt. Neither effort produced much in the way of increased trade or jobs, at least not before the 1935 election.

At home, Bennett raised corporate taxes and passed a series of annual Relief Acts, each as parsimonious as the year before, which set aside a small amount of federal funds for public works projects and direct relief for the unemployed (he also dipped into his personal funds to help individual Canadians). He was happy to leave responsibility for relief with the provinces, where it resided constitutionally, and the provinces in turn offloaded it onto the municipalities. But the constitutional question could not be ignored, and Dominion-Provincial Conferences were held in 1933 and 1934 to thresh out a comprehensive arrangement. Who was responsible for the unemployed? Which governments had the resources to do something about it? Ottawa had the financial power but not the constitutional authority; the provinces had the powers but lacked the financial resources to meet the challenges. Each blamed the others. The smaller provinces were more willing to hand over power to Ottawa, whereas Quebec and Ontario balked at relinquishing powers to the central government. Ottawa was reluctant to step in, but the federal government could not let the provinces default on their debts.

At the January 1934 Dominion-Provincial Conference, Bennett threatened to withdraw Ottawa from relief altogether, and the four Western provinces announced that such a move would force the West into default. In the end, all efforts to reach an agreement on relief and unemployment failed and the conference descended into acrimonious bickering.[10] No government had a solid plan other than, first, sitting tight and waiting it out until good times returned, and, second, blaming the other level of government for failing to do its job. The only result of these conferences was embittered relations between the provinces (regardless of which political party was in power provincially) and the Bennett government in Ottawa, a situation that did not bode well for Bennett in his search for provincial allies in the run-up to the 1935 election. In the meantime, the Canadian economy spun out of control.

There were areas in which the federal government could act to combat the Depression, and Bennett's government was increasingly active, especially in 1934–35, when some important – and constructive – legislation was passed. More funds were earmarked for direct relief through the earlier Unemployment and Farm Relief Act. The Farmers' Creditors Arrangement Act was introduced to provide farm debt relief to help families stay on their land through renegotiation of mortgages to prevent foreclosures. Similarly, the Canadian Farm Loan Act set up a system of low-interest mortgages for farmers. The Natural Products Marketing Act was passed as a way to offer federal help with the marketing of products and to maintain prices, short of government intervention to take control of the entire marketing process.[11] Finally, the Public Works Construction Act sought to create jobs by pumping money into infrastructure projects. To its credit, the Bennett government also created the Canadian Radio Broadcasting Commission (CRBC), a national broadcasting body and precursor of the Canadian Broadcasting Corporation (CBC) to regulate broadcasting, and the Canadian Wheat Board, a broader federal effort to stabilize the marketing of the annual Canadian wheat crop.

Equally important, the Conservatives passed the Bank of Canada Act, which established a central bank to regulate currency and credit. It meant that all currency would be produced by the Bank of Canada, not individual banks. It was a popular act, but the government faced some criticism. Under the Conservative plan, the new institution would be a kind of private national bank, in that private shareholders would buy shares and they would have the right to participate in the selection of the bank directors. Bennett argued that the new bank would therefore be beyond "political" control, but the Liberals opposed leaving it in private hands.

In addition, several prominent Quebec MPs who had long complained about the lack of francophones in the federal public service demanded changes to the bill. Ernest Lapointe, the influential

Quebec Liberal and Mackenzie King's close confidant, introduced an amendment calling for bilingual currency (even though the previous Liberal government had done little to introduce such currency). In rejecting the idea outright, Bennett exhibited a degree of tone-deafness, which only added to his government's growing unpopularity among Quebecers.[12] Nevertheless, the Bank of Canada began operations in March 1935, with Graham Towers from the Royal Bank as its first governor.

At the same time, Bennett vigorously revived section 98 of the Criminal Code (first passed in 1919), which made it illegal even to merely advocate the overthrow of the system of government in Canada. Section 98 could be applied unevenly and at random by the authorities against Canadians who had done nothing revolutionary, and left it up to them to prove their innocence. In 1931, Bennett used section 98 to arrest the leaders of the small Canadian Communist Party, and several of its leaders spent a few years in jail. This draconian provision had been denounced by people of all different political stripes, but in the early 1930s it was still in force and maintained by Bennett. To make matters worse, in 1933 Bennett restored the granting of aristocratic titles in Canada, something that his Conservative predecessor Sir Robert Borden had outlawed back in 1919. It made him an easy target for his detractors, who pointed to, on the one hand, his willingness to deport alien agitators and arrest working Canadians under section 98, and, on the other, his support for reintroducing the trappings of a Canadian aristocracy. If nothing else, it reinforced the sense that he was indifferent to the ravages of the Depression and its impact on average Canadian families.

At the beginning of 1935, the Canadian economy remained stagnant; unemployment had dropped from the record levels of 1933 but remained stubbornly high; farm incomes had not revived; urban demand for relief continued to rise; several provinces teetered on the brink of bankruptcy; and the imperial trade agreements had yielded little in increased trade, while the Americans had not even agreed to talk about tariff reductions. Bennett still saw himself as the captain of the ship, whose role it was to steer it through balanced budgets, tariff revisions, and the provision of relief. But now, after four years in office, he faced a re-election campaign that would force him to defend his record to the Canadian voter. The issues that would dominate the campaign – trade and tariffs, unemployment and relief, section 98, the Constitution – were already coming into focus.

Mackenzie King and the Liberal Opposition

For Liberal leader William Lyon Mackenzie King, 1935 started off well. On New Year's Day, he sat with his confidant Joan Patteson at the "little table" for about an hour, "with the following wonderful result for the first night in this momentous new year": Lorenzo de' Medici, a fifteenth-century Italian statesman and patron of the arts, came from beyond to greet King and offer his forecast for the coming year. He predicted that King would have a long life, be a peacemaker, make people happy, and, perhaps most importantly, "will be Prime Minister this year."[13] King had long believed in spiritualism and in his conversations with those who had passed from this world. His conversation with the Italian statesman likely only confirmed what he already hoped and maybe even believed, for the signs for the Liberals were all good as the year began.

King was already one of Canada's longest-serving prime ministers. He had been in politics since 1908, when he was recruited by Sir Wilfrid Laurier to serve as minister of labour. In the wilderness for most of the decade following the disastrous Liberal defeat in 1911, King was elected prime minister in 1921 and remained in office, save for a few months in 1925–26, until his defeat by Bennett in 1930. He had good political instincts, intuiting what might work and what would or could be acceptable to the greatest number of voters. He could sense political danger and where the dangers lay;

After losing the 1930 election, the Liberal Opposition was quick to leave the responsibility for the Depression at the door of the government. | "Blaming It on Bennett," March 21, 1931, *Montreal Star*, Library and Archives Canada, C-141243

he had a nose for politics that worked well over the years and made up for his lack of charisma, warmth, and the kind of personality that attracted followers and inspired loyalty. He was also lucky, even in defeat. In 1917, he remained loyal to Laurier and went down in defeat with his mentor, despite his own feelings in support of conscription. That defeat – or, more precisely, his loyalty to Laurier – served him well with the Quebec wing of the Liberal Party and helped win him the leadership in 1919, a position he held for almost thirty years. Similarly, his defeat in 1930 ensured that the Liberals would be out of office for most of the economic crisis, and the Depression would be forever linked to the Conservative Party, enabling his return to office in 1935. Once back in power, he remained until 1948, and his party continued on until 1957 – an astounding twenty-two years in office.

King saw Canada as a linguistically, religiously, and geographically diverse nation that it was his job to unite or at least keep from falling apart. In his view, the vehicle for this national unity was the Liberal Party; the Conservatives were the party of British colonials and big business, whose demands for high tariffs threatened that unity.[14] He fought long and hard against Tories – real and imagined – wherever he found them.

Ironically, he had a rather conservative view of the Depression, believing that it was caused by the collapse of world trade and exacerbated by the erection of protective tariffs. The solution was not to overthrow the system but to end the tariff wars and to restore world trade by reducing tariff barriers. Negotiations to reduce tariffs became his main proposal to end the Depression; in the meantime, the federal government had to keep things going – keep governments and people afloat until trade was restored. Bennett, like Tories everywhere, had raised tariffs and made things worse; the Liberals would reverse that trend and, the thinking went, things would improve. To this slim list of policy alternatives he added caution, hesitancy, and limited action, for there was no sense in leading the country where large parts of it might not want to go.

As a leader, King often appeared to worry more about making mistakes than doing what was right. He tended to put things off, avoid decisions, and extend negotiations, and then call it compromise; the 1935 election would be a perfect fit – he could sit tight and watch as the government disintegrated on its own. Although he could be overbearing and moralistic, his sympathies often lay with the average person over the plutocrats; he had a real disdain for armaments manufacturers and was closer to being a pacifist than any previous prime minister. He was intelligent and one of the hardest-working politicians of his, or any other, era.

He had few vices – at least of this world – and devoted his whole life to his party. He claimed to have a fundamental belief in Parliament and parliamentary government, was often disturbed by the poor attendance and lack of decorum in the House of Commons, and was critical of his own team as well as the Conservative government. "It was shameful the members in the House yesterday," he complained in his diary shortly after a debate on several new pieces of legislation introduced by the Bennett government in the last parliamentary session before the 1935 election:

> The Quebec men and many others desert Friday afternoon – [J.L.] Ralston and [Ian] MacKenzie's [sic] absences were particularly to be deplored, but the benches were only 1/3 filled on our side – not that – a little better on the other, and yet the greatest issue since Confederation was assuming definite shape and being joined by the parties. The men that are off thro colds, flu etc. are many – drinking I think the main cause – others helpless as children.

The government benches were no better: "It was pathetic to see the mechanical following applaud Guthrie's & Bennett's indefensible position as they must know it is indefensible." Charles Cahan "sat there while Bennett was speaking looking annoyed beyond words he gave no applause – held an order paper in his hand. Perley came in and out but did not stay, he too dislikes it all ... The other ministers sit like dummies. The spectacle is a shocking one." It was sad to think, King concluded, "how little the public know of what Govt. amounts to, how their liberties hang on a thread, but for one or two upright men who are ready to sacrifice themselves all would vanish over night."[15]

King's own speeches often descended into cliché and platitude, perhaps *because* he worked so long on them – trying to get the phrasing just right, trying to say something without really committing to anything, being careful to avoid any hint of controversy while at the same time attempting to appease one part of the country without alienating the other. And he could do this in speeches that lasted several hours, a feat that could test the goodwill of any member of the House of Commons, including R.B. Bennett. The two leaders irritated each other regularly. Liberal MP Charles "Chubby" Power recalled how Bennett "often indulged in petty squabbles with King, who had a similar belief in his own importance and that of the position he held as leader of the opposition. At times the arguments between them, even on minor procedural points, were interminable."[16]

Like Bennett, King was a childless bachelor who was devoted to politics and determined to win, but the similarities ended there. Bennett was forthright and volatile, while King smouldered and schemed; Bennett was public, while King was private; Bennett was decisive and liked to act, while King preferred to wait and avoided decisions until the very end; Bennett barely looked beyond tomorrow, while King played a much longer game. Perhaps most important, Bennett lost as much as he won in politics, whereas King was the perennial victor. In the run-up to the 1935 election, it looked like history was about to repeat itself.

The Rise of Harry Stevens

For Bennett, there were always Liberals to fight and Mackenzie King was a formidable opponent, but as 1935 began, the prime minister faced a greater threat to his leadership from within his own party, in the form of H.H. "Harry" Stevens. Henry Herbert Stevens was a British-born immigrant who was raised in Peterborough, Ontario, before he and his family moved to Vancouver. As a young man, he travelled and worked various jobs, including a stint as a miner in

British Columbia and as an office worker for a trust company. He also briefly ran a local newspaper and owned a small grocery business. He entered Vancouver municipal politics in 1909 before running and winning a seat (Vancouver East) in the House of Commons as a Conservative in the Tory win of 1911. Stevens is most often remembered as a virulent anti-Asian crusader before and after the *Komagata Maru*, a ship bearing hundreds of potential Asian immigrants, docked in Vancouver harbour in 1914.

In Ottawa, Stevens shared a parliamentary office with Calgary's R.B. Bennett, another rookie MP from the 1911 election. They developed a close friendship and worked together through the war years and into the 1920s. Stevens served briefly in Arthur Meighen's cabinet in 1921 and 1926 but lost his seat in 1930 even as the Conservatives were returned to power. Bennett, the new prime minister, found him a safe seat in Kootenay East, British Columbia, and brought him into cabinet as minister of trade and commerce.

Stevens was both a member of a Conservative Party that had strong ties to big business and a minister whose cabinet colleagues included several wealthy and successful businessmen. On top of it all, of course, was Bennett, also a very wealthy man. As a former small grocer, Stevens was also a businessman, but he had faced serious economic difficulties in the past and never attained the comfort or wealth of many of his colleagues. His lack of business success compared unfavourably with several of his colleagues, and he believed that this failure hurt his political career and that he was even looked down upon because of it.[17] Whether it was true or not, he resented it and it likely affected his relations with some of his more successful colleagues, such as Charles Cahan, Sir George Perley, and even, to some degree, Bennett himself. If nothing else, it heightened his awareness of the problems facing small business owners in Canada, and he became determined to fight for the "little guy."

Stevens increasingly devoted his attention to the difficulties facing small business owners and retailers in Depression-era Canada,

H.H. "Harry" Stevens as a rookie Conservative MP in Ottawa, 1912.
By 1935, Stevens had become one of the most popular Conservatives in
the country and a potential challenger for the prime minister's job. |
Photographer William James Topley, Library and Archives Canada, PA-043015

especially serious competition from the big chain stores, which were
threatening to squeeze out smaller retailers by undercutting their
prices. The big retailers used their power and influence to force
manufacturers to sell to them in bulk at much-reduced prices, and
they used loss leaders in their stores to lower prices to levels that
small retailers could not match. Manufacturers had to cut their costs
to make a profit, and their workers were caught in the middle,
working at reduced wages in sweatshop conditions, especially in
the production of clothing and textiles. At some point, the workers

could not afford to buy the clothing they produced. For Stevens, the culprits in this economic free-for-all were the major retail chain stores, particularly the two largest retail chains, Eaton's and Simpson's, and the major meat packers.

Trouble started on January 15, 1934, when Bennett asked Stevens to stand in for him at a meeting of the Retail Shoe Merchants and Shoe Manufacturers Association at Toronto's Royal York Hotel. In a speech that was broadcast simultaneously on a local radio station, Stevens condemned the large retailers for their purchasing practices, low wages, and big profits. He focused on what he believed was the crux of the problem: the "price spreads," the difference between what businesses paid for products and what they sold them for – or, more precisely, the huge disparity between what producers were paid for producing their goods on one end and what consumers were forced to pay for them on the other, and how much of the profit went to the powerful retailers and manufacturers sitting in the middle. "There must be action taken of some kind to face the evils that have developed like a canker," he declared. "I warn them that unless they are destroyed, they will destroy the system."[18] This was a matter close to Stevens's heart. He did not single out any company, but everyone knew to whom he was referring. And he went a step further, promising government action to rein in the power of the giant retailers. It was one thing to raise an issue of importance to shop owners but quite another to get ahead of where the government wished to go, and Stevens had discussed this proposal with no one in cabinet. To make matters worse, the small retailers and business leaders in the audience loved what Stevens had to say, and they fully expected action to follow.

Stevens made a name for himself with the speech, and he nurtured it with a series of speeches in which he set out the bad conditions facing workers and small businesses in Canada. His message quickly became very popular, attracting a lot of national attention as well as, increasingly, the ire of his leader, Bennett. From the head offices of Eaton's and Simpson's came demands that Stevens produce some evidence to support his charges of unfair competition – or be fired from cabinet if he could not. In addition, Stevens had broken one of the basic rules of this Conservative government by making promises on his own without Bennett's approval. Bennett demanded that Stevens stop saying such things; Stevens refused.

Stevens offered a letter of resignation from cabinet, but it was ignored by Bennett. Nevertheless, the two men's friendship had taken a serious hit, and the trouble between them was not ameliorated by their characters: both men could be stubborn and indignant, and neither was willing to concede an inch to the other. Stevens, however, had struck a nerve not only in the country but also in the Conservative Party, and even with the prime minister himself. Backbenchers sympathized with the plight of the small business owner, Stevens gave a plausible explanation of the deplorable economic conditions in the retail sector, and voters might be interested in hearing more about it.

Such was the popularity of Stevens's initial attack on vested interests that rather than sack his insubordinate minister, Bennett gave him his own Commons committee to examine the issue. On February 16, 1934, the Special Committee on Price Spreads and Mass Buying was established with Stevens in the chair. Better known as the Stevens Committee, it began a series of public hearings one week later in a committee room in Parliament. Over the next eighteen weeks, it attracted huge public attention, in the process turning Stevens into a household name as someone who appeared to actually be doing something about the Depression. In hindsight, Bennett might have wished that he had accepted Stevens's resignation right at the start, instead of giving him what he wanted – a national platform from which to launch his investigation into the problem of price spreads. What that decision almost guaranteed was a steady stream of commentary, criticism, and outrage emanating from within his own party – and often directed *at* his own party – as it prepared for a general election.

Stevens was a committee chair on a mission, as he set out to prove his allegations of price fixing and unfair competition by defending his friends and attacking large business owners, examining witnesses like a prosecuting attorney, and producing enough bombast, accusations, and heated exchanges with well-known businessmen to ensure steady publicity in the press. To critics, Stevens saw the problems facing small business in a simple way and he sought simple solutions. One contemporary observer noted that he had been "touched with the mental habits of a promoter to whom many propositions look rosy when they are really not so."[19] Vincent Massey, a leading Liberal, was even less charitable. "Stevens can hardly be acquitted of using the technique of the demagogue in his handling of the problem," he wrote to a British friend. "The Parliamentary inquiry has the air of a police court case with Stevens himself acting as police constable, judge, jury, and executioner."[20]

When the spring 1934 parliamentary session ended, Bennett could have allowed the Stevens Committee to expire, but instead, because of its popularity, he launched a full-fledged Royal Commission – the Royal Commission on Price Spreads and Mass Buying – with Stevens at its head. As a Royal Commission chair, Stevens might have been expected to remain quiet about the results of the commission at least until after it had researched and reported on the issue, but he could not, and he began speaking about what needed to done long before the commission was scheduled to meet for the first time in October.

In a private speech delivered on June 27 to a group of MPs at the Conservative Study Club, Stevens levelled accusations against the meat-packing industry and the large retail stores, particularly Simpson's, and spoke of his work in the Stevens Committee. He then launched a much-publicized personal attack on the aging

Toronto businessman Sir Joseph Flavelle, one of the major owners of Simpson's, for price fixing and unfair business practices. The published version of the speech was, according to one observer, "brutally frank, and, in the opinion of some people, somewhat indiscreet and not wholly accurate."[21] Flavelle, an important banker, philanthropist, supporter of many good causes, and major supporter of the Conservative Party, was outraged.

There is some debate concerning whether Stevens meant to release the speech to the public, but he did have copies printed and distributed. He claimed they were printed without his knowledge or consent and were solely for the information of other Conservatives who were interested but unable to attend the Study Club meeting. Critics charged that by printing three thousand copies he intended it for a much wider audience.[22] Regardless, one copy landed in the hands of journalist Grant Dexter of the *Winnipeg Free Press*. No friend of R.B. Bennett, the *Free Press* published it. The story was picked up by other papers and soon became a national sensation, angering many, including Simpson's. Bennett was livid. He threatened to sue the paper for libel and tried to stop further circulation of the contents of the speech.[23] Stevens was unrepentant, and the rift between him and the prime minister broke wide open. So began the "Stevens Affair."

It was a delicate situation for Bennett, who usually preferred decisive action. But he was soon to call five by-elections when the Stevens pamphlet appeared, and he likely did not want the speech to influence the outcome of those campaigns. Calling the by-elections also signalled that there would be no federal campaign that year, which, as it turned out, was fortunate given that the Liberals won four of the five by-elections, with only former Toronto mayor T.L. Church winning for the Conservatives in Toronto East. Bennett was also about to leave for England before going to Geneva to head the Canadian delegation at the League of Nations Assembly in September, and he was happy to avoid controversy in advance of his trip. Furthermore, during his absence he would need to rely even more on the popular Stevens to campaign in the five by-elections.

More important, what Stevens had to say was very popular, and it would do Bennett and his party no favour to discipline the one Conservative who was rising in public consciousness. Bennett saw himself as a supporter of the small business owner, but nationally he was seen as the champion of corporate Canada and the major business elites. It was Stevens who appealed to the "man on the street" – the small business owner who was a natural Conservative but who couldn't catch a break from the financial powers that controlled his fate. Bennett needed the support of such voters, and he was more likely to keep it with Stevens inside the party than on the outside as a critic, or even as a potential rival to his leadership. Stevens was widely popular with small business people and many in the agricultural sector, and he offered solutions of a non-socialist nature that were likely to attract Conservative voters as well as some Liberal voters. Even many Quebecers might be attracted to the non-socialist aspect of his proposed reforms. Already there was talk of Stevens as a potential prime minister or party leader and as a man who, if he replaced Bennett, could prove to be a more formidable challenge to the Liberals in the upcoming election.

Consequently, Bennett did not sue the *Winnipeg Free Press* or demand Stevens's resignation; instead, he left for Europe as planned. In his absence, the Conservative caucus began to break up, with many supporting Stevens for breathing some life into a moribund government while others opposed him and felt that he should wait until the Royal Commission had at least *begun* its work before revealing what it had determined. Those on the party's left wanted to stand with Stevens and small business; those on the right maintained their support for the business elite. There were diehard Bennett supporters, but a growing number believed that Bennett was on his way out, and Stevens presented himself as a winning future leader. With the cracks in the party becoming wider, there was rising speculation in the press over Stevens's future. For example, the *Toronto Daily Star,* which traditionally maintained an attitude of "studied contempt" regarding Bennett and had once congratulated him for "walking up to the very verge of doing something," openly wondered how long Stevens and Bennett could stay in the same government.[24]

By the time Bennett returned from Europe, cabinet was openly divided between Stevens on one side and, on the other, Minister of Finance Edgar Rhodes, the old-school veteran Sir George Perley, and, in particular, Secretary of State Charles Cahan, the mouthpiece of St. James Street (the Montreal financial establishment) and spokesperson for the older Tories who eschewed the radicalism suggested by Stevens and his inquiry. Last-ditch efforts were made to keep Stevens in the government, but the controversy came to a head on October 25, at the first cabinet meeting following Bennett's return. There was much criticism of Stevens's actions, especially from Cahan (who was also known as "Dino," short for dinosaur), and few ministers came to Stevens's defence. No resignation was demanded, but the cabinet requested that Stevens make a public apology to Sir Joseph Flavelle. The decision was leaked to the press and Stevens refused to toe the party line. Apologizing would have been the easy way out, Stevens concluded, but he reportedly told Bennett, "I prize my liberty of action and my sense of duty to the public of Canada more." He submitted his resignation for the second time, and this time Bennett accepted it.[25]

Stevens was out of the cabinet but he was still an MP and a member of the Conservative caucus, so the tension remained and the public feuding continued through the fall. He also resigned as chair of the Royal Commission, which had not even been convened, but remained a member and the focus of considerable national attention. The commission held its first hearing on November

1, 1934, with W.W. Kennedy, the Conservative MP for Winnipeg, as its chair. It continued until February 2, 1935. By then, Stevens was regularly pointed to as Bennett's rival and potential successor.

By the end of 1934, Stevens, no longer a cabinet minister and Royal Commission chair, had more time to travel the country crusading for the recommendations of the earlier Stevens Committee, and he faced the open hostility of several former cabinet colleagues. It remained to be seen whether the split with Bennett was irreversible, but the conflict had clearly spilled out into the open. On December 5, Bennett announced that he was staying on as leader to fight the election that had to be held in 1935, and it was clear to many that it was his personal dislike for Stevens that led him to continue as leader and prime minister. "In 1935 I had intended, as you know, to retire and had hoped to take up residence in England," Bennett wrote in 1938 to his old friend Max Aitken, now Lord Beaverbrook, in London. "But Stevens' action made that impossible and I had to remain."[26]

On New Year's Eve, *Winnipeg Free Press* editor John Dafoe opined on the coming election:

> The whole play will be on emotions, prejudices, appetites, hopes and what-not, with promises of a new Jerusalem for them as a reward for electors if they vote right. R.B. will be in the coming campaign the outstanding demagogue of Canadian history. Poor Harry Stevens will have to go way back and sit down, his ineffectual fires paling in contrast with R.B.'s effulgence.[27]

Few held out hope for reconciliation; more were worried that the split would completely fracture the Conservative Party and pave the way for a Liberal victory; still others silently longed for Stevens to replace Bennett as leader. Over the next year, the relationship deteriorated even further and Stevens evolved in two ways: first, from a minor nuisance into a major disruptive influence in the party, and second, from a potential rival to Bennett's leadership into an existential threat to his re-election.

Bennett had to respond to the challenge from Stevens both as party leader and as prime minister. Digging in his heels as an old-style Tory capitalist likely would not resonate well with the Canadian public. He believed – and was hearing from several close sources – that a bolder, more dramatic plan of action was necessary. It is perhaps not that surprising, then, that at the beginning of 1935 and facing an election that year, Bennett, as captain of a ship quickly taking on water, would be so receptive to the idea of sailing off in a bold new direction by launching a "New Deal" for Canadians – one filled with ideas and proposals that he could at least claim to have supported at some time in his past. The election campaign was on.

2

What's Left and Who's Right?

It is an accepted commonplace of politics – accepted by all sides – that the socialist C.C.F. would sweep the province if an election were held to-morrow.

– Bruce Hutchison, July 1935[1]

THE 1935 ELECTION WAS national in scope but it played out against a backdrop of provincial turbulence. One after another, provincial governments faced bankruptcy, while municipal governments felt the full weight of the Depression and ran out of money for relief. The old order was challenged as one provincial government followed another into political exile; in its place, new provincial governments were elected and two entirely new political parties were created at the national level. All claimed to have solutions to the economic and social devastation of the Great Depression. The two new parties, in particular, had different interpretations of the crisis and offered voters seemingly radical change to combat its worst aspects. When the dust settled after the election, there were some questions about which of the new parties was the most radical or innovative, but to understand the 1935 federal election, it is necessary to begin at the provincial level.

The Rise of the
Co-operative Commonwealth Federation

All political parties had to respond to the growing electoral power of Western Canada. In 1911, the Maritime provinces had 35 seats to the West's 34 in a House of Commons of 221 seats. Given Ontario's 86 seats and Quebec's 65, elections were won or lost in Central Canada. In 1935, however, Western Canada would cast over 1.15 million votes, more than double that of the Maritimes. By then the Maritimes had slipped to 26 seats while the West had gained ground, rising to 71. Western Canada combined now had more seats than Quebec and could not be ignored in a national campaign. And discontent was everywhere in the Canadian West in the months leading up to the 1935 federal election.

Canadian farmers had been organizing long before the Depression. There were grain growers' associations in each of the Prairie provinces, non-partisan leagues, and a variety of other grassroots organizations often inspired by populist developments in the American west. There were wheat pools and cooperative organizations, and the *Grain Growers' Guide* spoke for agrarian producers. There were also numerous socialist parties in the West, spanning the political spectrum on the Left, and independent labour parties regularly nominated candidates in provincial and federal elections, although the mainstream parties were still the most popular.

The defeat of reciprocity in the 1911 election was a serious blow to the West, as Prairie governments had consistently pointed to the high tariff wall as the most serious impediment to Western prosperity. The First World War only exacerbated regional tensions as the Liberal Party became increasingly focused on Quebec and its opposition to conscription, while Western Liberals generally

favoured conscription but argued that the Conservative government's wartime policy seemed to work against Western interests.
In the 1917 federal election, the choice was between a Union
government, which promised conscription and high tariffs, and
the French Canadian–dominated Laurier Liberals and their anti-
conscription promises. The West generally supported the Unionists,
for reasons having to do with the war, but shortly after the Armistice,
thoughts turned to independent political action. Several new parties
emerged across the Prairies and in Ontario. The United Farmers of
Ontario (UFO) were elected to office in 1919 and the United Farmers
of Alberta (UFA) were elected two years later.

In 1920, a small group of federal MPs led by T.A. Crerar, a former
Liberal who had bolted the party over conscription before the 1917
election and served in Robert Borden's cabinet as minister of agriculture, left the Union Government after it failed to deliver on tariff
reform. They formed the National Progressive Party, which was
soon endorsed by most farmers' organizations and became the focus
of rural discontent in Ottawa. In the 1921 federal election, sixty-
five Progressives were elected, virtually all from Western Canada
(only one candidate won east of the Ottawa River). They formed
the second-largest group in Parliament but declined the role of
official opposition, leaving it to the third-place Conservatives. This
decision reflected the view that they were in Ottawa to achieve
reform rather than create a new party. For some, like Crerar himself,
there was a lingering desire to reform the Liberal Party rather than
start a new rival party.

The number of Progressives declined to twenty-four in the 1925
election and, thanks to further accommodation with the Liberals,
only nine remained after the 1926 election. This rump formed
the core of what became known as the "Ginger Group." Over the
following years, an alliance emerged between the Ginger Group
and two independent MPs: James Shaver Woodsworth and William
Irvine. Both men represented urban ridings – Winnipeg and

Calgary, respectively – and together they formed a labour group in Parliament. "Mr. Woodsworth is the leader," Irvine said. "And I am the group."[2] From this alliance emerged a new political party.

Conferences of labour groups and agrarian organizations became more common as the Depression deepened, and a sense of commonality emerged between groups that otherwise might not have been seen as potential allies, such as small producers and landowners who preached independence and self-reliance based on land ownership, and labour groups who demanded the nationalization of property, government regulation, and legislation establishing minimum hours of work. Common ground was found on key issues: the nationalization of the banks and railways, the regulation of monopolies, tariff reform, and the provision of relief. By the early 1930s, there was more agreement than difference among the various farmer, labour, and socialist groups – each with its provincial distinctiveness – leading to calls for a wider, more inclusive conference to seek common solutions to the mutual problems caused by the Depression.

On May 26, 1932, about a dozen labour and independent MPs and various other progressives met in William Irvine's parliamentary office to discuss the creation of a new party. Besides Irvine and Woodsworth, those present included members of the moribund Ginger Group; M.J. Coldwell, president of the Saskatchewan Labour Party (and future Co-operative Commonwealth Federation [CCF] MP and party leader); Agnes Macphail of the United Farmers of Ontario, who was given responsibility for promoting the cause in Ontario; and a few members of the recently formed League for Social Reconstruction (LSR), a loose group of eastern university-based academics who hoped to make intellectual contributions to the new party along the lines of President Roosevelt's "brain trust" in Washington.[3] They agreed to stage a national convention with the goal of establishing a new political party, tentatively named the "Canadian Commonwealth Party."

At the convention in Calgary later that summer, the new party was officially created: the Co-operative Commonwealth Federation. The convention brought together an impressive array of farmer-labour-progressive groups, including the United Farmers of Alberta, the Dominion Labour Party of Alberta, the Socialist Party of Canada (from British Columbia), the Canadian Labour Party, and the United Farmers of Canada, Saskatchewan Division. They were joined by a myriad of provincial branches of socialist parties, economic reconstruction clubs, independent labour parties, and other agrarian-progressive organizations. An eight-point program was approved, calling for, among other things, the nationalization of banks and railways, economic planning, social welfare, and land tenure for farmers. The CCF was born.

J.S. Woodsworth was the obvious choice and popular favourite to lead the new party. Born on a farm in Etobicoke, near Toronto, he was a pacifist and former Methodist minister imbued with the views of the Social Gospel and its desire to do good works in this world – through devotion to social activism and service – rather than waiting for the next. He resigned from the church during the First World War and subsequently devoted his life to labour and socialist causes, arriving in Winnipeg for the General Strike of 1919, where he was arrested for sedition. More missionary than preacher, he worked in several industries and gained numerous contacts while speaking to large numbers of progressive, socialist, farmer, and labour groups all across the country. He was first elected an MP for Winnipeg in 1921 and assumed the leadership of the labour group in the House of Commons. By the early 1930s, he was an experienced politician who had learned how to succeed in Parliament. More than anyone else, he brought together what in many ways was a disparate collection of labour, socialist, and agrarian forces.

A man of intelligence and integrity, he had a positive view of human nature. Revered by his followers and colleagues, and described by his biographer as a "prophet in politics," Woodsworth also shared reprehensible views on race, eugenics, and immigration, which, although not uncommon at the time, have tarnished his reputation. "He was not an angel or a saint," David Lewis, a young CCFer (and future NDP leader), recorded in his memoirs. "He possessed an ego and a temper. He was demanding and sometimes impatient, even authoritarian. He had his likes and his dislikes and they were as irrational as those of most people. In short, he was human; but he was one of the finest human beings I have known."[4] In any event, it was enough to earn Woodsworth the role of national chairman, making him de facto leader of the party, although, given the nature of the CCF, his control did not extend over all the different groups that the federation comprised.

The new party needed a platform, and one was debated, revised, and adopted at the CCF convention in Regina in August 1933. On the table was the Regina Manifesto, a document produced by the LSR and often largely credited to historian Frank Underhill of the University of Toronto. It was described by one observer as "a mixture of Christian, Fabian, and Marxian socialism, shot through with progressive reformism," which infused the CCF with the "strong underlying belief that man is both a rational and social creature, capable of creating a perfect society by abolishing the corrupt social order."[5]

The purpose of the new party was to create a "cooperative commonwealth" in which "the principle regulating production, distribution and exchange will be the supplying of human needs and not the making of profits." To achieve this goal, a CCF government would aim to "replace the present capitalist system, with its inherent injustice and inhumanity, by a social order from which the domination and exploitation of one class by another will be eliminated, in which economic planning will supersede unregulated private enterprise and competition, and in which genuine democratic self-government, based upon economic equality will be possible." More specifically, the new party advocated state planning of the

The new party in action. Members of the Co-operative Commonwealth Federation in June 1938, from left to right: T.C. Douglas, Angus MacInnis, A.A. Heaps, J.S. Woodsworth, M.J. Coldwell, Mrs. Grace MacInnis, Grant MacNeil. | Photographer Yousuf Karsh, Library and Archives Canada, PA-181423

economy; nationalization of banks and all financial institutions, utility companies, and transportation companies; removal of the tariff on agricultural goods; security for farmers; a national labour code to regulate wages, hours of work, and working conditions; a national system of health insurance; a more equal tax system; abolition of section 98 of the Criminal Code; promotion of peace abroad and freedom of assembly at home; and amendment of the British North America Act to give the federal government power to deal with the urgent problems of the Depression. "No CCF government," the Regina Manifesto concluded, "will rest content until it has eradicated capitalism and put into operation the full programme of socialized planning which will lead to the establishment in Canada of the Co-operative Commonwealth."[6] This party platform would take the CCF through its first federal election in 1935.

As its name suggests, the CCF differed from the traditional parties in that it was a federation of different groups and these groups remained somewhat distinct. Indeed, the CCF's official name included the tag "(Farmer, Labour, Socialist)" as a reminder that not all members or their respective groups supported all the goals and platforms of the others. But there were broad areas of general agreement. It was also a political party that was both idealistic and radical: idealistic in that it held an almost evangelical belief in the perfectibility of Canadian society and shared a desire for converts to the movement to remake Canadian society; radical in that it called for the replacement of capitalism with socialism – or at least more cooperation – to achieve the co-operative commonwealth. "Labour Party, agrarian party, Marxist socialist, Christian socialist," wrote historians John Herd Thompson and Allen Seager. "The CCF continues to baffle theorists because it fits no single model." Or, as Woodsworth himself put it, the CCF was "a distinctly Canadian type of socialism."[7]

Distinctly Canadian perhaps, but there were many groups that resisted the social democratic appeal of the CCF. There were some 150 delegates at the Regina convention but no representatives from the major labour organizations. A.A. Heaps, a member of the Independent Labour Party of Manitoba and the MP for Winnipeg North, for example, maintained a somewhat ambivalent relationship with the CCF. He participated in its creation but was never part of its inner circle (and he had not been invited to the early meeting in Irvine's office). He was more a trade unionist and doctrinaire socialist than the farmer-labour type found in the CCF. As the decade wore on, he opposed the party's shift to pacifism in the face of rising fascism in Europe, and he was well aware that pacifism was a political liability in his European multi-ethnic riding.[8] Nevertheless, he supported the party in the House of Commons and ran as a CCF candidate in the 1935 election.

At the other end of the political spectrum, the United Farmers of Ontario also failed to attend the Regina convention and remained suspicious about the socialist aspects of the party's platform. Attacking capitalism was one thing, but they were small landowners and it was affluence, not socialism, that they sought. The UFO officially withdrew from the CCF in 1934, meaning that MP Agnes Macphail – who was present at the creation of the CCF – ran as an independent/UFO candidate in the 1935 election, although she usually supported and voted with the CCF in Parliament. Finally, neither the Protestant nor Catholic churches endorsed the new party, despite its clear spiritual overtones. In Quebec especially, the CCF was attacked for its radical ideas, both by influential newspapers such as *Le Devoir* and by the Church hierarchy. It was a dangerous movement, declared Archbishop Georges Gauthier of Montreal in February 1934, based upon "a materialistic conception of the social order which precisely constitutes the anti-Christian character of Socialism."[9]

The creation of the CCF was a turning point in Canadian federal politics in that it permanently upset the traditional balance between the national Liberal and Conservative Parties. Earlier third parties, such as the National Progressive Party, tended to be more regional in nature and caused more limited upset to the political system. The CCF, in contrast, was playing a much longer game and had decidedly national ambitions. Now a Conservative defeat no longer meant – almost by definition – a Liberal victory, or vice versa. Canadian voters had another choice. The CCF's roadmap to a socialist Canada could now be compared to and contrasted with what the other parties had to offer. At the same time, having a clear set of proposals posed a problem for the CCF as it forced the party to defend those proposals, even if they were unpopular, while allowing the other parties to shift with the political winds, offering all things to all people.

The CCF also introduced the issue of class into Canadian politics, or at least it offered a voice for the working class and presented a serious critique of, and alternative to, the prevailing capitalist system – something neither traditional party had ever done. This was to be a particular problem for the Liberals. The Conservatives had staked out their traditional position as the defenders of order, business, and small government, and offered conservative economics and the defence of the establishment. The Liberals, however, had been willing to rest on tariff reform as their basic platform and then allow the Conservatives to self-destruct. The CCF made this scenario more problematic. Whereas the Liberals could contemplate the absorption of the earlier Progressives, this was not to be the case with the CCF. The new party was more than merely a collection of Liberals lost in the political wilderness; it was a direct challenge to Liberalism (as well as Conservatism). The CCF was here to stay.

Electoral success followed swiftly. Several Western cities elected CCF mayors. In British Columbia in 1933, the CCF ran on the proposition that the older parties' day had come and gone and it was time for something new, and it emerged as the official opposition. It also became the official opposition in Saskatchewan the following year. It had less success in the Ontario election held on the same day, winning only one seat, but activist parties were clearly on the rise. The CCF would be a force in the 1935 federal election, and the threat to the traditional parties was clear.

William Aberhart and Social Credit

Something completely different was emerging in Alberta, where the traditional parties faced perhaps their greatest challenge. Alberta likely suffered during the Depression more than any other Canadian province. Despite the image of independent farmers as small landowners in control of their own destinies, the opposite was actually true. Rural Albertans experienced great insecurity thanks to a dependence on eastern bankers, grain elevator companies, and the international price of wheat. Springs and autumns that were too cold and summers that were too hot combined with periods of drought, flood, dust, and pestilence. Thanks to its isolation, political impotence, and unique political culture, Alberta already had a lengthy history of rural activism, radicalism, reformism, and progressivism. In the 1930s, these forces were tapped into by a new movement under the banner of Social Credit and its prophet, William Aberhart. Aberhart didn't create these conditions; he embraced them. He gave Albertans a plan and offered himself as a new leader.

William Aberhart was born in Ontario in 1878 and moved to Calgary as a young man, where he worked as a teacher and ultimately became a school principal. A fundamentalist Baptist, he took up preaching as the head of the Prophetic Bible Institute in Calgary, and by 1925 had gained considerable attention and a wide audience thanks to his regular Sunday broadcasts on a Calgary radio station. The line between Aberhart's evangelical rhetoric and political activism became increasingly blurred in the Depression, and he emerged as a kind of Social Gospeller who increasingly embraced a political radicalism that ran parallel to, rather than being submerged by, his fundamentalism.[10] Like CCF leader J.S. Woodsworth, he increasingly prioritized social activism in this life over his faith in salvation in the next, moving readily from the pulpit to the campaign trail.

Aberhart quickly became a convert to the ideas of Social Credit after his introduction to the theories of British engineer Major C.H. Douglas on how to ameliorate the inefficiencies of modern technological society, particularly the problems of purchasing power. Based on Douglas's "A + B theorem," in which the total cost of production (C) comprised the wages of the workers in any industry (A) plus all the other costs (raw materials, taxes, etc.) (B). In this scenario, the total wages paid to the workers (A) was never enough to cover the total cost of the goods (C). That difference would need to be made up by the introduction of a "social credit." This appeared to be a commonsense solution to the problems of modern capitalist society: gain control of the money supply so as to regulate it efficiently and control prices to ensure fairness, and then supply social credit or dividends to individuals to make up the gap between wages and the total cost of production. It was a simple solution, to be sure, but at its heart it offered the one thing that was widely called for in the West: inflation. By pumping money into the economy, or just printing and distributing more currency, it would stimulate purchasing and raise prices, and for many it was the way out of an otherwise impossible situation. It was especially attractive to rural Albertans (among others) because social credit wasn't about overthrowing capitalism or nationalizing land ownership; it was a call to reform the monetary system.[11]

Aberhart introduced social credit philosophy and political talk into his Sunday afternoon radio broadcasts, mixing social credit with Christian fundamentalism and attracting tens of thousands of listeners, not only in Alberta but also in British Columbia and Saskatchewan. A talented orator, he came across as devout and sincere; in other words, he was believable and offered some optimism to people in desperate need of hope. He included skits in his broadcasts from October 1934 to February 1935, such as a "Man from Mars" series in which a foreign-sounding Martian would arrive on the set asking pointed questions about why earthlings had been unable to solve their own economic problems. The solutions were provided by Aberhart or his collaborator, future Alberta premier Ernest Manning, and the listener would be exposed to some hard truths about Depression-era Alberta. One political scientist called it "the opening guns in the most successful political campaign that Canada has ever seen."[12]

Social credit study groups were organized to spread the word. Speaking tours and social credit gatherings – part political rally, part revival meeting – were staged across the province, and what

A teacher turned preacher turned successful politician: William Aberhart addressing a rally in St. George's Island Park, Calgary, in July 1937. | Library and Archives Canada, C-009339

began as a movement swiftly transformed into direct political action. Demands for reform grew, as did criticism of the provincial government. The refusal of the governing UFA to endorse any social credit doctrine at its annual convention in January 1935 was the final straw. Organization accelerated, and Aberhart announced that social credit would run a full slate of candidates in the upcoming provincial election. The inaugural convention of the new Social Credit Party was held in April 1935, and Aberhart was chosen as the party's first leader. Its platform featured a mix of education reforms, health insurance, law and order measures, improved government efficiency, tax reform, help for the agricultural and dairy sectors (action to prevent foreclosures, interest-free loans), and regulation of prices and enhancement of purchasing power through the distribution of "basic dividends" so Albertans could meet their needs for food, clothing, and shelter. It also included the right of recall of political candidates "if they fail to carry out the proposals made prior to election."[13]

Aberhart's new party was rejected by the business class, including, not surprisingly, the banks and other financial institutions, as well as by the federal government and the traditional political parties, most economists, and a majority of newspapers. It did not matter; if anything, being rejected by the very groups of people who were the main villains who had created the corrupt system in the first place likely enhanced the party's popular appeal. It was the eastern-dominated federal government and its financial supporters – the bankers, the railway companies, and others like them – who benefited from the existing system and would protect it as long as they could.

Aberhart used the Prophetic Bible Institute as Social Credit headquarters and religion was never far from the surface, but the deeper he delved into social credit, the more he wandered from Bible prophecy. A few church members claimed that "when Social Credit entered the front door of the church, the Holy Spirit left by the back door."[14] Moreover, as the provincial election approached (and the provincial election overlapped with the federal campaign), Aberhart increasingly diverged from the philosophy of Major Douglas and the campaign focused more on Aberhart himself. Aberhart asked voters to have faith in him to do the right thing once in office. There was no need to explain the theory, he explained; it was only necessary to elect Social Credit candidates and then leave it to Aberhart and the "technical experts" to implement it. As he explained at a rally in Edmonton on August 16, 1935: "You don't have to know all about Social Credit before you vote for it; you don't have to understand electricity to use it, for you know that experts have put the system in, and all you have to do is push the button and you get the light. So all you have to do about Social

Credit is to cast your vote for it, and we will get experts to put the system in."[15]

On August 22, the Social Credit Party won fifty-six of the sixty-three seats in the Alberta legislature, wiping out the UFA, defeating all the labour candidates, and reducing the opposition Liberals to a handful of seats. The election had been as much about the party's leader as it was about social credit, and the sweeping victory of Aberhart and his personally selected candidates ensured his domination of the new Social Credit government in Edmonton. In the short run, it also meant that Aberhart would wield considerable influence in the federal election held just weeks after his provincial triumph.

The Triumph of Provincial Liberalism

When R.B. Bennett was first elected prime minister, he could call on the help of five Conservative provincial governments. By the time the 1935 federal election was called, however, there were Liberal or Liberal-Progressive governments in every province except Alberta. Something had gone wrong for Conservatism, at least on the provincial level, and this did not augur well for the party's chances in the federal election. Interestingly, at the same time that Canadians welcomed the creation of new national parties advocating more radical change, they turned their backs on socialism at the provincial level and returned to the more comfortable and safer confines of Liberalism. This suggested a volatility in Canadian politics, and the resurgence of provincial Liberalism not only foreshadowed what was about to happen nationally but also introduced new provincial players who would help shape how the federal election unfolded.

In British Columbia, the Depression hit the forestry, fishery, mining, and pulp and paper sectors particularly hard. Agriculture, especially the fruit industry, was also devastated. Thanks to its milder climate, Vancouver attracted tens of thousands of unemployed men, who drifted through, looking for work. Some estimates put the number of homeless men at over 100,000. Hunger and poverty were widespread. In Victoria, the provincial government of S.F. Tolmie had been in office since 1928. By the early 1930s, it faced numerous accusations of corruption, including at the work camps and in the distribution of relief, but the Liberal opposition remained in a state of disarray.

Into this mix stepped the self-confident, outgoing, and flamboyant Ontario-born Thomas Dufferin "Duff" Pattullo, who went west in search of adventure, first to Yukon before landing in British Columbia. Elected to the British Columbia legislature in 1916, he took over as Liberal leader in the late 1920s and promised health insurance, lower taxes, and an economic council to examine unemployment. Pattullo presented himself as very much an activist leader, arguing that the state had a role to play in bettering the lives of the average British Columbian who was suffering through the Depression. His agenda promised more government services; it was not the socialism of the far left but more the progressive liberalism of President Roosevelt's New Deal. His goal was not to overturn the system but to make the existing one work better; state intervention could be used to make capitalism work more efficiently and improve people's lives. If nothing else, he would at least do *something*. He coined a new term for his vision of a more vigorous, interventionist state: "socialized capitalism."[16]

The inability of the Conservatives to handle the economic crisis opened the door for a Liberal sweep in the 1933 provincial election, with the party winning thirty-five of the forty-eight seats in the legislature. Responding to Pattullo's campaign slogan – "Work and Wages" – British Columbians chose action over complacency, innovation over orthodoxy. Pattullo was an activist at heart, and just days after his election victory he announced: "We must be up and doing." As his biographer explained, Pattullo "was always more inclined to action than to reflection, and now was the time to get on with it."[17]

The architect of the "Little New Deal," Thomas Dufferin
"Duff" Pattullo, premier of British Columbia. | Louis Laurier
Lyonde collection, Library and Archives Canada, PA-053714

The Pattullo government immediately introduced legislation to
raise the minimum wage, reform the tax code, and initiate a public
works program. It also increased funding for schools and unemployment relief, and established committees to investigate health insurance, unemployment insurance, and the education system. People
were soon referring to Pattullo's plan as the "Little New Deal."

Patttullo's victory had national implications, and in Ottawa
Liberal leader Mackenzie King was quick to see an opportunity. He
wrote immediately to congratulate Pattullo on his success, which
King saw as evidence of "a nation-wide desire for a belief in the
necessity of a change from Tory to Liberal principles and methods
of administration." He then suggested setting up a Royal Commission to investigate the sins of the previous provincial Conservative

government. Such an act, King believed, "would unearth so much in the way of scandal that, when it comes to the federal elections, Bennett's Administration would suffer in your province, as effectively as Tolmie's did on Thursday last."[18]

Nevertheless, even though they had known each other since childhood, the two men never really got along well. Pattullo and King came at Liberalism from opposite directions, and the British Columbian was soon demanding action from the federal government, including an unemployment insurance scheme and improved old-age pensions, both of which King was reluctant to support. Robert Cromie, the editor of the *Vancouver Sun,* wrote Pattullo in February 1935: "You think you will get a lot of action from Mackenzie King; you will get nothing except evasions and promises and procrastinations. So, if the whole Pattullo programme is tied to the time we will get action from Mackenzie King, we are sunk."[19]

Federal-provincial tensions are an inevitable part of the Canadian political system, and British Columbia was no exception. Pattullo turned to Ottawa for loans and loan guarantees but never received as much as he demanded. His reform agenda came into conflict with federal powers, and his complaints soon escalated into demands for modifying the terms of British Columbia's place in Canada. Pattullo emerged as a champion of provincial rights, one of several provincial premiers who were looking to Ottawa for help in solving enormous economic problems and were beginning to question the basic structure of Confederation. The provinces asked for more; Ottawa was less than forthcoming. Still, in the short run, the election of Duff Pattullo gave a great boost to Liberal fortunes in British Columbia in the run-up to the 1935 federal election. It was also clear that federal-provincial relations, taxation powers, and the Constitution would be part of the looming national debate.

It was a similar situation in Saskatchewan, where the provincial Conservatives won in 1930 but, after four years in office, proved

unable to combat the effects of the Depression. The government of
J.T.M. Anderson was in disarray and now faced a well-organized
Liberal opposition led by James Gardiner. Like Pattullo, Gardiner
was an Ontarian who moved west to seek his fortune. He entered
Saskatchewan politics in 1914 and served as a minister in the government of Charles Dunning in the 1920s. He became premier from
1926 to 1929 after Dunning left for Ottawa to serve as Mackenzie
King's finance minister (until his electoral defeat in 1930). Gardiner
was a veteran and partisan Liberal and was well liked by King. When
King was defeated in the 1925 election, Gardiner found him a seat
in Prince Albert, Saskatchewan. King won the seat again in 1930,
and, quite happy with being the sitting member for Prince Albert,
he planned to run there again in 1935.

In the Saskatchewan election on June 19, 1934, the Liberals won
fifty of fifty-five seats and 48 percent of the vote. The Farmer-Labour
group – one of the groups affiliated with the CCF – won five seats
and 24 percent of the vote, while the incumbent governing Conservatives were wiped out, with no seats and only 27 percent of the
vote. Even rising Conservative politician John Diefenbaker was
defeated in the riding of Prince Albert and left politics for several
years. In 1934, Saskatchewan remained a two-party province, but
now it had a Farmer-Labour/CCF opposition.

As the new premier, Gardiner worked with the Bennett government in Ottawa to put together an aid package for his devastated
province, and a federal-provincial relief agreement was signed.
Meanwhile, the federal Liberals were the big winner in Saskatchewan
– Mackenzie King now had a staunch ally in Regina and knew he
could count on him for support once the federal campaign began.
Gardiner may have already set his sights on a federal appointment
should the Liberals sweep back into office nationally.

Manitoba was an outlier in provincial politics – the only province where the governing party was not thrown out of office at some
point during the decade. Throughout the 1930s, the government

was led by John Bracken, another Ontario-born Westerner, who had taught at the newly created University of Saskatchewan. In 1922, the United Farmers of Manitoba (UFM) won a surprise victory in the provincial election. Perhaps the most surprised of all were the UFM members, who had not yet bothered to select a leader. After some soul searching, they invited Bracken, who was not a member of the party, to take over as premier. Thus, without a seat in the legislature and with no political experience, Bracken became premier of Manitoba, a job he held for the next twenty-one years.

The UFM soon changed its name to the Progressive Party of Manitoba, but the quiet teetotalling Bracken led a rather conservative, rural-focused government, although he did introduce a provincial income tax and various other reformist measures. Less charismatic or outgoing than Pattullo or Gardiner, he maintained his majority throughout the decade, but in 1932, facing a resurging Conservative opposition, he engineered a coalition with the Liberals and won the provincial election later that year. What emerged in Manitoba was largely a Liberal government in all but name, and by 1935 it was focused on ejecting from Ottawa the Bennett Conservatives and their high-tariff policies.

However outgoing and colourful Pattullo and Gardiner may have been, they paled in comparison with Ontario's Mitch Hepburn. First elected to the House of Commons in 1926, Hepburn was re-elected in 1930, making him a rare Ontario bright spot in what was otherwise a bleak Liberal outcome. His standing in the party rose quickly, but he chafed in opposition and felt overlooked by King, and at the end of 1930 he announced that he would seek the provincial Liberal leadership. King was less than enthusiastic about Hepburn's prospects or about having to fight a by-election to preserve Hepburn's seat in the House of Commons.[20] In the event, Hepburn retained his federal seat until the Ontario provincial election was called for June 1934. By then, Liberal prospects were much improved.

King also disapproved of Hepburn's colourful lifestyle and considered him unstable and unpredictable. "Mitch Hepburn was unique," wrote his biographer. "Hot and impulsive, incapable of imposing restraint on his private life, and hyperbolic in speech and behaviour, he lived on the edge of his physical and emotional resources."[21] He was also self-confident and informal, erratic, and a populist politician and demagogue. Or, as described by Toronto's *Mail and Empire*, Hepburn was "a Hitler, a Mussolini, a Napoleon, a Caesar and an Alexander the Great all rolled into one."[22] For Mackenzie King, such qualities did not lend themselves well to sober and thoughtful political leadership.

The Ontario Liberal Party inherited by Mitch Hepburn had been out of office and wandering the political wilderness since 1905. At Queen's Park, Conservative premier George Henry ruled, having replaced Howard Ferguson in 1930 when the latter left Ontario politics to become Canada's High Commissioner in London. Henry was a political veteran with considerable executive experience, but he was largely ineffective in dealing with the Depression, and by 1934 Ontario voters were looking for change. Hepburn was able to overcome the Conservative stranglehold on Ontario, attracting support from various non-Conservative sources, including the United Farmers of Ontario, labour groups, and progressives. He was young and dynamic, and he promised action at a time when action was felt to be necessary. In the 1934 election, his party swept the province, winning seventy-one of ninety seats; only Toronto remained in Conservative hands.

As premier, Hepburn is perhaps best remembered for auctioning forty-seven Tory automobiles in Toronto's Varsity Stadium before a cheering crowd of eight thousand on August 27, 1934. The stunt earned approximately $34,000 for the province and a good deal of notoriety, applause, and popularity for Hepburn. He was a populist showman, but more important for the 1935 federal election, he was also now in charge of the most populous province, and for the first time in decades, the federal Liberal Party could rely on the support of the governing party in Toronto. Moreover, the provincial wings of the Liberal Party were essential to party organization, especially when it came to fundraising. Hepburn would have his say and play a critical role in the 1935 Liberal victory.

Things were reversed in Quebec, where Liberals had been in power for as long as anyone could remember. The Conservative opposition roamed the political wilderness while the Liberals took the heat for their failure to alleviate the worst effects of the Depression. Louis-Alexandre Taschereau's Liberal government, in office since 1920, was very much under attack for lack of action, for corruption, and for selling out the province's economy to American capitalists. The pulp and paper industry – central to Quebec's resource-based economy – was devastated, along with other key sectors of the economy. The birth rate was falling, immigration was down, and rural depopulation, already a chronic issue, was accelerating. People were looking for solutions in all sorts of places.

At the same time, progressive elements in the Quebec Liberal Party, along with some Catholic leaders, issued a more progressive platform calling for widespread social reforms, but of a non-socialist nature. The initial goal was to reform the party, but by early 1935 this seemed unattainable, and a more formal break was made, leading to the creation of a new political movement, the Action Libérale Nationale (ALN), led by Liberal Paul Gouin, son of the former premier, Sir Lomer Gouin. The ALN called for an end to political corruption, support for rural Quebec, colonization schemes, the protection of French Canadian culture and way of life, and action against the foreign domination of Quebec's economy. While technically still within the Liberal Party, the ALN appealed to a small group of younger, more nationalistic Liberal reformers, many of whom were disappointed with Taschereau and his government.

The wildcard in this developing situation was Maurice Duplessis. First elected as a Conservative in Trois-Rivières in 1927, he immediately rose to prominence in what was a very small party. He was temporary leader of the opposition in the Quebec legislature by 1932, and became official leader of the Conservatives in 1933, replacing Camillien Houde, the colourful mayor of Montreal, who had lost his seat in the 1931 provincial election. Duplessis took over a party that had been in opposition since 1897. Although never closely allied with the federal Conservative Party, Quebec Conservatives had a difficult time distinguishing themselves from the former in the mind of the average Quebec voter. Nevertheless, Conservative fortunes were on the rise in the province, first in the 1930 federal election and then in the 1931 provincial campaign. There was reason for optimism: business circles in English Quebec were staunchly Conservative and the party could count on a handful of seats in the Montreal region; in addition, there was still considerable Conservative support in the agricultural regions of the province.

Despite differences in policy and style, and even mutual suspicions, an alliance of convenience emerged in 1935 between the ALN and Duplessis to challenge the entrenched, powerful Liberal government. The ALN provided new ideas and fresh faces; Duplessis provided financial backing and organizing experience. By November that year, this informal alliance had sparked the creation of the Union Nationale; within a year, Duplessis had solidified his position as leader and swept the 1936 provincial election, inaugurating the Duplessis era, which would dominate Quebec politics until his death in 1959. For most of the 1935 federal campaign, however, he sat on the sidelines, even as his flirtation with the ALN caused considerable concern, and Quebec politics remained very fluid.

For the federal Liberals, a Quebec victory in the approaching election was almost certain, unless their campaign was dragged under by the unpopularity of the provincial government or the party was split between rival factions. There were concerns that the rift between the ALN and Taschereau would turn into a major rupture before election day, forcing many federal Liberals to choose sides, something they were reluctant to do. For example, despite his close connection with Taschereau, leading Quebec Liberal MP Ernest Lapointe did not want to break with the ALN before the federal election, even as the ALN grew closer to Duplessis and the Conservatives.[23] Premier Taschereau insisted, however, that there was only one Liberal Party – his – and the federal wing ultimately agreed.[24] Fortunately for the federal Liberals (but not for Taschereau), the breach in the Quebec wing did not occur until a few weeks *after* the national campaign.

In the Maritimes, the tough times and regional disparity of the 1920s continued through the even tougher years of the 1930s. As with the prairies, the east coast economy was more dependent than Central Canada on primary production and the export of fish, lumber, pulp and paper, and agricultural products. Coal and steel production fell to historic lows, and municipal governments proved unable to handle the demands for local relief. By 1933, some 12 percent of the Maritime population was on relief.[25] The voices of these smaller provinces were drowned out by those of the larger ones, which only made things worse.

The Conservative Party's luck ran out in the Maritimes. Holding office in all three provinces at the height of the Depression but being unable to do very much about it ensured a political backlash at the polls as blame for the Depression was distributed across the region. Being associated with the federal Conservatives, whose popularity was falling just as rapidly, did not help either. All three provincial governments implemented various old-age pension schemes, public works programs, and other relief projects, and all pointed out the inequities and injustices of the current state of affairs and called for better terms within Confederation. As in the other provinces, however, the political trend was Liberal.

In Prince Edward Island, the Conservative government, first elected under James D. Stewart in 1931 and now led by William MacMillan, had run out of steam by 1934 and was defeated by farmer-turned-politician and former premier Walter Lea. Lea's Liberals swept the province, leaving the Conservatives without a single seat in the legislature. In Nova Scotia, following the federal election of 1930, Premier E.N. Rhodes departed for Ottawa to join Bennett's cabinet, leaving Gordon Harrington in charge. It was Harrington who bore the brunt of the Depression, and when he failed to deliver, his government was defeated by former Dalhousie law professor and rising Liberal star Angus L. Macdonald. Macdonald himself had entered provincial politics only after his defeat in the 1930 federal election, but once in office he went on to win re-election in 1937. The Conservative government in New Brunswick went through several leadership changes in the early 1930s, but even the eminent L.P.D. Tilley – grandson of Sir Leonard – could not hold on to power and was defeated in June 1935 by Liberal lawyer Allison Dysart, who reduced the Conservatives to only eight seats and became the province's first Roman Catholic premier.

By the summer of 1935, on the eve of the federal election campaign, one provincial government after another had switched from Conservative to Liberal control, except Quebec (which was already Liberal) and Alberta. The significance for the federal contest was clear. As Mackenzie King wrote in his diary after listening to the provincial electoral returns from New Brunswick, "this victory, on top of British Columbia, Saskatchewan, Ontario, and Nova Scotia, makes five provinces in succession in which Tory governments have been overthrown and replaced by Liberals with overwhelming majorities." R.B. Bennett had no one but himself to blame, King concluded; it was a fatal error to have put off for so long the calling of the federal election. "It makes practically certain a Liberal sweep for the whole Dominion."[26]

The advent of Liberal provincial governments gave a huge boost to Liberal fortunes nationally in the months leading to the 1935 election. The federal wing of the party was in many ways reliant on the provincial wings for organization, fundraising, and constituency matters. There were still a few areas of concern: the party in Quebec was facing growing turmoil with the split between Taschereau and the ALN; Pattullo in British Columbia was moving in a noticeably different direction from his federal counterparts; in Ontario, Hepburn was a bit of a wild card who, if not handled properly, could play spoiler in the most populous province; and in the rest of the provinces there was always the question whether loyalty to the national party would transcend more local politics. But there were now allies in almost every province who could be counted on for at least some campaign support; this was of enormous value for the Liberal challengers in the 1935 election – and something that the Conservatives, CCF, and Social Credit could only dream of.

The emergence of the CCF and the victory of Social Credit in Alberta also complicated the federal election campaign. The origins of the two new parties differed: the CCF began with national ambitions and dreams of forming a federal government, whereas Social Credit began as a provincial party and its national dimension was largely an extension of that provincial reality. A national party in the usual sense had no time to emerge since the federal election followed Aberhart's victory by only a few weeks. Its federal candidates would benefit from the enthusiasm in the air and could rely on the support and the work of the thousands of Albertans who kept the faith during that summer, but Social Credit's scope would be more limited, with the party having less time or even desire to expand on a national scale. There is some doubt as to whether Aberhart's appeal would have extended beyond rural Alberta or Saskatchewan in any event, but without national or other regional leaders, Social Credit was destined to play a less dynamic role in the 1935 federal campaign.

If the CCF made a misstep – and it was a misstep only in hind-sight – it was affiliating with the United Farmers of Alberta in 1932. On the one hand, it made sense to form an alliance with the party that had been in power since 1921, because it brought the new party close to the centre of power. And at first it seemed to work, with UFA-CCF candidates contesting and winning a couple of provin-cial by-elections in Alberta before the 1935 federal election. On the other hand, the CCF bet on the wrong horse by allying itself with what was by then a fairly conservative and moribund UFA govern-ment that had drifted far from its more socialist origins. The CCF ran no candidates in the 1935 provincial election and threw its support behind the UFA, but as the political winds shifted in favour of the Social Credit Party, the UFA slid into oblivion and the CCF found itself shut out of Alberta – a province where under normal circumstances its platform might have been received with consider-able sympathy.

As with the "radicalism" of the new provincial premiers, it is not always easy to pigeonhole the two new parties. There were differ-ences in style, of course. The CCF seemed intent on educating people, asking them to join teams, clubs, and associations as well as a political party, all in an effort to convince them of the evils of modern capitalist life. Social Credit was based more on faith and asked people to follow a leader; you didn't need to understand it, you just needed to put the right person in charge. Moreover, whereas the Social Credit Party wanted to make the existing system work better, to make it work for the average Albertan and Canadian, the CCF wanted to change the system itself.

Beyond these, however, there were great similarities. Both the CCF and Social Credit advocated more government involvement in managing the economy and money supply, both offered protec-tion from the malevolent economic forces in society, and both of-fered potential solutions to the worst economic crisis in Canadian history. Both promised dramatic action that hinted at a fundamental radicalism. Both parties targeted similar villains – the "big shots" who had created the mess Canadians found themselves in during the Depression. Both attacked big business, the financial interests, the callous disregard in Ottawa for the suffering of the average Canadian, and, of course, the biggest big shot of all, R.B. Bennett. When the federal campaign began, one of the new parties issued a series of pamphlets condemning the Liberals for starting the Depression and portraying Mackenzie King as the office boy of the "big-shots." The heading of one pamphlet read: "Bank Robbers Get Billions but the BIG-SHOT BANKER IS A BIGGER CRIMINAL THAN THE GUNMAN because the banker's greed hurts all the people all the time." The question is whether most Canadians would have been able to distinguish whether such rhetoric came from the campaign literature of the CCF or the Social Credit Party.[27]

As the federal campaign switched into high gear in the summer of 1935, there were Liberal premiers almost everywhere and two new Western-based parties in the contest. A number of things were yet to be determined. What impact would these provincial premiers have on the election campaign? What relationship would the new parties have? Would they cooperate or would they compete for the few ridings that might be open to a third-party candidate? Did the advent of the parties portend a sea change in Canadian electoral politics, or would it produce needless vote splitting, leading to the re-election of Liberals and Conservatives? The winds of political change may have shifted, but it remained to be seen how far these new parties and new premiers could sway public opinion. They now faced their greatest task: convincing the Canadian public to vote for them.

3

It's Time for a New Deal

Not in thirty years have pre-election trumpets sounded so
uncertainly, or has there been as much doubt about who
shall go forward to battle, or under whom, or about what.
The whole thing is a jig-saw puzzle, pathetically confusing.

– *Maclean's,* July 1, 1935[1]

ON THE SECOND DAY of January 1935, Prime Minister R.B. Bennett
walked into an Ottawa radio station to announce a new direction
for his government, for himself personally, and, he hoped, for the
people of Canada. Bennett knew that – barring a constitutional
amendment to the contrary – there would have to be a federal
election in the coming year. Five years of Depression had taken an
enormous toll on Canadians, and he and his party would likely be
held accountable. It was time for bold action if he was to save his
government and to have any future as prime minister. He could not
say how the year would end but, if nothing else, he would have his
say about how it began.

The new course that he launched that night would be given a
label he never actually used himself: Bennett's New Deal. Bennett

was well known for spontaneity in his public pronouncements – facing down both hecklers on the campaign trail and opposition MPs in the House of Commons – but there was no shooting from the hip when it came to his New Deal. The speeches were well planned – he had been working on their content for weeks with the help of two confidants, Rod Finlayson and William Herridge. Finlayson, a Winnipeg lawyer, was enticed to Ottawa to serve as Bennett's executive assistant and speech writer. Herridge was Bennett's brother-in-law and Canada's minister to Washington, where he had a first-hand look at President Franklin Roosevelt's New Deal. He liked what he heard of Roosevelt's fireside radio chats and sent Bennett a steady stream of positive reports on Roosevelt's successes. The Americans were suffering from the Depression as much as Canadians, if not more, and Roosevelt's New Deal seemed to speak to the desperation of millions of Americans who turned to their government for any kind of leadership and action that promised to alleviate the dismal economic conditions. Perhaps, Herridge argued, a dynamic plan of action, containing sweeping reforms and clear goals, set out by the prime minister on radio – in other words, a Canadian version of the New Deal – might work similar magic on the Canadian electorate.

The Bennett New Deal unfolded through a series of five radio broadcasts spread over ten days, from January 2 to 11. The broadcasts were made from Ottawa's CRCO studios beginning at 9 p.m., and the air time was paid for out of Bennett's own pocket. Each lasted approximately thirty minutes. The speeches were picked up and broadcast simultaneously on thirty-eight other stations across the country, from Vancouver, British Columbia, to Sydney, Nova Scotia. Just about every Canadian could listen in.[2]

Bennett began with a sweeping examination of the difficult challenges facing Canadians after five years of Depression. It was a "critical hour in the history of our country," he began, and "momentous questions wait your decision. Our future course must now be charted." He claimed to know that future course and confirmed that he would captain the ship. "The old order is gone," he announced. "It will not return. We are living amidst conditions which are new and strange to us." He then reviewed the situation he had inherited and what his government had been able to accomplish in the past five years. In 1930, the country was in crisis and needed decisive action to "avert shipwreck," he said, maintaining the nautical metaphor; the system needed saving and support, not experiment. At that time, it was too dangerous to introduce radical reforms; recovery was needed first, then reform. Then he added, as if anticipating future questions about his sincerity and why he had waited five years to do all these things that were now self-evidently necessary, "We had to defer reform until the time for reform had come." Well, the time for reform *had* come, and there was much work to be done.

Veteran Winnipeg journalist Grant Dexter commented on the first speech that Bennett had "made rather a mess of this speech as he became nervous in the middle of it, believing he lacked time to complete the manuscript. He began to race, stumbled and fumbled and, in the latter passages, was not his usual rhetorical self." Mackenzie King feigned disdain but was drawn to his radio like a moth to a flame, convinced that Bennett had stolen his ideas from *Industry and Humanity,* King's own book. "It is plagiarism of the most obvious kind, with the most nauseating self-sufficiency & egotism," he wrote. "He is pretty sure to divide his own party, and neutralize his efforts in a campaign."[3] Clearly, though, Bennett was on to something, and letters of congratulations and support flooded into his office from across the country. People wanted to hear what he had to say, and his delivery improved with each new broadcast.

In subsequent speeches, the prime minister addressed the problems of income inequality and called for sweeping legislation introducing minimum wages and a maximum work week; for an end to all child labour and sweatshop working conditions; for unemployment insurance and an improved old-age pension system; for health insurance and civil service reform; and for more support for farmers beyond what was contained in bills passed the previous year.

> Our task – simple in theory, difficult in performance – is to replace in the old system those elements which are worn out, broken down, obsolete, and without further utility, so that the system may work. Perhaps some would call that "radicalism." If it is, it is the sort of radicalism you will have a lot more to do with, so long as we live under a well-ordered system.

Nothing can cool Canadian passions for radical reform or dampen enthusiasm for social transformation faster than someone asking the question: Is it constitutional? This question, however, sat like a stone at the bottom of the New Deal proposals. Minimum wages, child labour laws, health insurance, and so on were known to fall under provincial jurisdiction; how could the federal government do all these wonderful things without either provincial support or fundamental constitutional change? The "provinces had a prior right re: property & civil rights & that I believed such legislation wd be declared ultra vires," King complained privately, "as Bennett time & again has said himself it would be."[4] Any move to change the Constitution in Ottawa's favour would face an uphill battle in Quebec, against both the provincial government and the church hierarchy, and there would be a backlash from other provinces as well. It was the classic political debate in Depression-era Canada, and it was a question Bennett was forced to address.

Bennett faced the issue squarely, arguing that he could implement these proposals without undermining the Constitution. Section 132 of the British North America Act (BNA Act) gave Ottawa the responsibility for implementing foreign treaties. This section had little relevance in 1867, but by 1935 Canada had signed a few treaties independently of Britain and joined a variety of international organizations, and Ottawa was responsible for implementing the international conventions and other agreements arising from those treaty obligations. As a signatory of the Treaty of Versailles, for example, Canada committed itself to maintaining good working conditions within its borders, controlling disease, and ensuring the "just treatment of the native inhabitants of territory under their control" (article 23). Canada had also joined the International Labour Organization and thereby committed itself to the various employment standards set out in its charter. These may have been matters of a local nature under the BNA Act, Bennett argued, but Canada's growing international responsibilities made it necessary for the federal government to intervene and legislate in these areas. If the government of Canada, through international agreement, committed itself to the setting of wages, hours of work, and other social reforms, it then fell to the government of Canada to implement them.[5]

In addition, in 1932 the Judicial Committee of the Privy Council (JCPC), the highest court in the British Empire, ruled in favour of the federal government in two important cases, one dealing with aeronautics and the other with radio broadcasting, and supported the federal government's role in both fields. The decisions were based on section 91 (residual clause) of the BNA Act, which granted Ottawa jurisdiction in areas not covered in the act. The courts appeared to be moving towards supporting federal power over provincial power; would this not also apply to the responsibility for relief, unemployment, and fair wages? For Bennett, the answer was self-evident; for others, considerable doubt remained.

In the later addresses, Bennett shifted to a more partisan, political tone. All his new plan, he explained, would be left to the Canadian people to decide:

If you say yes, then I will not rest until I have put it into operation. But if you say no – if you are satisfied with conditions as they now are, if you think that there is not need for reform, if you feel that the Government is not required to do anything more – then I am not willing to continue in this office. For if you believe that things should be left as they are, you and I hold contrary and irreconcilable views. I am for reform.

In what was beginning to sound like a campaign speech, he concluded: "Your country's future is at stake. This is no time to indulge your personal prejudices or fancies. Carefully and calmly, look well into the situation. Then pick the man and the policy best fitted to deal with it. And resolutely back that man and that policy." If you opposed his reforms, believed in inaction and in laissez-faire in the marketplace, then you must support the Liberal Party; but if you wanted progress, reform, and the mitigation of the abuses of the capitalist system, then you must vote Conservative. "Do you want reform, or do you not want reform?" he asked. "If you do not want it, back the Liberal Party. If you do want it, back my party." In asking Canadians to make that one clear choice, he held out one last glimmer of hope for his re-election.

The New Deal and Its Critics

The initial reaction to the New Deal broadcasts was favourable. Bennett could be dynamic and enthusiastic when he wanted to, he was an effective orator, and the speeches had sufficient evangelical flavour to capture people's attention, if not their imagination. Radio was still new enough to heighten public interest, and thousands of Canadians tuned in each night to listen to the prime minister. Those without radios joined friends who had one – everyone wanted to play their part in what had become a national event. The term "Bennett Parties" was soon used to describe groups of people who gathered around a radio to listen to the popular New Deal broadcasts,[6] which came at a time when Canadians were willing to listen to new ideas – any ideas – that might help alleviate the Depression. How long that popularity would last remained to be seen.

Bennett's cabinet colleagues were likely more surprised than upset at the broadcasts because the prime minister had divulged none of his plans to them, even at a cabinet meeting just a few days earlier. That the whole New Deal emerged from Bennett's brain, with the help of Herridge and Finlayson but with no consultation or input from the Conservative Party, the Conservative caucus in Parliament, or cabinet members was not, at first, of much concern. This omission would, of course, have serious political ramifications. Robert Manion, the minister of railways and canals, supported the thrust of Bennett's new plan but recorded his initial reaction: "R.B. Broadcast 9 p.m. Jan. 2, 1935 – new policy of reform – never submitted to council." Later he added: "R.B.B. giving his third broadcast tonight ... Has not mentioned the matter in cab. Insulting!"[7] It was typical of Bennett's style.

Some government members liked what they heard; others were horrified. Justice Minster Hugh Guthrie was very enthusiastic and suggested dissolving Parliament immediately and going to the country, using the broadcasts as a springboard into a spring election campaign. An election had to be fought that year, so why not go now and ride the enthusiasm sparked by the speeches? Many other Tories across the country came out in support; if nothing else, the New Deal broadcasts sparked a little enthusiasm in the party and galvanized the troops. Conservative newspapers – from the *London Free Press* and Toronto *Mail and Empire* in the east to the *Winnipeg Tribune* and *Calgary Daily Herald* in the West – were guarded but not opposed. The Vancouver *Daily Province* was pleased that Bennett had at last turned the tables on the Liberals; it editorialized that Bennett "has stolen Mr. Mackenzie King's thunder, and all the possible planks of his platform. He bids fair, even, to steal Mr. King's horses and not a few of Mr. King's men."[8]

Still, there were concerns about how the business community and financial interests would respond, and worries about how the New Deal would be received in Quebec, where the Catholic Church was likely to oppose anything that even remotely smelled of socialism. Several of the old-guard Conservatives were not pleased: Finance Minister E.N. Rhodes disapproved, Minister without Portfolio Sir George Perley and Revenue Minister Robert Matthews were unimpressed, and Secretary of State Charles Cahan considered resigning from cabinet.[9] In Montreal, the *Gazette* had its own spin: Bennett was less the reformer and more the raider as he appealed "to the people of Canada for support of his proposed further invasion by the state into the field of private rights." It was the "opening of the election campaign," the *Gazette* pronounced, and the speeches were "devised to make up for the time lost by a tardy establishment of the party organization for the coming campaign."[10]

Bennett was immediately criticized for pilfering the ideas of the Canadian left, even though he argued that he was trying to *save* capitalism and the free market, not overthrow it or replace it with socialism. Everyone listened to Bennett speak of the need for unemployment insurance, minimum wages, and shorter work hours, but almost everyone remembered an earlier time when he railed against such policies, claiming that they were impossible to implement. Speaking in Newmarket, Ontario, Agnes Macphail denounced the entire thing. Bennett was "five years too late with his speeches," she said. "Those speeches show how powerful the C.C.F. has become."[11] CCF leader J.S. Woodsworth sent Mackenzie King a clipping of an editorial cartoon depicting Bennett driving off in an automobile with a woman representing the New Deal, while King chased after them, yelling that Bennett had stolen his material.[12]

Bennett had also been saying for five years that the economy was improving, that things were getting better, and that prosperity was just around the corner; now he seemed to be saying the opposite, that the whole system needed to be turned on its head. Was it just coincidence, many commentators asked, that this deathbed conversion occurred during the run-up to an election? Historian Frank Underhill wrote in the *Canadian Forum* soon after the broadcast: "Of course Mr. Bennett is sincere when on the eve of a general election he suddenly announces a new policy which is a reversal of all the past record of himself and party. He possesses in a supreme degree the politician's greatest asset, the capacity for auto-intoxication." Others were just left scratching their heads. "The man who only a few weeks before had intervened personally to prevent [communist politician] Tim Buck speaking in an Ottawa theatre, was speaking as Tim Buck himself might have spoken in his less violent moods," concluded a *Maclean's* columnist. "A curious contradiction, surely, is our Prime Minister."[13]

In Quebec, the New Deal was seen as a Trojan Horse: promises of progressive social legislation with the seeds of centralization of power in Ottawa buried within. Even if they liked some of what they heard, for Quebec nationalists, "Laurentian" separatists, and progressives, including some of the disgruntled Liberals who had recently bolted the party to form the fledgling Action Libérale Nationale (ALN), there were concerns that the New Deal would infringe upon provincial jurisdiction.[14] The provincial Liberal government of Louis-Alexandre Taschereau was equally unimpressed, as were, for the same reasons, many federal Quebec Liberals, such as Ernest Lapointe. Even if they were sympathetic to the New Deal policies, defending provincial rights was always good politics in Quebec.

In Toronto, Vincent Massey, president of the National Liberal Federation of Canada, mocked Bennett's deathbed conversion to liberalism in a letter to a British colleague. Bennett "is as versatile as ever," he noted, "and has now discovered that he has always been an ardent reformer and as a self-appointed St. George is out to slay the dragon of 'uncontrolled capitalism,' of which until a few months ago he was the leading defender." Massey was even moved to express himself in verse with a lengthy poem deriding the New Deal, for circulation among friends. It included these lines:

> *More verbal thunderbolts the earth to shake,*
> *But honest citizens will not mistake*
> *The glib and unctuous for something real,*
> *Old dealer's junk for genuine "new deal."*[15]

Mackenzie King was beside himself over what he had heard. He described the scene in his diary: on the eve of final broadcast, he "had a bath, then dinner, and read paper awhile then read Bennett's 4th speech over the radio. Listened to most of it after concluding the reading of the press releases." His anger grew:

I felt humiliated to think of the country being in the hands of such a man. I uttered spontaneously the words "what a buffoon." It was really pathetic, the absolute rot & gush he talked – platitudes – unction, & what not, a mountebank and hypocrite, full of bombast & egotism – talk of <u>my</u> reforms, wishing to see it all under way before passing off the scene etc. – no mention of the government or colleagues, or parliament – sickening and disgusting. If the people will "fall for" that kind of thing, there is no saving them, they will deserve all they will get.[16]

King's political instincts quickly reasserted themselves, however, and his thoughts turned to his counterattack and, more importantly, the upcoming election. Most observers predicted an April or May campaign; King reasoned that Bennett might introduce a few pieces of New Deal legislation, dissolve Parliament, and then go to the country on his reform platform. The announcement could come at any time, and the Liberal opposition had to be ready. The day after the final broadcast, King began preparing his response to Bennett's speeches.

What to make of the Bennett New Deal immediately became a bit of a historical parlour game. Did Bennett really plan to reform the capitalist system? What did he hope to achieve? Clearly there was an element of political expediency about the New Deal; after five years in office, his party could hardly boast of success in bringing Canada out of the Depression, and all the signs pointed to Bennett's government being blamed for this failure. A new plan with new ideas might be a way to shift the national focus in another direction. It is easy to speculate that this kind of thinking made it much easier for the rest of the Conservative Party to embrace the new proposals and to embark on this uncharted course of government action and intervention. Bennett's swift embrace of the New Deal, however, was also a testament to how far the Depression had shifted the political centre of gravity in Canada away from its traditional moorings. Bennett may have felt that he had to make an honest attempt to reform his party – even to redefine Canadian conservatism – to address the crisis in the country.

Most critics would not go that far and instead focused on the timing of the speeches. Were they broadcast solely to set out an agenda – *the* agenda – to be followed by appealing to the country for a mandate to bring in these reforms? Journalist Grattan O'Leary certainly believed so; after meeting with Bennett, he had the "clear impression that Bennett proposes to accept any challenge from King to go to the country." In other words, Bennett had only a general plan and few specifics, and the speeches were simply a broad overview of what he hoped to do. He told O'Leary "that he really could not be very specific as not one of the proposed measures had been drafted, or even reduced in broad terms to paper. He had the general outlines in his head. What he is talking about is his election platform."[17] But for the plan to work, it would be necessary for King and the Liberals to play along and come out swinging against the proposals. That way, Bennett could champion the cause of reform and challenge the "stand-pat" Liberals. Would the Liberals take the bait?

If enacted, the New Deal proposals would have situated R.B. Bennett, if perhaps not the entire Conservative Party, to the left of the Liberal Party in terms of campaign promises. It was an area of the political spectrum that was growing more crowded by the week. One joke circulating in Ottawa was that in the past one could find federal politicians who were Liberal, Conservative, or something else; now they were all "Reformers." By the time Canadians voted in October, there would be five major political parties and a host of smaller, independent groups, all advocating "reform" of some sort – to the banks and monetary policy, to capitalism, to trade policy, to the retail industry, to the railways, to foreign policy, to the role of government in Canadian lives, and to society itself. Many promises were made; far fewer were kept. If nothing else, Bennett at least regained the political initiative. But another thing was certain: it was the opening shot in the 1935 federal election campaign. The announcement of Bennett's New Deal was the "end of the beginning" of the national contest; it was also the beginning of the end for R.B. Bennett.

The Politics of the New Deal

On January 14, Prime Minister Bennett hosted a lavish dinner at Ottawa's Château Laurier. It was a farewell dinner for Japanese Minister Iyemasa Tokugawa, who was leaving his Ottawa posting to return with his daughter to Japan. After some pleasantries, Tokugawa remarked to the assembled Ottawa elite that he might one day like to come back to live in Canada. But then, taking a dig at Canada's restrictive immigration laws, he added that he was not sure if he would be allowed back into the country; maybe he could make it as an agricultural labourer? At his table in the audience, Mackenzie King felt a little uneasy and was in a reflective mood. "It was a sumptuous gathering," he wrote. "I could not help thinking that the starving proletariat looking in at the gathering would have thought it a strange sort of beginning to the reform of the capitalistic system."[18]

It was clear to anyone who cared that Bennett's New Deal marked the unofficial launch of the election campaign, but no one knew for sure exactly when the election would be called. Bennett had postponed making the call – likely because of his party's bleak prospects – and the loss of five of six by-elections in 1934 only encouraged further delay. The New Deal speeches, therefore, were intended to rally the party and the country and then be used as a campaign platform for the long-awaited election. Things did not work out as planned, however.

In the days following the radio broadcasts, Bennett took to the road to sell his new proposals, repeating his message in Ontario and Quebec to the Montreal Board of Trade, the Canadian Construction Association, students at Queen's University, and the Young Conservatives Club in Toronto, and to a gathering of Canadians in New York City. He also made an effort to mend his relationship with H.H. Stevens. Cabinet ministers Robert Manion and Richard B. Hanson, who replaced Stevens as minister of trade and commerce, were called on to bring the two former colleagues together, and Stevens and Bennett met and exchanged correspondence outlining their divergent opinions. The halting movement towards reconciliation did not get very far, however. Neither man had had a change of heart. Had Bennett announced his retirement, Stevens would have happily stepped into the prime minister's office, but Bennett appeared more determined than ever to stay on as leader. Stevens was equally adamant.

The parliamentary session – the last before the election – opened on January 17. The Governor General read the Throne Speech laying out plans for sweeping social and economic reforms, new policies and regulations, help for the needy, and protection for masses. One of the first acts of the government was to ratify six draft conventions of the International Labour Organization, dealing with hours of work, minimum wage standards, and other labour protections, in an effort to buttress Bennett's contention that the

The major contenders in the 1935 election: R.B. Bennett and Mackenzie King (March 6, 1934). | Photographer Nelson Quarrington, Library and Archives Canada, PA-148532

federal government had the constitutional authority, under section 132 of the BNA Act, to implement the thrust of the New Deal. In addition, and as promised in the New Deal speeches, the government introduced the Employment and Social Insurance Act, which proposed to establish a national commission leading to the implementation of unemployment insurance in Canada. Over subsequent weeks, additional bills were introduced, dealing with minimum wages, a weekly day of rest, and the eight-hour work day.[19]

Bennett's plan was set out in broad terms in his New Deal proposals. It was expected that the Liberal opposition would do what oppositions do – oppose the plans – and if, as expected, they voted against the proposed reforms, Bennett could call a spring election with his campaign platform in hand. The Conservatives would go into the campaign not defending their past record but rather arguing in favour of the new set of reform proposals. But there was one serious catch: they needed the Liberals to play along.

Within days of the New Deal speeches, King had developed a new strategy to spoil Bennett's plan. At first, he thought the Liberals should come out swinging against Bennett's proposals, but he changed his mind after a long talk with the veteran Liberal Sir William Mulock (who was soon to celebrate his ninety-first birthday). After four or five "full" whiskeys, Mulock started talking about Bennett and warned that it would not be a good idea to obstruct his New Deal – "that it would be better to have Bennett bring in his measures and wait till we saw them before opposing." If Bennett expected Liberal opposition, perhaps the best strategy would be to do the opposite: cooperate. "This will take the Govt. unawares," King wrote in his diary that night. "No doubt Bennett expects a fight, strong opposition & hopes to score on that score." The Liberals would call his bluff and make Bennett produce the reform legislation, then offer to cooperate and to see the legislation passed swiftly through Parliament before the election was called. That way, "Bennett's bubble would be pretty effectively pricked. He will be like a flattened tire in trying to make headway with his reforms."[20]

King decided not to tell the Liberal caucus of his plans to cooperate with the Conservatives, likely from fear of leaks. "We are now in the campaign & must not hand over our tactics to the enemy," he wrote (at the time, he believed the election would come in April). But the Liberal MPs were instructed to speak little in the House and not delay measures, so as to force the Conservatives to introduce the New Deal legislation, which King believed the Tories did not have ready. The Liberals sat back and voted in favour of the Throne Speech, supported the establishment of various committees, and remained silent during private members' resolutions. It seemed to work. By January 25, King was recording that Bennett "is certainly terribly embarrassed. He has not his legislation ready – he was really lying about it, in the presence of his ministers."[21]

Throughout January, there was constant speculation over when the election would be called, and things became even more complicated as Bennett's health began to fail. Late in the month, not long after the resumption of Parliament, he came down with a very bad cold. He refused to rest, and by mid-February the cold had developed into a serious respiratory infection, confining him to bed for several weeks. King had already noticed Bennett's deteriorating condition but remained suspicious. Bennett looked "very tired" in Parliament and had put on weight. "I am amazed he has not collapsed before this; he may do so at any time," King confided to his diary. "We must watch for a dissolution at any time." Then on March 7, while still convalescing at home, Bennett suffered a heart attack. He was believed to be on the mend and was preparing to return to Parliament when he had a seizure.[22] As Charles Cahan told King, "the nurse had gone into his room and found him in a chair unconscious; that his forehead was out in beads of perspiration, and his face as white as a sheet. She did not know whether he was alive or dead and was greatly alarmed."[23] A heart specialist was called in and Bennett was bedridden again, for several more weeks.

With the prime minister not expected back in Parliament for some time, it was left to Deputy Prime Minister Sir George Perley to oversee the government's reform program. The aging Perley faced a number of immediate problems: first, he was never a big supporter of the New Deal to begin with, and second, Bennett had kept everything to himself and within the Prime Minister's Office, and even the cabinet did not know what his plans were. "The matter is very urgent and everyone [is] worried about it," wrote cabinet colleague Robert Manion. The whole Conservative team was "greatly inconvenienced," as Bennett "has kept so many of these reform matters in his own hands, not having discussed many of them with his colleagues." And what if this was the "first step towards retirement" for Bennett – where would that leave the party?[24]

Much of the daily work in the House of Commons fell to Finance Minister Rhodes, but he was handicapped from the start. "The situation in the House is most curious," he wrote former prime minister Robert Borden. "My colleagues are taking up various Bills which stood in the name of the P.M., but, as was his custom, he had kept the contents of the Bills and the material to be used with them, entirely to himself, with the result that we are now in the position of having different Ministers coached by his Secretary."[25] Manion captured the dilemma succinctly in his diary: "R.B. now ill two weeks – are much embarrassed as *he has in his own head* much, if not most, of the leg. proposed."[26]

The uncertainty continued into spring. By April 16, Bennett was well enough to greet the press in his hotel room at the Château Laurier. However, he had earlier pledged to represent Canada at King George V's Silver Jubilee, scheduled for May 6. On April 18, he left for New York and then London, and did not return until May 17. This meant three things: (1) there would be no spring election; (2) the campaign for the New Deal was largely over; and (3) as long as Bennett – the one man in a one-man government – was incapacitated or missing, the government continued to drift, legislation ground to a halt, and plans were left unfinished.

The big question now was whether Bennett would be able to return at all, and if not, who would replace him. Many believed this was Bennett's long goodbye – he would make one last official visit to England and return to announce his retirement. Rumours circulated in Ottawa that Bennett was finished and that Stevens might step into the job; there were other rumours that a national unity government would be formed, again under Stevens's leadership, although some mentioned Charles Dunning, the former Liberal finance minister. Finance Minister Rhodes was also given serious consideration as a replacement, as was the popular but less known Robert Manion. At one cabinet meeting in early March, Rhodes openly speculated on the need for a national unity government to deal with the country's financial problems. He insisted that it was something the country "must have," wrote Manion, who opposed the idea.[27] All the speculation led to the creation of a League for National Government – an organization that claimed a membership of 35,000 – dedicated to the formation of a national unity government following the upcoming election.[28]

King, who was convinced Bennett would retire, even thought that he might be approached to lead a national unity government, but the idea made little sense when the party was already on the verge of an electoral victory – better to sit back and watch the Tories disintegrate. But once Bennett announced he was going to London for the Jubilee, everyone knew the election would not be held until late summer at the earliest. Early in April, King spoke with Perley, who mentioned the first Monday after Labour Day as a possible date.[29] No decision was made, but the talk was now of late summer or early fall for the election campaign.

Bennett seriously considered retirement, especially after his heart attack. In London, he wrote his old friend and Canada's High Commissioner in the United Kingdom, Howard Ferguson: "I doubt very much whether I will be able to go on. If I get half a chance to rest for six months, I will be all right, but as there is an election before that time, it looks to me as though I might have to retire."[30] But there were a number of factors to be considered. His first choice to succeed him was Rhodes, but Rhodes himself was near retirement and declined. Bennett also approached Senator Arthur Meighen, the former prime minister, about returning as leader of the party, but Meighen also – wisely – declined.[31] To further complicate matters, Bennett knew that many of his cabinet colleagues were likely not to run in the next election, let alone stand for the party leadership, so the pool of possible candidates was shrinking rapidly. Whom could he trust? The road to the leadership appeared to be opening wide for H.H. Stevens – a prospect that Bennett considered intolerable.

When Bennett returned from England, the government made one last legislative push before calling the election. On April 12, the Royal Commission on Price Spreads and Mass Buying had issued its report, and Bennett accepted it and was determined to move ahead on its recommendations. The report revealed the enormous wage gaps in manufacturing industries between unionized employees and the non-unionized, in home work and workshops, between men and women, and between provinces; more generally, it revealed just how low wages were, especially for the non-unionized and home-workers. Many Canadians had to work extremely long hours just to make ends meet, and the few labour laws and regulations were regularly evaded, if not completely ignored. The report made several recommendations to protect consumers and the rights of labour, and it advocated the establishment of a government trade commission to regulate competition across the country.

The government enacted a flurry of legislation in June 1935, many of which, though potentially effective, were quickly overshadowed by and forgotten in the election campaign, including the Dominion Housing Act (to help first-time homebuyers with mortgages); the Dominion Trade and Industry Commission Act (a recommendation of the Price Spreads Royal Commission to grant more power to the Tariff Board); and amendments to the 1934 Natural Products Marketing Act (to set up domestic marketing boards for various natural products) and the 1934 Farmers' Creditors Arrangement Act (to remove, in British Columbia, the application of this law in order to enable government officials to negotiate new terms for mortgages to keep farmers on their land). The final bill established the Canadian Wheat Board, a marketing agency to oversee the purchase and distribution of the Canadian wheat crop.

The Liberals were split on the Wheat Board bill (i.e., whether it should be compulsory for farmers to participate), but they supported it in the end. On most of the others, their strategy was to support the bills in principle – for what they hoped to accomplish – but to oppose them on constitutional grounds, namely, that the federal government was intervening in provincial matters through extensive social legislation. King was certain that the Conservatives' plan was to paint the Liberals as opponents of these reforms and thus frame the election campaign, and he was determined to not let it happen. He condemned the Conservatives for politicizing what was a constitutional matter that could be settled only in the courts. "We believe the attempt of the government to make a controversy over provincial rights a major issue of the coming elections would, if successful, endanger the unity of the dominion," he announced in the House of Commons. "If parliament possessed the jurisdiction, we would vote for the measures of social legislation thus far introduced." He then concluded with a double negative typical of the man: "The position at present, therefore, is ... we do not know that parliament does not possess the jurisdiction."[32] On this, and on many aspects of Bennett's New Deal, the CCF agreed. It supported much of the reforms in principle, but on the constitutional question it backed the Liberals and called for an amendment of the BNA Act to give the federal government more powers to deal with these serious economic issues.

The Rise of the Reconstruction Party

The question of Bennett's future lingered throughout the parliamentary session, but it was his relationship with H.H. Stevens that brought matters to a head. Bennett's health had not completely recovered, and he had other good reasons to retire. After meeting with him on his return from Britain, King described Bennett as "a very sick man ... his breath was bad, his eyes are very contracted, looks like a man who had suffered some great fright – or was being hunted with fear. He said to me 'they said I shouldn't be here' now." But King also understood why he could not leave: "It is only because of his hatred of Stevens and his determination not to allow him to succeed to the leadership, and his inability to find any other leader, that he now finds it necessary to stay with the party through the campaign." King turned it into a backhanded compliment, adding that Bennett was right to stay on as leader because he "is the man the people rightly wish to defeat."[33]

Throughout Bennett's illness and absence in England, Stevens continued what had become an unofficial campaign for Bennett's job. He had returned to Parliament in March and repeatedly attacked the government, particularly Charles Cahan. "He was very demagogic," King later wrote in his diary. "I shall not soon forget the scene. The Ministers looked chagrined beyond words, Perley crouched beside Guthrie both with their heads down, others were in similar attitudes ... Stevens clearly is making a brazen attempt to secure leadership of the party." Relations deteriorated so badly that a few weeks later, Cahan told King that if Stevens ever took over the leadership of the Conservative Party, he and the financial and commercial interests he represented would throw their support behind King and the Liberals.[34] By then, Cahan was referring to it as a crisis in the Conservative Party.

All of this made Stevens a bit of a wild card. There was open speculation in the party about the leadership, and MPs began taking sides. Many questioned whether Stevens should be embraced so as to ensure a united Conservative Party on the campaign trail, while others believed the gap had grown too large. Stevens did not challenge Bennett directly, but in the Conservative caucus, there was growing support for Stevens to stay in the party and even to become leader, and this group included several cabinet ministers. There were also whispers about breaking with the party altogether to form a rival organization, and rumours circulated that Stevens had discussed with a couple of wealthy and influential Montrealers (including Sir Edward Beatty of the Canadian Pacific Railway and long-time Conservative Sir Herbert Holt) the formation of a new National Party with Stevens at the helm.[35]

The appearance of the Price Spreads Royal Commission report and Bennett's efforts to implement aspects of it only gave Stevens more ammunition. On June 5, before a crowd of three thousand in Toronto's Massey Hall, he attacked Bennett's bill to create a trade and industry commission under control of the Tariff Board. The speech drew a strong rebuttal from Bennett in the House of Commons on June 10, and the split between the two men broke wide open in Parliament. Stevens was demanding far too much, according to Bennett, who, perhaps unintentionally, played right into the hands of the Liberals by claiming that what Stevens demanded was unconstitutional – precisely the argument the Liberals were making about his New Deal legislation. "This country has a constitution," Bennett thundered in the House on June 19; "it is a federal union." Any disregard for this fact was "the first step towards fascism."[36]

Few Conservative MPs expressed support for Stevens following Bennett's outburst, and most remained silent when the former minister spoke (most of those who applauded were Liberals). Stevens must have been surprised at how quickly his support from within Conservative ranks evaporated. Days later, he accused his colleagues of dereliction of duty in "not long ago resisting the domineering attitude of their Leader." He wrote to a Toronto friend: "They will talk, as most of them did, very freely behind his back, but for some reason or other, with a few exceptions, were afraid to express their views to his face. Had they done so things would have been much different today."[37] Mackenzie King quickly noticed the changing mood:

> It was apparent, in the House, that Stevens had lost out, with the probability that Bennett was going to continue as leader. Practically all the applause was given to Bennett; very little to Stevens, revealing what a lot of sycophants the members of the Tory party are. When they thought Stevens was going to become the leader, they were three-quarters for him. Now that Bennett had asserted his authority, they are wholly for him ... They lie down like a lot of whipped curs.

I cannot imagine a party in a more uncomfortable position than they are.[38]

That night, the Conservative caucus toasted Bennett, who hinted that he would lead the party again in the next election. There was no one left whom Bennett trusted or saw as a replacement if he retired, and it seemed that Stevens would be the likely – perhaps the only – choice to take his place, which he found unacceptable. All efforts to rein in Stevens had failed, and the personal relationship had descended into bitterness, aggravated by Stevens's continuous attacks on the party in the House of Commons. For someone of Bennett's temperament, these were acts of betrayal and disloyalty that could not be walked back. Stevens could not become leader of the party and prime minister. Bennett would have to stay on despite the risk to his health. Stevens had lit a fuse and Bennett came out swinging, and the party rallied behind him.[39] He made his decision official on July 5, informing his caucus that despite his heart condition and other health worries, he would be staying on. "I'll die in harness rather than quit now," he announced.[40]

The break between Bennett and Stevens was final. Stevens had briefly attended a Conservative caucus meeting in June but left when he was ignored by Bennett. He later claimed he had not even been invited to the meeting, which he took as a sign of his ouster from the party. If Bennett had instructed the chief whip to withhold the invitation, "it is tantamount to saying that as far as he is concerned, and as far as the Party is concerned (if there is no protest) the individual thus treated is considered to be no longer a member of the party. No other interpretation is possible."[41]

Stevens formally left the Conservative Party on July 7. He held a press conference to announce the formation of his own party, soon to be dubbed the Reconstruction Party of Canada. Bennett's actions were leading to the "ruination of the Conservative Party," he wrote three days earlier, and under his leadership the party had not the "remotest chance for success at the coming election." Like Caesar, he had resisted the "very strong demand for me to lead a third party,"[42] but the pressure soon became irresistible. Stevens claimed to have in his possession twenty thousand letters from all the provinces, from sitting MPs, local boards of trade, Conservative associations, clergy, and university professors, and a cross-section of workers, small business people, farmers, fishers, and professionals, urging him to break out on his own. The tipping point was a delegation of supporters that presented him with a resolution from a conference of small business people meeting in Hamilton, calling on him to launch a new party.

Stevens claimed that he based his decision on his dissatisfaction with the government's lacklustre plans to implement the recommendations of the Royal Commission, although it was likely more than a coincidence that he made the announcement just days after Bennett confirmed that he would stay on as Conservative leader. As the Reconstruction Party campaign literature put it, this was to be a new party, one "completely separated from the old parties that had so grossly failed the people of Canada."[43] Both old parties were "indissolubly involved in the present system of concentration of control of wealth,"[44] and Stevens's goal, and the goal of the new party, would be to implement the Royal Commission's recommendations. He also promised a number of related actions, from a public works program and housing initiative to a reforestation project, and vowed to nominate a candidate in every electoral riding.[45]

Bennett was heard, on at least one occasion, referring to the new party as the "Deconstruction Party"; another critic referred to Stevens as the champion of "the masses and the asses," Ontario premier Mitch Hepburn labelled him "Sanctimonious Harry," and others referred to his supporters as "Stevists," while *Maclean's* could not seem to decide whether Stevens was the "the evil conscience, or accusing Angel, of the Conservative party."[46] But there was no denying the threat Stevens and the fledgling Reconstruction Party

posed to Conservative chances for re-election. The Reconstructionists made a direct appeal to the small business community and
middle-class consumers, especially in Ontario, who felt they were
getting a bad deal from the large retailers. These were traditionally
Conservative voters in the heartland of Canadian Conservatism,
and dozens of Ontario Conservative ridings were instantly jeopard-
ized. King believed Stevens to be a bit of a demagogue but had also
seen him as a formidable contender for the Tory leadership; however, he gave the new party little chance in the election. He understood well the implications of the Reconstruction Party for the
Liberals. "The effect of his action will be mostly to split the Tory
party worse than ever," he wrote in his diary, "and make the path
the surer for the Liberals. He will injure the C.C.F. already they
amount to very little."[47]

If nothing else, the rupture within the Conservative Party and
between Bennett and Stevens brought the Liberal campaign strategy
more clearly into focus. King was determined to "let the cleavage
between Bennett and Stevens widen itself and become more apparent to the country." Part of the plan was to avoid complicating
matters or confusing Canadian voters with a lot of new policies or
promises of action. King had broadly set out Liberal policy two
years earlier, on February 27, 1933, in a parliamentary speech that
he referred to throughout the 1935 campaign. The closest he came
to an election manifesto, it called for an unemployment insurance
scheme of some kind, greater government control over credit and
banking (through such things as a central bank), spending cuts,
a balanced budget, support for the Canadian National Railway,
increased international and internal trade through the easing of
trade restrictions, and support for peace and harmony in the world.
To all of these, he might have added: condemning all Tory governments for their inaction in alleviating the Depression.

There had been calls from within the Liberal Party for a bolder
plan of action. Alberta Liberal leader W.R. Howson, for example,

annoyed King by proposing a conference in the West to talk about Liberal policies. The last thing King wanted to talk about was policy and principles in advance of an election the Liberals were likely to win. And now, with the likelihood of Stevens and Bennett attacking each other on the campaign trail, he was even less inclined to let any new ideas interfere with his chances for victory. At a June 26 caucus meeting, he said that he "did not intend during the campaign to propose any plan or any ism as a cure-all." He warned against making the Liberal Party a target by giving its enemies something to shoot at, concluding that "the main thing from now on is to realize that the people vote against, rather than for something and to keep their mind focused on Bennett and his mismanagement of things."[48]

International Developments and Domestic Turmoil

There were always concerns that international developments might disrupt Liberal planning. Foreign affairs were always an intangible in Canadian politics: usually beyond Canadian control, as unwelcome as they were unavoidable, and liable to provoke deep divisions in Canadian society. In 1935, two issues of growing importance straddled the election campaign. The first, trade, was the perennial Canadian election issue, and there were concerns that Bennett might be able to turn the tables on the Liberals. The second, Ethiopia, raised the spectre of war and, even worse, conscription.

In the aftermath of the largely unsuccessful Imperial Economic Conference of 1932, Bennett began searching for a trade deal with the United States. The Roosevelt administration (especially Secretary of State Cordell Hull) was more open than previous Republican administrations to trade deals, and Bennett made clear his desire for negotiations during his April 1933 visit to Washington. The US Reciprocal Trade Agreements Act of 1934 authorized the president to undertake trade deals without Senate approval, but even then the two sides merely exchanged proposals through early 1935, with the official negotiations beginning only in August, just as the Canadian federal election date was announced.

Bennett wanted a deal signed before the election, thinking it would give him an electoral bounce; King and the Liberals were hoping he would fail. King was beside himself with outrage, seeing how Bennett, who fought bitterly against reciprocity in 1911, was now selling himself as the prophet of freer trade. Ironically, the two parties had clashed over trade agreements with the United States in previous elections, especially in 1911; now both of them desperately wanted one.

The Liberals had one real advantage in that the Roosevelt administration, especially the State Department, likely believed the United States could get a better deal with King than they could with Bennett. Bennett had displayed an unwillingness to offer concessions to the Americans, but King was known to favour a much broader and more comprehensive agreement – something that had long been a part of Liberal policy. In June, before the official discussions began, Harvard University professor William Elliott visited King to discuss a trade deal. It was unusual for an American representative to be talking with the leader of the Canadian opposition. Even though Elliott never claimed to be an official spokesperson for Washington, he had met with the president, he was invited by (and stayed at) the US Legation in Ottawa, and he promised to meet with (and inform) the president upon his return. Elliott told King that Washington had just about completed a trade deal with Bennett (which was not completely true); King hoped that whatever deal was agreed to might be open for revision – and even expanded to bring in the United Kingdom – after the election. King also impressed on Elliott his hope that the president would wait until after the election to sign any new deal and again emphasized his desire for a wide-ranging agreement. The larger concern for King, at least in the short term, was the boost a trade deal would give to Bennett and the Tory election platform during the campaign.[49]

The second international development looming on the horizon concerned the fate of Ethiopia, one of the few independent African states and a fellow member of the League of Nations. In his desire to re-establish an Italian empire, Fascist dictator Benito Mussolini clearly had his eye on Ethiopia and was threatening hostilities. There had been sporadic fighting, and by mid-1935 an Italian invasion appeared imminent. The League of Nations established a committee of members to discuss the application of sanctions against Italy either to prevent an invasion or to punish Italy in the event of one. A Canadian was a member of the committee. The situation deteriorated over the summer, and sanctions – and even war – appeared to be a distinct possibility. If the League and/or Great Britain became directly involved in a war with Italy, Canada might be dragged into the conflict as well. To make matters worse, the United States was not a member of the League or bound by its decisions, and a confrontation with the United States was also possible if one of the League's sanctions was applied to Italy's oil imports from the United States. All the old issues of conscription, relations with the British Empire, and Canada's autonomy versus its international responsibilities threatened to resurface and disrupt domestic politics, particularly within the Liberal Party. No one in Canada wanted war, but throughout the run-up to the election campaign, news of the worsening international situation competed with domestic electoral politics on the front pages of Canadian newspapers.[50]

Otherwise, the Liberals appeared to be cruising to victory, and just when it looked like things could not get any worse for the Conservatives, they did. There had been unrest in some of the work camps set up by Bennett's government to house unemployed men, and in several of them, the men began organizing and demanding better wages and work conditions. In Vancouver early in June, close to a thousand unemployed men launched the On-to-Ottawa Trek, intending to go to Ottawa to present the government with their demands. Thus began one of the most memorable events in the history of Canada's Depression.[51] Hopping on freight trains, the protesters made their way east, gathering considerable local support en route and stopping in most of the major towns along the Canadian Pacific rail line. Large crowds formed when they arrived, and the whole thing took on the air of a great popular event in the bleakness of mid-Depression Canada. At first, Bennett announced that the trekkers would not be stopped unless a request came from a provincial government, but Ottawa increasingly came to view the trek as communist-inspired and decided to prevent it from continuing to Ottawa.

The RCMP stopped the trekkers – now numbering over two thousand – in Regina. There they sat while several of their leaders proceeded to Ottawa to present their demands to the federal government. On June 22, eleven trek leaders met with Bennett and his cabinet on Parliament Hill. They explained their demands, Bennett responded negatively, tempers flared (or at least Bennett's did), accusations flew, and Bennett dismissed each of the demands, arguing they were either unreasonable, not within his power to grant, or unnecessary. If anything, Bennett seemed more focused on the fact that most of the trek leaders were foreign-born.[52]

In the meantime, in Regina the federal government took over the responsibility of feeding the protesters, but this stopped after Bennett refused their demands and their leaders returned from Ottawa. In addition, the authorities demanded that the trekkers remove themselves from Regina to a nearby work camp. They refused and trouble broke out. On the evening of July 1, the trekkers held a meeting in Regina's Market Square, and RCMP officers arrived with warrants to arrest their leaders under section 98 of the Criminal Code. The officers attacked the crowd and the riot was on, spilling into neighbouring streets. Barricades were raised, cars overturned, rocks thrown, windows smashed, and there was sporadic fighting. When it was all over, one Regina police officer and one protester were dead, dozens of trekkers had been jailed, considerable property had

The Regina Riot, which broke out when RCMP officers attempted to arrest leaders of the On-to-Ottawa Trek (July 1, 1935). It couldn't have come at a worse time for the government as it prepared to call the election. | Royal Canadian Mounted Police, Library and Archives Canada, e004666103

been damaged, and the rest of the rioters were interned under police guard at the Regina exhibition grounds.

Bennett had stood his ground, but his rough handling of the trek leaders was another black eye for his government and his reputation, just as Parliament was about to be dissolved for the election. The Liberals were once again the beneficiaries of Tory mismanagement, even though they said little about it when it came up in the House of Commons. Ernest Lapointe and other Quebec Liberals did not want to upset opinion in Quebec by appearing to be sympathetic to these "communist-inspired" rioters in Saskatchewan. For the Liberals, the best option was to leave it to the CCF to bring it up, and it fell to J.S. Woodsworth to place the blame for the whole messy affair squarely on Bennett and his government.[53]

The Election Is Called

On July 5, 1935, Parliament was prorogued, ending the session begun in January. Bennett left for a seaside holiday, and King retreated to Kingsmere, his country home outside Ottawa, for a rest. Woodsworth travelled west, leaving behind his manifesto "ripping capitalism and the social order fore and aft."[54] On August 15, Parliament was dissolved and the election was set for Monday, October 14. That date came as a bit of a surprise as most observers had believed an earlier September date more likely. Also, the fourteenth was Thanksgiving Day, and the holiday had to be rescheduled for later in the month. The ostensible reason for the late election date was that it was important to wait until the harvest was finished before going to the polls; some critics speculated that the government was delaying as long as possible to let the dust settle from the Liberal provincial wins over the summer.

Either way, the election call was long overdue. The government had waited until the very end to make the call, and by then it was perhaps already too late. Bennett would probably have preferred to resign if he could have found someone other than Stevens to take over the Conservative leadership. His party was largely disorganized and unprepared, even though everyone knew the election was coming. The Conservatives had lost all the battles at the provincial level right through the summer of 1935, and they had lost most of the by-elections since 1930, including five of the six held the previous year. At dissolution, there were an additional four ridings with no sitting MPs for which Bennett had avoided calling by-elections.

Bennett was also losing an assortment of MPs and other allies. Up to twenty Conservative MPs were unlikely to stand for re-election, and sixteen left for patronage appointments before the election – to the new Wheat Board, the Tariff Board, positions as deputy ministers, and elsewhere. There were also sixteen vacancies in the Senate waiting to be filled, and the list of competing candidates grew daily. Bennett also lost a handful of cabinet ministers (in addition to Stevens) and needed to reshuffle the deck as the campaign began. The trusted E.N. Rhodes (finance) left for health reasons and was not replaced before the election; R.C. Matthews (national revenue) also retired because of ill health and was replaced by J. Earl Lawson; J.A. Macdonald (fisheries) quit, citing no special reason, and was replaced by William G. Ernst, the MP for Queens-Lunenburg; Hugh Guthrie (justice) announced his retirement and was soon appointed chair of the Board of Railway Commissioners and replaced by G.R. Geary, MP for Toronto South. From Quebec, Onésime Gagnon was appointed minister without portfolio; Alfred Duranleau (marine) retired to take up a position on the Superior Court of Quebec, and his spot was filled by L.-H. Gendron; Arthur Sauvé (postmaster general) also retired, and Samuel Gobeil, MP for Compton, took his place. Sauvé, Rhodes, and Donald Sutherland (national defence) were all appointed to the Senate.[55]

The Conservatives were clearly a party in trouble. The government now faced four challengers in the election, including one that sprang directly from within their own party. And with the Reconstruction Party in the east and Social Credit in the west sure to eat away at Conservative support, the Liberals appeared to have the most to gain. "What with four major parties (or should it be five?) where we used to get along with two, not to mention the minor prophets promising ale with the steaks, Ottawa hasn't blinked at such a scrambled election since it ceased to be Bytown," one *Maclean's* critic concluded. And thanks to "Mr. Bennett raising the ante on Mr. King, and Mr. Stevens raising it on Mr. Bennett and Mr. Woodsworth raising it on all of them, the political landscape has become utterly unrecognizable."[56]

What was not clear was the impact the new parties and their reform pledges would have on the electorate. "Mr. Stevens and Mr. Woodsworth," noted one observer in the *Canadian Forum*, "have both issued manifestos very similar in language though fundamentally different in policy and the public, so far as they have reached the public, know in general they stand for a change."[57] But would the Reconstruction Party eat into Conservative support or attract working-class and rural voters away from the CCF? Would the new parties in both the east and west help or hinder the Liberals in their effort to return to power, or did the provincial trend to Liberalism portend a Liberal sweep? Social Credit, like the Reconstruction Party, was a largely unknown factor, and for all three new parties, the upcoming election would be their first test at the national level.

No one could forecast how the election would turn out, but many believed it would be seen from hindsight as a turning point in Canadian politics, or at least as the end of an era. John Dafoe of the *Winnipeg Free Press* editorialized at the end of the parliamentary session on July 5: "We are virtually at the end of one of the most remarkable episodes in Canadian history: the dictatorship of Mr. Bennett. It was a dictatorship with the consent – willing or enforced – of a parliamentary majority, but it has been a dictatorship just the same with all the characteristics and defects of that kind of government." A new era was about to begin, he added, and the upcoming election would enable Canadians to pass judgment on the old: "The parliament of robots and automation ... is now shorn of power, which has now reverted to the electors; and we shall see what they think about the Bennett dictatorship and about their representatives who submitted to it."[58]

4

The Campaign Begins

The whole tone of all the party programmes reveals a general
leftward movement in outlook and policy; and doctrines and
ideas, which isolated cliques a few years ago were discussing
in whispers, are now quite fashionable in all circles of society.

– "Canada: The Parties and the Election,"
The Round Table (September 1935)[1]

THERE WAS A SENSE that 1935 would be a historic election. The
advent of three new political parties, with more candidates than
ever and a greater diversity of campaign commitments, promised
to bring an enthusiasm to the campaign not seen in many years.
With the severity of the Depression and the deteriorating international situation as a backdrop, voters and candidates knew that
the winning party would face immediate and enormous challenges
in an increasingly dangerous world. It was also a long campaign,
from August to October, and it began slowly and did not really take
off until mid-September. But it was clear that this election would
matter.

The Party Platforms

Soon after the election was called, four of the major national party leaders (not including William Aberhart or any leader of the Social Credit Party) were approached by the editor of *Maclean's,* who offered space in the magazine for each leader to set out what they believed to be the key issues in the campaign. All the leaders accepted, and the four "The Issues as I See Them" articles appeared in the September 15 edition. Each party also produced platforms or manifestos that they tried to sell to the Canadian voter through radio, newspapers, pamphlets, and campaign events. It was impossible to do justice to all the issues in the election, Bennett wrote: "The issues here involved are so complex, so influenced by world affairs outside and beyond the control of any single government that a thorough, exact analysis might well fill a full volume or more." Over the course of the campaign, however, all the parties spelled out their plans for the future and by election day Canadians had a fairly clear idea of where they stood. "In my opinion," Bennett added, "this general election is one of the most significant in Canadian history."[2]

As the government of the day, the Conservatives knew they would have to defend their record, and their list of achievements became one of the main pillars of the Conservative campaign. The message was straightforward: in 1930, the Conservatives had inherited a very bad situation from the previous Liberal government (which had done nothing to prevent or alleviate the Depression), and now those same Liberal politicians were trying to get back into office. The Conservatives highlighted their successes, including the creation of the Bank of Canada and Canadian Wheat Board, amendments to the Bank Act to put an upper limit on interest rates on loans, the Natural Products Marketing Act, the Farmers' Creditors Arrangement Act, and other pieces of legislation. They did not dwell on the persistently high unemployment but pointed to all the jobs that had been created since 1930. Canadians were reminded of the government's social legislation – minimum wages, the eight-hour day and forty-eight-hour week, and others that came from the recommendations of the Royal Commission on Price Spreads and Mass Buying – and informed that the lingering constitutional cloud meant that no more could be done without amendments to the British North America Act.

One of the central issues in the 1935 election was trade, or, more generally, how to use trade agreements and tariff policy to increase Canada's balance of trade, create jobs at home, protect Canadian industry from outside competition, and improve the economy. The collapse of international trade was understood by many to be the root cause of the Depression, and for the Conservatives and Liberals especially, the revival of trade was key to getting Canada out of it. To that end, the Conservatives pointed to the higher tariff introduced in 1930, which they claimed protected Canadian jobs from unfair and unscrupulous outsiders. They declared the Ottawa trade agreements from the Imperial Economic Conference of 1932 to be of great benefit to Canada – agreements, they warned, that King and the Liberals would dismantle. They also pointed to Canada's improving trade balance and promised a trade deal with the Americans.

Unfortunately for Bennett and the Conservatives, the American trade talks continued into early October, ending just days before the election, and no deal was reached before the vote.[3] Bennett would have welcomed one but the negotiations had stalled. The question would later be asked whether the Americans had purposely held back on reaching a deal (as Mackenzie King had recommended), knowing that they might get a better one if they waited until after the anticipated Liberal victory. In any case, there was no deal on the table and therefore no debate on the contents of any proposed agreement.

Another issue brought together the themes of leadership, strength, and law and order. Over the course of the campaign, the Conservative message was that Bennett was a strong leader (and a strong leader was needed now more than ever) and that his Conservative government had saved the country from economic disaster – that capitalism itself had been saved. Great progress had been made to end the Depression, trade was going up, and unemployment was going down. It was clearly not the time to hand the reins of power back to the weak, indecisive, and corrupt Liberals. Canadians were asked to choose between the law and order of the Conservatives and the laissez-faire policies and attitudes of the opposition. Only Bennett could prevent the revolution that was brewing in the country – and now allegedly promised by the Co-operative Commonwealth Federation (CCF).

The Conservatives hammered away at the theme of anti-communism, and more often than not it was wrapped around a discussion of section 98 of the Criminal Code (making it illegal to advocate, publish, or promote the use of violence to overthrow the government), which the Liberals and CCF promised to repeal and which the Conservatives promised to preserve and defend. According to the Conservatives, the Liberals would allow radicals and revolutionaries to run freely around the country and do little to stand up to sedition and lawlessness, while the CCF, despite its denials, would actively support a socialist revolution. Banks would be nationalized, property confiscated, and so on. As Bennett put it at one campaign stop in Vancouver, the choice for Canadians was between "drift" and "violence" on the one hand and "national progress" on the other.[4]

This issue resonated well in Quebec, where section 98 remained more popular than in the rest of the country. Quebecers were reminded repeatedly that all the parties except the Conservatives had promised to abolish section 98; only Bennett stood in the way of a gradual slide towards communist domination. As one Conservative ad in *Le Canadien* explained, if you wanted to protect your family, traditions, morality, and both natural and divine rights against communism and the overturning of section 98, you must vote for Bennett.[5]

A campaign theme that played a smaller role than might have been expected was Bennett's New Deal. "Last January I told you that I was for reform. I am still for reform," Bennett explained to the readers of *Maclean's*. "All that is evil, all that is entirely selfish, all that is deliberately wicked in our present economic system must be swept away."[6] But as the campaign unfolded, the message of the New Deal faded. It could hardly be expected that individual Conservative candidates would campaign on the basis of a policy that had not been discussed or endorsed by either the caucus or the cabinet, but by the latter part of the campaign, even the prime minister had largely dropped the rhetoric of dramatic change promised in the New Deal and reverted to more standard Conservative fare: strong leadership, tariff reform, balancing the budget, law and order, preserving section 98, strengthening the Empire, and attacking the Liberals for their sins, past and present.

In their campaign slogans, the Conservatives played on these ideas of strength and decisive leadership with phrases like "Canada wants a fighter – vote for Bennett," or the more succinct "Stand by Canada" and "Vote Bennett." In some cases, a more targeted approach was used: "Women of Canada: think of your future before you vote." In Quebec, the Conservatives had a tough uphill battle and took a different approach. Rather than attacking King or Ernest Lapointe directly, they focused on the less popular Liberal provincial government with the slogan "A vote for King is a vote for Taschereau."[7] An ad in *Le Canadien,* one of the few francophone papers to support Bennett, portrayed the prime minister as the leader best suited to defend the country from radicalism on the left and right, making the vote "Un Choix Facile à Faire."[8] In both French

Canada and English Canada, the focus was on Bennett, not the Conservative Party.

For their part, the Liberals also focused much attention on the record of the sitting government, but what the Conservatives portrayed as accomplishments, the Liberals condemned as failures. The government had promised work and wages and provided neither; it had made extravagant promises and failed to deliver on any of them. A list of these promises from the 1930 campaign was compiled in a pamphlet dubbed *The Book of Promises*, which was used during the campaign.[9]

On rare occasions, the Liberals referred to Bennett as a dictator. On one evening, for example, at a campaign rally in Montreal, Bennett was pilloried as a dictator, an enemy of democracy, a humbug, a blunderbuss, and the cause of all of Canada's ills.[10] More often, the words "dictatorship" and "fascism" were only hinted at as being where the country was headed (the inclinations of the CCF and the Reconstruction Party were included here as well). Only the Liberals stood for liberty, responsible government, and the authority of Parliament. It was in this context that the Liberals argued for the repeal of section 98. The Liberals' anti-communist credentials were clear, but the Conservative government had used the present crisis to infringe on free speech and individual rights, making the repeal of section 98 and the ending of arbitrary deportations a necessity. "Arbitrary and autocratic methods," King wrote, "are no substitute for British justice."[11]

The Liberals also brought out the traditional Liberal playbook and campaigned on national unity (which Bennett had harmed), democracy (in a world where democracy was under threat and being undermined at home by Bennett), and cooperation and teamwork (in contrast to Bennett's one-man show) – and as the only party that could provide a strong, national majority government (something the CCF, Social Credit, Reconstruction Party, and even the Conservative Party could not do). The Liberals made few bold promises, reflecting King's desire to let Bennett lose the election rather than trying to woo voters with new, elaborate proposals. The Liberals were not promoting a "last-minute programme drafted to catch the passing breeze of a particular day or hour," King wrote.[12] But it was also important not to appear opposed to reform, and so promises were made, but usually they were sufficiently vague to mean anything to anyone. Work would be done to help agriculture and industry and reduce the cost of production, policies would be introduced to create jobs, the Bank of Canada would be brought under firmer government control, support for the Canadian National Railway would be maintained, the government would seek to reduce taxes, and so on. One concrete promise was to set up a national commission to oversee unemployment and to cooperate with the provinces in the administration of relief, all leading to the future introduction of unemployment insurance. But above all else, Liberals would offer "good government."

Like the Conservatives, the Liberals focused a lot on trade and tariffs as the way to create jobs, balance the budget, and alleviate the Depression. They generally supported freer trade than the Conservatives, and promised to remove Bennett's 1930 tariff increases and to implement some recommendations of the Price Spreads Royal Commission to reduce internal trade barriers. The differences between the two main parties were not as significant as in past elections, however: Conservative support for "protection" had waned and now both parties advocated tariff reform, more extensive trade agreements (especially with the United States), and a general lowering of international trade barriers. Both parties argued that the expansion of trade was the key to future prosperity.

The general thrust of the Liberal campaign was to offer confidence and stability, two aspects of Conservative failure that only the Liberals could rectify. While the Conservatives had split into two parties, the Liberals offered a united front and could count on the support of the eight provincial Liberal governments – a point they emphasized by having Liberal premiers appear on stage alongside King at every opportunity. Bennett's government was even criticized for the fracturing of political life into rival political groups, including the CCF and the Social Credit and Reconstruction Parties. In the difficult days ahead, only a strong Liberal majority (with the cooperation of its provincial allies) could restore the confidence of the Canadian people and make the hard choices government would need to make. There would be no need for minority or national unity governments with a Liberal victory. No one could predict the future or the challenges Canada might soon face, making "stability and an unmistakeable majority ... more essential than ever."[13] In this way, the Liberals hammered away at the things they did not want – dictatorship, rule by a radical third party, national unity government, and so on – rather than what they stood for. It also went without saying that these things could be achieved simply by voting Liberal, without the Liberals having to actually promise to do anything.

All these things were captured in the campaign's most memorable slogan, "King or Chaos." For various reasons, magazine publisher Colonel John Bayne Maclean had lost faith in Bennett, even though his publications – from *Maclean's* to the *Financial Post* – had benefited from Bennett's high tariffs on imports of American magazines. In 1935, he threw his support behind King and the Liberals, and in September there were discussions over placement of a Liberal ad in *Maclean's*. The magazine hoped for a double-page spread, whereas the Liberals didn't have the cash to pay for it and hoped that Maclean might donate a little free advertising space in his flagship magazine. Maclean refused. In the meantime, two *Maclean's* advertising staffers worked up an advertising spread with a strong message to sell to the Liberals, and it was here that the slogan "King or Chaos" was born. The Liberals bought the ad and immediately used the slogan on billboards and in pamphlets and speeches, so much so that the slogan was in common use long before it appeared in the October issue of *Maclean's*.[14]

The CCF and Social Credit released their platforms in July. Running only in Alberta and neighbouring British Columbia and Saskatchewan, the Social Credit Party had few thoughts of national victory, and the federal wing was largely an extension of the provincial party that swept into power just as the national campaign began. For many it was a matter of faith, and Social Credit was more a movement than a political party; it was, one historian wrote, "like an irresistible army," sweeping to victory first provincially and now seeking it at the national level.[15] If there were any questions, voters could be directed to the widely circulated *Social Credit Manual,* which set out the basics of the Social Credit plan. Most voters, however, simply relied on party leader William Aberhart himself. As one journalist recorded:

> In Mr. Aberhart's words, Social Credit had swept Alberta like a prairie fire. Under him, the people, in a radio-wide fraternity, had appealed to God against all their alleged oppressors. Some, no doubt, were genuine converts to Social Credit theory. Some, perhaps, hailed the second coming of ready cash. Others said: "We do not think he can do it, but he says he can and we'll let him try."[16]

Premier Aberhart had played down the theoretical side of Social Credit during the provincial campaign, and this theme continued in the federal campaign. Nevertheless, Social Credit appealed to a broad cross-section of the population, not just the rural folk, including urban workers, small business leaders, labour and social activists, women's groups, the unemployed, and even some professionals. Only later did the Social Credit government reveal its conservative nature; in the election of 1935, both provincially and federally the Social Credit Party – with its critique of the Depression and in its proposed solutions – could claim a radical element that challenged the CCF as the leading progressive party on the left.[17]

The CCF platform differed little from the Regina Manifesto, the party's founding document. The party called for the abolition of capitalism, and promised to nationalize the banks, utility companies, and other important industries, and to raise taxes on the rich in an effort to redistribute wealth within Canada. The CCF would not ban private property, only *bad* private property, the kind that allowed one person to exploit another. Much less concern was shown to the tariff and trade policy, except to condemn economic nationalism, but the CCF did join with the Liberals in calling for amendments to the BNA Act. The stand on capitalism was often embedded in a critique of Bennett the "reformer" and his radical rhetoric demanding change – change that could come only from the eradication of capitalism.

The CCF also condemned section 98 and promised to repeal it, which opened the party to charges of being communistic and anti-religion, something the Liberals were able to avoid for the most part. The CCF was anti-communist, leader J.S. Woodsworth explained, but not anti-Christian; in fact, he labelled the CCF platform as "applied Christianity."[18] Still, the CCF was repeatedly forced to respond to accusations of communist influence and to remind voters that everything it promised to do would be done with fidelity to Parliament, the Constitution, and the ballot box. However unfair, it was a charge that lingered and likely cut into support for the party. CCF pamphlets with calls to "Smash the Big Shots' Slave Camps and Sweat Shops"[19] may have helped express the party's anger at bankers, governments, and capitalism, but probably hurt rather than helped the party's image and made it easier for their opponents to tag the party with the red, radical, communist label.

One last issue that played out primarily in British Columbia was Woodsworth's stand on giving Asian Canadians the right to vote. It caused controversy in the province where anti-Asian racism was deepest, as well as in the three Vancouver ridings where the CCF had the strongest support (Vancouver East, Vancouver North, and

New Westminster). Some of the opposition came from organized labour, a group the CCF looked to for support, but it was used primarily as a wedge issue by the Liberals, who played on racist sentiment to sway some votes. About a week before election day, the British Columbia Liberals took out a large ad in the *Vancouver Sun* with the headline "C.C.F. and the Orientals." The ad condemned Woodsworth for stating that he would give the vote to East Asians, and proclaimed that "a vote for ANY C.C.F. candidate is a vote to give the CHINAMEN and the JAPANESE the same voting right that you have." A vote for the Liberals meant the opposite, of course, and the ad featured photographs of the Vancouver-area Liberal candidates, including Ian Mackenzie and Vancouver mayor G.G. McGeer.[20]

"They were willing to sacrifice some minor scruples," one observer wrote, "if there were some votes to be gained by doing so."[21] The effectiveness of the anti-Asian campaign is uncertain, as the CCF ultimately got more votes in British Columbia than the Liberals, but it was an issue in Vancouver until the end of the campaign. At the final local CCF rally, for example, Wallis Lefeaux, the party's candidate in Vancouver Centre, denied that giving the vote to Asian Canadians was even CCF policy, but added that, even if it were, there were only about eight hundred Asian Canadians in British Columbia who would be eligible to vote.[22]

H.H. Stevens issued the manifesto of the Reconstruction Party on July 11, and there was a greater gap between the new party and the Tories than one might have expected, given that the party consisted mainly of former Conservatives. Dubbed the "New National Policy of Reconstruction and Reform," the Reconstruction Party's fifteen-point program promised to restore prosperity to the Canadian economy and social life through a broad public works program, economic development in the oil and mining sectors, higher taxes on the rich, and the establishment of a federal trade and industry commission – to act as regulator, negotiator, conciliator, and referee – to help solve industrial and commercial disputes. Similar kinds of boards and commissions would be established to undertake similar kinds of work in the agricultural and financial sectors.

The prime issue for the party, not surprisingly, was the concentration of economic control in the hands of a small number of individuals and corporations. Stevens was out to defend the average Canadian from these malevolent and powerful forces: farmers whose prices for their produce were set by powerful corporations; workers whose wages were reduced by powerful employers; small borrowers who could not get loans from powerful financiers; independent business people who faced prices dictated by powerful merchandizing institutions. It was these conditions that led to labour unrest and rural protest, and ultimately to the rise of radical parties and calls for the overthrow of capitalism. The two old parties had shown themselves unwilling to address this situation; indeed, they had nurtured it. It was the goal of the Reconstruction Party to intervene and bring about such conditions "as will hold the balance in equity between the great mass of people and [the] powerful corporations which control credit, industry and commerce."[23] Beyond that, as Stevens's biographer noted, the party had almost no ideological base. "It was led by a dissident Tory ... They had no long-range plan other than to forge through enough broad legislation to protect the little man."[24]

Brief mention should also be made of one final issue that applied to all the parties in September and October 1935: the Italian-Ethiopian crisis. The threat of war was in the air throughout the campaign; in fact, developments in Africa regularly pushed election news off the front pages of Canadian newspapers. The crisis did not become a major election issue, however, as none of the parties was keen on Canadian involvement and all were happy to avoid it altogether on the campaign trail. When it was spoken of, the leaders' comments were fairly similar in nature. "In peace, the Conservative Party stands for Canadian rights, and stands against the economic aggression of any foreign country," Bennett announced early in the campaign. "We will not be embroiled in any foreign quarrel where the rights of Canadians are not involved." The Liberal position was set out in Quebec City by Ernest Lapointe on September 7: "In my opinion no interest in Ethiopia, of any nature whatever, is worth the life of a single Canadian citizen." At the same rally, Mackenzie King added: "You can trust the Liberal Party to see to it that, as regards the great questions which involve the lives of men and women, any Liberal Government will see to it that not a single life is unnecessarily sacrificed in regard to any matter beyond what affects the safeguarding and rights of our own country." Both comments were received with thunderous applause.[25]

Stevens took a similar stand for the Reconstruction Party, calling it "an unthinkable thing that Canada be dragged into a war involving obscure things in Europe or Africa." The CCF was even less enthusiastic about foreign interventions. Woodsworth said little of the growing conflict, but when it looked like war might break out between Italy and Ethiopia, he declared that a CCF government would hold a plebiscite before any decision was made on Canadian participation. And if Canadians voted to go to war, Woodsworth, a confirmed pacifist, stated that "I think any C.C.F. government, would resign rather than lead them."[26]

The Italian-Ethiopian crisis did not wait for the Canadian election, however, and fighting broke out in Africa just days before election day. Bennett had originally given orders to follow the lead of the British and French in any discussions, but when Italy invaded Ethiopia, the issue of sanctions arose in the League of Nations. With Parliament dissolved, Bennett was inclined not to make any statement and to abstain on the League vote on whether Italian aggression had occurred. The Canadian team at the League headquarters in Geneva, led by Howard Ferguson, the former Conservative premier of Ontario, and Walter Riddell, the advisory officer in Geneva, were upset because by abstaining on a sanctions vote they would be perceived to be siding publicly with Italy and its allies. Ferguson made plans to go golfing rather than abstain, but Lester Pearson, a young external affairs officer, suggested a transatlantic telephone call to the prime minister for clarification. It was the first time they called Ottawa from the Geneva office, and the call reached Bennett at breakfast in his railway car in Lindsay, Ontario, en route from Ottawa to Toronto. Pearson recorded part of their conversation: "How is the campaign going, R.B.?" asked Ferguson. "Fine, Fergy, we have them licked," Bennett replied.[27] Bennett gave Ferguson permission to vote with the League majority on the issue of aggression and to use his own judgment as events unfolded. The crisis continued beyond the election – and became more dangerous from a Canadian standpoint – but the timing could not have been worse for Bennett and the Conservative campaign.

The Voters

There were a little under 11 million Canadians in 1935, and it was estimated that 6 million of them were eligible to vote. The overwhelming majority of Canada's population was of either French or British origin, and the proportion only increased in the 1930s thanks to the Depression and the severe immigration restrictions, which led to the collapse of immigration into Canada, from 1,166,000 immigrants in 1921–31 to only 140,000 in 1931–41.[28] There were almost 3 million French Canadians and almost 5.5 million of English, Scots, Welsh, and Irish backgrounds. These were followed, according to the 1931 census, by Germans (473,000), Ukrainians (225,000), Dutch (148,000), Poles (145,000), and thousands more of various other European backgrounds. There were also a little over 150,000 Jewish Canadians and fewer than 20,000 Black Canadians.

In the groups excluded from voting (except in a few rare cases) were approximately 85,000 Asian Canadians and a little over 125,000 First Nations and Inuit peoples. Technically, Asian Canadians were not excluded from voting nationally, but thanks to the 1920 Dominion Elections Act, racial restrictions on who could vote provincially were to be respected at the federal level, meaning that South Asian, Japanese, and Chinese Canadians in British Columbia (where most of them lived) and Chinese Canadians in Saskatchewan would not be able to vote in 1935. As for Indigenous peoples, only Métis and those who had been enfranchised were eligible to vote.

In the 1930s, the participation of recent immigrants or ethnic minority communities in political life was still rather limited and ineffectual, and it varied between different groups and in different parts of the country. There were a few exceptions: German Canadians had long been influential in the Ontario ridings around Berlin/Kitchener, and federal politicians of German origin were not unusual. Mackenzie King, as a young Liberal running in Berlin in 1911, found it wise to try his hand at speech making in German to attract votes – unsuccessfully, as it turned out.

Several mayors and aldermen, and a handful of provincial politicians had emerged from "ethnic" communities, primarily in Western Canada, where the population of new Canadians was relatively greater. But in 1935, even in Western Canada, most non-British communities were either too small or too dispersed to play a significant role in federal politics. The Jewish community had a little more influence in a few ridings, and several Jewish MPs had been elected, including Sam Jacobs from Montreal, Sam Factor from Toronto (both Liberals), and A.A. Heaps from Winnipeg (Labour/CCF).

In addition, in some newer communities, political interest and activity were focused more on recently departed homelands than on Canadian politics. This was partly because many new Canadians were relatively recent arrivals who were not yet Canadian citizens and therefore could not vote; for others, inability to speak English or French made it more difficult to follow Canadian politics or navigate the voting process itself. Due to discrimination and sometimes outright hostility from the majority population, political action could be a daunting and unwelcoming adventure. In addition, minority communities themselves were often divided over political issues back home. Like other Canadians, they held diverse and often competing views on political issues, and their voting behaviour was divided as well. For example, despite contact with mainstream Canadian political parties, Toronto's Italian community in the early 1930s was more focused on political developments in fascist Italy than in Ottawa. Similarly, significant ideological divisions within the Ukrainian Canadian community seriously hampered hopes for political cooperation.[29]

The traditional parties made efforts to attract the votes of minority communities. The Liberals in particular gained the strong allegiance of many groups of new Canadians. Even the Conservatives, despite their historical promotion of a British Canadian style of nationalism, which was less appealing to many communities, supported various groups and clubs, minority-language newspapers, and the distribution of publicity material in several different languages. However, the Borden government's 1917 Wartime Elections Act, which disenfranchised many new Canadians who had immigrated from enemy countries, solidified support for the Liberals in these communities. For the most part, the Chinese, Japanese, and South Asian Canadian communities and the First Nations People could not vote, and there was no need for any of the political parties to seek out their votes in the 1935 election. If anything, the possibility of these groups being given the vote became an issue in the election.

The new parties – the CCF, Social Credit, and several other socialist and communist groups – were much more open to newcomers, both in their willingness to welcome non-British Canadians into their ranks and through platforms demanding economic justice, agricultural reform, and so on, which had greater appeal to many immigrant workers, refugees, and new working-class Canadians. Finnish, Ukrainian, and Jewish immigrants in particular gravitated to socialist and communist parties (much more so than immigrants from Catholic countries, who rejected socialism, communism, and the left in general), to the point where many British and French Canadians responded with an outburst of nativism, equating these parties with "foreign" radicalism and unfairly casting suspicion on their radical ideas.

Despite the appeal of the newer parties, the political tilt of non-Anglo-French voters still favoured the traditional parties in 1935, particularly the Liberals. In Montreal, for example, the Jewish community could rely on one provincial seat, the riding of St-Louis, where approximately one-third of voters were Jewish. Despite internal divisions within the community, the rise of the Union Nationale, and the emergence of communist candidate Fred Rose, support for the Liberal Party remained solid through the provincial election of 1935. Likewise, in Saskatchewan, despite the rise of the CCF, the non-Anglo-Saxon population continued to back the provincial Liberals – who had favoured immigration and denounced the Ku Klux Klan, which had been instrumental in the 1929 provincial Conservative victory – leading to the Liberals' sweeping victory in 1934.[30] It would have been surprising if the federal Liberals had not looked to both groups – Jewish voters in Montreal and the non-Anglo-Saxon voters in Saskatchewan – for similar support in the 1935 federal campaign.

Women in Canadian Politics in 1935

By 1935, more and more women were becoming involved in Canadian political life, not just in political parties but through community activism, women's clubs, church organizations, study groups, international organizations, and university groups such as the Student Christian Movement of Canada and the Antigonish Movement. Many Canadian women participated in the interwar peace movement or channelled their energies through traditional organizations such as the National Council of Women of Canada, the International Order of the Daughters of the Empire, the Women's Christian Temperance Union, and the Young Women's Christian Association, or through newer groups such as the Federated Women's Institutes of Ontario, Pioneer Women's Organization, the Women's Section of the Grain Growers Association, and L'Alliance canadienne pour le vote des femmes du Québec.

Through the 1920s, the struggle for women's political rights continued not only for the provincial vote in several provinces but also against legal discrimination, for the right to hold various political offices, and for other social reforms. By the 1920s, several women had been elected to provincial legislatures, city councils, and school boards. The most consequential development was the famous Persons Case. Not long after women got the federal vote, the Federated Women's Institutes of Canada put forward Judge Emily Murphy to be Canada's first female senator. Prime Ministers Arthur Meighen and Mackenzie King both rejected the suggestion, pointing to the BNA Act, which they claimed precluded the appointment of women because membership in the Senate was reserved only for "qualified persons." This rejection sparked years of litigation on this question. In April 1928, the Supreme Court of Canada ruled that women were not "persons" according to the act and could therefore not be appointed to the Senate, only to be overruled by the highest court in the Empire, the Judicial Committee of the Privy Council (JCPC), in October 1929. The JCPC ruled that section 24 of the BNA Act included women and they were therefore eligible for Senate membership. But Murphy was a Conservative, so King appointed Cairine Wilson, one of the founders of the National Federation of Liberal Women of Canada, as Canada's first female senator.[31] Senator Wilson went on to campaign vigorously for the Liberals in 1935.

Close to a dozen women ran in the 1930 federal election, the vast majority as members of a smaller party or as independents. Virtually all were defeated. The most prominent female MP at the time and

Agnes Macphail, the first woman elected to the House of Commons
(May 15, 1934). | Photographer Yousuf Karsh, Library and Archives Canada,
PA-165870

during the course of the 1935 election was Agnes Macphail, who
was first elected as a United Farmers of Ontario candidate in 1921
and remained in Parliament until 1940. She was a steady voice in
the House of Commons, an activist in the peace movement, and a
leader in the drive for prison reform during the 1930s. She knew
first-hand that it was not an easy journey for women in politics;
they were expected to support the party and its policies but were
often left on their own at election time, facing all the barriers,
stereotypes, and resistance along the way. As feminist author and
reformer Nellie McClung wrote in 1930 to Irene Parlby, a member

of the Alberta legislature with the United Farmers of Alberta from 1921 to 1935, "It seems that the hostility to women in public life is not lessening, but rather growing."[32]

Winning the right to vote was no longer the issue for most Canadian women, except those mentioned above who were denied the vote and in Quebec, where women were not granted the provincial franchise until 1940, but having the vote had not led to any kind of unity among women voters. Indeed, just the opposite occurred as the female vote split along lines of class, religion, language, region, and ethnicity. Women didn't start voting for one big women's party; they voted for all kinds of parties. "There has never been a campaign like the suffrage campaign," recalled Agnes Macphail in the early 1930s. "But when all was over, and the smoke of battle cleared away, something happened to us. Our forces, so well organized for the campaign, began to dwindle. We had no constructive program for making a new world ... So the enfranchised women drifted. Many are still drifting."[33] There was little talk of forming a separate women's party, but there were new opportunities for political action and it was now more a question of shaping the issues through the vehicle of the existing party structure.

The traditional parties had women's auxiliaries such as the National Federation of Liberal Women of Canada (ca. 1928), but they were aimed primarily at harnessing women to work for the party organization – answering phones, licking stamps, distributing literature, and doing other party work – rather than as an avenue for women to enter political life.[34] Much has been written and speculated concerning Bennett's and King's attitudes and relationships with women, and little of it suggests that either was anything but traditional in his views about women in politics. The two men revered their mothers, and both claimed to support rights for women, but these rights were understood within the context of the home and family. In family life, women played a central role as wives and mothers, but in the public sphere it was a different story. Politics was the preserve of men. King's diaries are filled with references to male colleagues living hard and dying young, but they are presented without reflection concerning the difficulties men faced in political life. But when MP William Kennedy died and his wife announced that she would contest his seat in Parliament, only to die soon herself, King was quick to draw conclusions. Her death was "very sad, it reveals wherein women were not meant for politics," he confided to his diary. A few days later, after speaking to the National Federation of Liberal Women of Canada in Ottawa, he wrote: "Women do not know what they miss by not being what above all they were meant to be (like mother)." It was patronizing, even by King's standards, considering that most of the audience knew exactly what it meant to be a woman and what they might have been missing.[35]

Some of the smaller independent parties were more open to women, especially those parties that had relatively little chance of winning. A fair number of women were involved in organizing and supporting Social Credit, at least on the provincial side, and Aberhart's sweep in 1935 brought two women to the Alberta Legislative Assembly. The CCF also had several women in positions of influence, and its reform platform contained several key women's issues, but female CCF candidates were few in number and often relegated to unwinnable ridings and offered little party support,[36] while behind the scenes, women ended up doing primarily the same things as women in other parties. "Whatever their background, once active in the party the majority of women gravitated toward 'female' areas of political work," historian Joan Sangster has written, "revealing the existence of a political sexual division of labour within the CCF similar to that in Canadian society."[37] There were several leading feminists in the party, but there is little evidence, for example, that they had influence on either the contents or adoption of the Regina Manifesto. There was still much work to done. Agnes Macphail recalled speaking with CCF leader J.S. Woodsworth in the

House of Commons and being told, "I still don't think a woman has any place in politics."[38]

Fifteen women ran in the 1935 election, and most had little chance of victory. Macphail was a sitting MP, but due to redistribution her riding was amalgamated with parts of a neighbouring riding into Grey-Bruce (Ontario). She faced two opponents, both doctors: Walter Hall, the sitting Liberal MP for Bruce, and Lewis Campbell, the Conservative whom she had defeated in Grey Southeast in 1930. Macphail was forced to deny allegations that she had received funds from the Liberal Party and that she was somehow anti-Catholic; for her part, she denounced the "terrible economic conditions" in the country, while "Mr. Bennett sat pat and talked much," and King "sat pat and said nothing – which he does superbly."[39]

On the other side of the political spectrum was Martha Black, whose husband, George, was MP for Yukon and a former Speaker of the House. Black was a northern businesswoman with traditional views of the role of women in politics, but in 1935, when her husband became seriously ill, she stepped in and ran – and won – as an Independent Conservative. It was an uphill struggle in a riding where it was said there were only two political parties, "the Liberals and the Blacks." In her memoirs, she reflected on the different kinds of roadblocks that political women faced, sometimes from unexpected sources. "I had other troubles too," she wrote. "There were the younger women, who said: 'What can this damned old woman do for us at Ottawa?' [Black was sixty-nine at the time.] That was hard to take, yet I hurled back, 'You'll be lucky when you reach my age if you have my sturdy legs, my good stomach, my strong heart, and what I like to call my headpiece.'"[40]

The CCF fielded seven female candidates (three in Ontario, two each in Alberta and Saskatchewan), and the Reconstruction Party fielded five (two in Ontario and one each in New Brunswick, Manitoba, and British Columbia). The fifteenth female candidate ran as

In Yukon, there were only two political parties, "the Liberals and the Blacks." Shown here is Martha Black, who succeeded her husband, George, as MP for Yukon and became the second woman elected to the House of Commons (March 25, 1936). | Photographer Yousuf Karsh, Library and Archives Canada, 4346038

an Independent in Quebec. The Liberals and Conservatives fielded no female candidates at all (although Black, while running as an Independent, was essentially a Conservative).[41]

Despite the small number of candidates and their marginalization from the political centre, women were actively involved in the campaign, through essential volunteer work ranging from driving cars and providing daycare to operating the telephones and preparing lunches. The various women's political associations were also much involved in campaign work, and it was common to have delegates from these associations on stage, presiding over rallies or introducing speakers, at railway stations greeting candidates, working behind the scenes at campaign headquarters, and contributing to the mechanics of elections as polling officers and enumerators.

It was expected that more women than ever would vote in 1935. "Women have stopped their bridge games to listen," wrote one journalist with a patronizing flourish, "and grandmothers have sat up beyond the stroke of 12 to hear all arguments concerning the platforms and the plans of the three major parties." Certainly, women were the target of much political advertising – a barrage of campaign literature aimed primarily at the home, the welfare of children, and general security. Not surprisingly, that was what all the parties, in their own ways, were promising. "I shall be sadly disappointed if we do not have a large women's vote," said the president of the Toronto Liberal Women's Association. "And I do not expect to be disappointed."[42]

Party Organization and Financing

Political campaigns require strong foundations, and political parties can only go as far as their organizations can take them; it was no different in the 1935 election. When R.B. Bennett took over as Conservative leader in 1927, the Tory organization was small, disorganized, and underfunded. Bennett handpicked Major-General Alexander Duncan McRae, the Conservative MP for Vancouver North, as national party director, who then created an extremely effective organization. McRae travelled the country, collected names and made contacts, distributed information, organized events, raised money (most of which came from wealthy party members, particularly Bennett himself), and created an Ottawa headquarters from which to control campaign news and publicity. Included in this was the Standard News Service, a propaganda organization that fed news stories and pro-Conservative information to hundreds of newspapers across the country. It was an effective office and team and went a long way towards ensuring Bennett's victory in 1930.

Once in office, however, Bennett allowed this organization to atrophy. The national headquarters was closed, the staff were laid off, the riding associations across the country all but disappeared, and Bennett's relations with McRae soured. McRae resigned and his position remained vacant for years; most of those who had engineered the Conservative victory in 1930 left for other things.[43] By 1935, the entire organization was crumbling and, because Bennett had paid for much of it from his own pocket, without further financial support from him there was little money to help rebuild the party. Bennett was in charge of the party, including its finances, and when he decided to neglect party matters, he effectively shut the party's organization down. It was all made worse as he dithered on whether or not to retire, and his serious health problems through the early part of 1935 only complicated matters as the Tory organization languished in uncertainty.

It was not until late 1934 that some action was taken, but even then Bennett remained reluctant to name a chief fundraiser. He must have known that as the major contributor to the Tory campaign in 1930 he would be expected to play that role again in 1935, but on this matter he was less than forthcoming. Bennett finally appointed Toronto Conservative MP Earl Lawson as Tory national organizer in December. Lawson was well known in Ontario circles but something of an unknown character in the rest of the country. With journalist Frederick Edwards as his director of publicity, he set up a small Ottawa office and began building the organization from the ground up. A fundraising campaign was launched and a Conservative mailing list, which had largely disappeared following the 1930 election, was reassembled (ultimately collecting over 400,000 names from across the country). The Conservative Party bulletin, *The Canadian,* was revived, but only four editions were published before election day. Soon the national office was preparing publicity material and planning the campaign, tours, and speeches. Bennett himself continued to rely on his confidants Rod Finlayson and W.H. Herridge for his speeches.

There were problems right from the start. The organizing activity was initiated early in 1935, but only after the New Deal broadcasts, and much momentum was lost as the organization scrambled into action. In addition, several of Bennett's cabinet colleagues decided not to run for re-election, and, unlike in 1930, there were no provincial premiers to support the party. Support from the provincial wings was much diminished and the access to patronage that came from holding office was gone. Campaign directors were appointed for each province, including Conservative senator Joseph Rainville, who was put in charge of the Quebec wing, but all these provincial directors suffered similar problems, and complaints flowed into Ottawa about the lack of funds and the general disorganization of the party and the campaign.[44]

Still, it is probably not sufficient to blame the Conservative weakness in 1935 on party disorganization and lack of funds. Indeed, by election day, and despite constant complaints about lack of money, the Tories had attracted almost as many donations as the Liberals. Party stalwart and wealthy former newspaper publisher Lord Atholstan (Hugh Graham) collected $458,306 for the party in Montreal, and a similar amount was raised in Toronto by provincial Conservative colleagues D.M. Hogarth and W.H. Price. Most of the cash came from the major banks, breweries, Dominion Textiles, and prominent individuals and wealthy benefactors like Atholstan himself.[45] Ultimately, the Conservatives could not blame their campaign problems on a lack of funds. In fact, they spent more on radio broadcasting than the Liberals, but the party never fully recovered from the slow start and growing pains from earlier in the campaign.[46]

In contrast, the Liberals were the clear front-runners in the 1935 election, but even they had problems raising money and organizing a national campaign. Mackenzie King was determined to keep out of the fundraising side of things. "This is the sordid side of politics," he recorded in his diary, "and win or lose, I am not going to concern myself in the least about campaign funds, except wherever possible to prevent our men from doing anything not wholly justifiable and right." True to his word, King sent a cheque for $150 to his riding association in Prince Albert "to help with organization purposes," but remained upset at having to pay any expenses out of his own pocket and being *expected* to do it. "The leader of the Party to pay the shot for himself & his followers! So much for appreciation and gratitude."[47] King subsequently refused to contribute any money towards his election expenses, leaving that burden to the Prince Albert Liberals. He even threatened to look for a seat elsewhere until the local Liberals agreed to foot the bill.[48]

The Liberals had been burned by scandal earlier in the decade, when the Beauharnois Light, Heat and Power Company gave money to the Liberal Party in return for help in its plan to build a hydro-electric power station. The Beauharnois scandal cast a pall of corruption over the entire party and even infected the prime minister, and led to significant changes in the way the Liberals raised money. The old guard was removed and a new National Liberal Federation of Canada (NLF) was created in 1932 as an independent entity within the party to oversee organization and fundraising. To lead the NLF, King turned to Vincent Massey, a wealthy Liberal, former politician, and patron of the arts with excellent connections in all the right places for a fundraiser. Massey represented the snobbish upper-class side of life that King railed against privately but was also drawn to. Although he told Grant Dexter, a reporter for the *Winnipeg Free Press*, that "all Massey ever did was to inherit a fortune and live a life of cultured ease,"[49] for King, Massey's wealth and connections made him the ideal person to head the NLF. And King could offer Massey what he really wanted: the position of Canada's High

Commissioner in London – provided the Liberals won the election. Massey had toyed with the idea of becoming lieutenant-governor of an Australian state but was warned by King that his absence from Canada would likely disqualify him from the position he desperately wanted. King wrote: "I felt that those who left the party in its time of need would get no recognition later. That I intended to leave to those who did the party's organization and publicity, the naming of persons for positions my approval being necessary, that I felt if he were away it wd be impossible to appoint him to London later on."[50]

Massey stayed. He became president of the NLF in 1932 and spent the next few years building the party's finances and speaking on the need for Liberal reform. He saw the new CCF as a growing threat to mainstream Liberalism and often came into conflict with King, who bristled at the ideas of the "new Liberalism" espoused by Massey and many of the younger party members. King felt it was up to him to decide on policy matters – certainly not Massey – and believed that too much policy might actually hurt Liberal chances. An already strained friendship deteriorated into suspicion and mistrust, especially on the part of King; he may even have seen in Massey an emerging rival for his job as Liberal leader (an idea that Massey had toyed with).[51]

Massey was King's handpicked choice for NLF president, but much of the actual fundraising was overseen by the NLF's secretary, former journalist and businessman Norman Lambert. In cash-strapped Depression-era Canada, it was hard to find the funds for Liberal publicity, distribution of literature, advertising, travel, telephone, meals, and so on. The NLF also provided a clipping service, produced a newsletter, undertook limited research activities relating to policy, and distributed speeches and other publicity material. By 1934, it was producing the *Liberal Monthly*, a magazine filled with Liberal news stories, which, despite its name, did not appear monthly in the months leading up to the election.[52]

More importantly, the NLF was essentially built upon the provincial Liberal parties. Its advisory council comprised seven representatives from each of the provinces (plus representatives from young Liberals and Liberal women), and the prime fundraisers were more than likely linked to the provincial associations, or at least worked for both. Financing of the campaign was overseen at the local level as well, as the national party had little money to disburse. National help came in the form of pamphlets and other campaign literature and, rarely, a visit from the party leader. Paul Martin, who contested a seat in Windsor, in southwestern Ontario, was lucky to receive a cheque for $1,500 from Massey, but was forced to rely on local fundraising – a challenge given that the presidents of the big automobile companies were all Tories. "The enormous cost of election campaigns always staggered me," Martin later wrote.[53]

In Quebec, the party ran a fairly autonomous organization and, given that the provincial Liberals likely knew what would or would not work, those involved were left pretty much on their own to raise funds, direct publicity, and so on in the Quebec region. Tensions surfaced between the provincial and federal wings of the party (discussed in Chapter 2). Premier Taschereau believed that the federal Liberals, led by Ernest Lapointe, were too radical; for his part, Lapointe dismissed Taschereau as the "worst type of old-fashioned Whig, if not a Tory."[54] But they agreed to cooperate during the 1935 election, and Chubby Power was unofficially made Liberal organizer for Quebec City, with P.J.A. Cardin in charge of the Montreal area.

Western Canada fell a little more under the direction of the central office, but on the whole the system was working smoothly. Reports from Edmonton were positive, even a little over-optimistic. "The Conservatives are dead here," reported George McLeod, the Liberal candidate in Edmonton East. The organization was solid and prospects were good. "The C.C.F. will be our strongest opposition, and they are not making much headway."[55] In Saskatchewan, Jimmy Gardiner expressed some concern about the lack of understanding in Western Canada "as to how things are being handled in connection with general organization," and he called for greater coordination of the work between east and west. Things needed "pepping up," he informed King. "I think it would be well if the central office kept us as fully informed as possible on every activity from now until election time. The feeling that the outside corners are always in touch with the central office is a good thing when an election is warming up."[56]

There were also tensions in Ontario between the provincial wing and the NLF, tensions that had been building since Mitch Hepburn's historic victory in the 1934 provincial election. Federally, the Liberals had not won a majority of Ontario ridings since 1874, but Hepburn believed he could deliver the province in the federal election. Meetings were held and agreement was reached to leave the NLF in a titular leadership position but with Hepburn and the provincial Liberal association really in charge on the ground, first for the series of 1934 Ontario by-elections and then for the federal campaign.[57] King was naturally suspicious of Hepburn's political intentions and saw a threat to his leadership of the federal party, believing that Hepburn had his eyes on Ottawa despite his denials of any such ambitions. To make matters more difficult for King, the national campaign, at least in English Canada, would rely on funds coming from Toronto – procured from mining companies, manufacturers, construction companies, and a long list of major resource corporations in the province. And Hepburn, having just enacted legislation easing the sale of wine and beer, could rely on the distillers, malters, and brewers to come to the aid of the party.[58] In the end, Hepburn and the Ontario Liberal Association essentially funded the national campaign in Ontario out of an office in Toronto's King Edward Hotel – just a few floors below Hepburn's own room.

Most of the money for the Liberal campaign was raised in Montreal and Toronto, although there was some local fundraising all across the country. In Montreal, Senator Donat Raymond was in charge; in Toronto, it was Frank O'Connor, a wealthy business-man, president and founder of Laura Secord Candy Store, and chief fundraiser for the Ontario Liberals (O'Connor anted up a fair bit of his own cash and was appointed to the Senate two months after the election). The usual suspects were approached for support, including Labatt Breweries, Imperial Oil, Canadian General Electric, Eaton's, Algoma Steel, and other corporations, as well as individuals such as Joe Atkinson of the *Toronto Daily Star* and, perhaps not surpris-ingly, given the controversy with H.H. Stevens and his Special Committee on Price Spreads, Simpson's president C.L. Burton. There were some 240 donors from Ontario alone,[59] but money was a problem throughout the campaign and efforts to secure donations continued right up to election day in October.

The money raised in Montreal went to help the campaign in Quebec and the Maritimes; the funds raised in Toronto financed the campaign in Ontario and the West. It is always difficult to be precise but it is estimated that the Montreal group raised a little over $625,000, with over $500,000 earmarked for the Quebec cam-paign, around $50,000 each for Nova Scotia and New Brunswick, and $15,000 for Prince Edward Island. In Ontario, the numbers were similar, with the Ontario Liberals raising in the range of $550,000, with $265,763.75 going to Ontario ridings and another $116,329.13 for publicity in the province. Saskatchewan received $65,600 and British Columbia $33,500, while Manitoba and Alberta received much less, around $8,500, perhaps reflecting the understanding that Liberals didn't have much of a chance in Alberta. The rest went to the national campaign and for miscellaneous expenses.[60]

It is not surprising, given the context of the Depression, that both traditional parties struggled to find sufficient funding for the 1935 election campaign. But it was even more difficult for the three new parties that emerged before the election, as they faced huge problems establishing themselves, nominating candidates, and mounting and paying for a national campaign.

Time quickly ran out on the Reconstruction Party, which began operations only days before the election was called. There was no time to build a party, and any organizing was largely handled by Stevens himself. Stevens came out of the Conservative Party and it is not surprising that many of his supporters and organizers did too. A few Tories were attracted to the new party, as were former Conservative candidates and an assortment of grassroots contributors and party workers. A weekly newspaper, the *Reconstruction Party*, was published beginning in August, and a number of "Stevens Clubs" were established in various parts of the country. In Leamington, Ontario, for example, the Young Canada Conservative Club dissolved itself and all but one of its members regrouped as a new Stevens Club.[61] During the election, these clubs did much of the work at the constituency level and attracted supporters to the party.

Stevens appointed Warren Cook as his second in command and party treasurer. Cook was not a politician but rather a wealthy Toronto manufacturer and one-time president of the Canadian Association of Garment Manufacturers who had helped Stevens with research in advance of the Price Spreads Royal Commission. Cook worked from his Toronto office and a group of provincial campaign organizers was selected across the country, including Jacques Cartier, who had organized for the Tories in 1930 but left to follow Stevens and take over organizing for the new party in Quebec. They all got off to a very late start and had even more trouble than the Conservatives raising money. The original plans were scaled back to the point where candidates were largely left to their own resources to finance the campaign (including their election deposits). Reconstruction candidates came from many different backgrounds, but all were essentially forced to share one characteristic in order to finance their campaigns: they had to have a job. One estimate put the total amount raised at a little over $30,000, most of which went to the "national" campaign. Stevens was able to pay for only one national broadcast, on October 12.[62]

For the Social Credit Party, the federal election was over-shadowed by the Alberta provincial campaign a few weeks earlier, but the party benefited from the publicity, radio broadcasts, and pamphlets, and the enthusiasm that had been whipped up in mass meetings and picnics during the earlier campaign. Party organization, such as it was, flowed from William Aberhart and his close associates, and the national party was largely an extension of the provincial party. Aberhart's imprint was everywhere. "I have been organizing all my life," he later explained. "There's nothing I'd rather do than organize."[63] In addition, as the governing United Farmers of Alberta disintegrated, Social Credit replaced it in many ways. UFA locals invited Social Credit speakers and distributed Social Credit literature, and many UFA supporters simply shifted their allegiance from the old party to the new. Social Credit study groups were refashioned as political entities, and Aberhart's mailing list of supporters of his Bible radio show served as the party's contact list for announcements, advertising, and campaign literature.[64]

Following Social Credit's provincial victory in August, federal candidates were selected for all ridings in Alberta and Saskatchewan and many others in British Columbia and Manitoba. Relatively little is known about the party's financing. Most businesses, the banks, and newspapers rejected social credit philosophy and were unlikely to support the party financially, although in later years considerable sums were collected from the Alberta business community, including some businesses that rejected the monetary theories of social credit.[65] In 1935, campaign fundraising was a local affair, and many campaign picnics began with an air of evangelical fervour and ended with the passing of the collection basket. Social Credit was a new and appealing political party, lacking the traditional trappings of a national political party and flourishing on the enthusiasm and largely volunteer contributions of local groups and individuals.

In 1935, the CCF set up a permanent office headquarters in Ottawa. David Lewis, a young lawyer and future leader of the New

Democratic Party (NDP), had just returned from three years in England and was eager to immerse himself in the new party. He moved to Ottawa just before the election and was soon deeply involved in the party's organization. The structure of the CCF was a little different from that of the other parties, which tended to be more centralized (the Social Credit and Reconstruction Parties were actually centralized around a single person). The CCF was a somewhat disparate federation of more than a dozen affiliated groups across the country, including branches of British Columbia's Socialist Party of Canada, locals from the fading UFA, the Farmer-Labour Party in Saskatchewan, and a variety of clubs in the Maritimes and Ontario.[66] This permitted a greater diversity of views but also meant that organizing for a national campaign would be a little more convoluted, with the provincial wings operating on their own. The CCF was moving in the direction of a more structured national party akin to the Liberals and Conservatives, but in 1935 they remained much less centralized.

The party actively established study groups across the country to educate and recruit new members, which was very important not only for party support but also for fundraising. It was not likely to attract many donations from Canadian businesses, and trade union support did not materialize until years later, meaning that in 1935 the party relied on the support of the rank and file.[67] This did not augur well in the run-up to the election. As J.S. Woodsworth wrote historian and League for Social Reconstruction member Frank Underhill at the University of Toronto, "under existing conditions it was almost impossible for us even to finance our own offices." Underhill had argued for a more "effective organization," to which Woodworth responded: "As a matter of fact we have very little real organization across the country."[68]

David Lewis recorded in his memoirs how he "had not realized how destitute the CCF was at that time." Woodsworth informed him about the lack of campaign financing and said that each CCF

The "prophet in politics," CCF leader James S. Woodsworth (June 17, 1938). | Photographer Yousuf Karsh, Library and Archives Canada, e010751658

candidate "must either finance himself or, like invading armies of old, live on the peoples it conquers. This may all seem like making bricks without straw – but somehow the bricks are actually being made!" Woodsworth added that "we are in the position where a man must show his qualities of leadership by leading, by drumming up a group and gradually securing support."[69]

There was some debate in the party over how to organize for the campaign. Frank Underhill, looking on from his Toronto office, called for a much stronger and more focused political party, with all the trappings of a traditional party – national headquarters, administrators, secretaries, and bureaucracy to oversee the publicity, and all the rest. Believing that success was on the horizon, Underhill urged the party to focus on victory in the election, and he grew frustrated with Woodsworth's tolerance of different voices in the party. "You have no idea how great masses of people are looking to you for a lead and how willingly they will accept from you a definition of exactly where the CCF is going and how it proposed to get there," he wrote Woodsworth in 1933. But the leader needed to speak out and "so crowd out the cranks and simpletons by laying down gradually a definite party line."[70] Others were less optimistic. One editorial in the *Canadian Forum,* a magazine usually sympathetic to the CCF, critiqued the new party in the run-up to the election:

> With a few exceptions, its political leaders lack the administrative capacity which would be so essential for carrying through their plans of wide government control. Furthermore, many of them have not weaned themselves from the point of view of the South West corner of the House. There they performed a spirited task of opposition, but Mr. Woodsworth and many of his colleagues have never really envisaged themselves actively and aggressively as a potential government. The CCF's day may come, but from present indications it will not come in 1935.[71]

Woodsworth realized that, despite some electoral success in British Columbia and Saskatchewan, the CCF was not going to win the election or even form the official opposition in the new Parliament. The best that could be hoped for was that the new party would have an influence on the direction of national affairs. To a supporter who asked whether the CCF could win a majority, he replied: "I do not think that at present it is at all possible that at the next election we could win the majority. In a great many parts of the country we have not the slightest organization."[72] He expressed growing frustration over such expectations in a letter to a colleague in May: "I confess that I am a bit tired of the mentality of our people who get discouraged unless they can delude themselves into the belief that we are going to be the government. There are more of this class of people in Ontario than anywhere else, and possibly, if they cannot see more clearly or have not more courage, they might as well turn back at this stage than later on."[73]

Nevertheless, from his vantage point in the House of Commons and given his deep understanding of how government worked, Woodsworth clearly realized the importance of winning elections. "I agree," he wrote in 1933, "that the main purpose of the CCF is not to get votes, that is, to get votes at any cost. But we are out to get votes, and the only way to do so is to constantly *recruit* fresh groups of people, many of whom, up to the present time have been allied with one or other of the old parties."[74]

THE CAMPAIGN WAS ON, and the candidates hit the ground running. Over the course of a few weeks, all the work in organizing, fundraising, manifesto writing, and candidate selection would be judged by one standard: winning the vote. Yet, as one contemporary commentator noted, "on the eve of the election, everybody was in the most profound uncertainty as to the outcome."[75] It seemed that most Canadians wanted change, but it was not at all clear what that change meant. The Liberal Party was the clear front-runner and it seemed that only an unexpected catastrophe could change that. There was less certainty about the other parties: no one could tell how far the Tories would fall or how much of their support would be siphoned off by one of the new parties. Would election day produce total victory for the Liberals, or would they be denied that triumph by unexpected wins for the CCF, Reconstruction Party, or Social Credit? The one point on which all the candidates seemed to agree was that in the run-up to the election of 1935, the campaign on the streets would be crucial.

5

King or Chaos?

It may be that we will have to go through the tragedy
of a slaughter all across the country because the attitude
of people everywhere seems to be to destroy existing
conditions without any thought of what may be the result.
No Opposition ever wins election, it is invariably the
Government that is defeated. In other words, Oppositions
don't have to have policies, all they have to do is to
encourage insurrection and rebellion.

– Howard Ferguson, 1935[1]

THE GREATEST NUMBER of voters were found, not surprisingly, in
the major cities. Vancouver had about 140,000 registered voters;
Ottawa had approximately 90,000; on the island of Montreal, there
were just under 600,000. The eleven Toronto ridings contained a
little over 434,000 voters. The numbers in each of those ridings
varied considerably, from Danforth on the low end (approximately
29,000) to Spadina on the high end (approximately 52,100).[2] On
the flip side, Yukon riding was the largest in terms of size but smallest
in terms of population, with only 1,805 registered voters.

Candidate nominations continued up to the week before election day. Although the numbers fluctuated slightly, in the end there were 891 candidates running for the 245 seats in the House of Commons. It was the largest number of candidates in Canadian history to that date (the previous high was 644 in 1921; there were only 546 in 1930), and no seats were won by acclamation. In Labelle, Quebec, it looked like Henri Bourassa, the aging political veteran, would again win his riding by acclamation, but at the last minute the Liberals nominated a candidate to challenge him for the seat. There were now only two ridings that were represented by two MPs: Queens in Prince Edward Island, and Halifax.

In fact, most ridings had four or more candidates. Of Saskatchewan's twenty-one constituencies, seventeen had four names on the ballot and two had five. The Liberals, the Co-operative Commonwealth Federation (CCF), and Social Credit fielded candidates in all the ridings, the Conservatives in nineteen, and the Reconstruction Party in three, and there was an assortment of independent candidates. Each of Vancouver's four ridings had five candidates. Only one was from the Social Credit Party (W.A. Tutte in Vancouver Burrard); the fifth candidate in the other three ridings was a socialist, communist, and independent, respectively. The old standard two-party contests were unusual – some two dozen in 1935 – and most of them occurred in Quebec, while all four party leaders faced three or four opponents. It was a similar story in Montreal Verdun, where there were ten names on the ballot. In addition to the Conservative, Reconstruction, and CCF candidates, there were two Independent Liberals, two Independent Conservatives, a Labour candidate, a Veterans candidate, and a member of the eponymous Verdun Party. The presence of three new parties competing for votes was the obvious explanation for the plethora of candidates, but there were also a large number of Independents (Liberal, Conservative, Labour, and even Reconstruction), twelve communist candidates, one anti-communist, eight Labour and Liberal-Labour, and one person who ran as a "Technocrat."

Only three parties fielded a sufficient number of candidates to form a government: the Liberals, Conservatives, and Reconstruction Party. It is also difficult to be precise about the affiliation of some candidates as there were Liberal-Progressives in Manitoba, Independent Conservatives, and so on, whose connection to their parties was not always clearly defined. The Liberals had the most candidates, 245, and they supported Independent Liberals in a few other ridings. There were even Liberals and Independent Liberals running against each other in some ridings. For example, in the large riding of Churchill, Manitoba, when T.A. Crerar won the nomination, his defeated opponent promptly declared that he would run as an Independent Liberal (he withdrew from the race before election day, however).[3] A couple of other ridings were left open for Independent candidates, including Montreal Verdun (mentioned above) and Yukon, but the Liberals were represented in all Ontario ridings except Hamilton East. The Conservatives ran 228 candidates, leaving at least five Quebec ridings, as well as others in Nova Scotia, Ontario, and Manitoba, with no Tory candidate. The Reconstruction Party put up 172 candidates, offering a fairly full slate of candidates in most provinces except Saskatchewan and Alberta.[4]

The CCF fielded 121 candidates, primarily in Ontario and the West, with only five running in Quebec and none at all in the Maritimes. A majority CCF government was therefore impossible. The party's only hope was to win enough seats to wield some influence in the next Parliament or, perhaps, in a very unlikely scenario, form a minority government with the help of one of the other parties.

One of the most serious campaign problems for the CCF, however, came from the Left, not the Right. In advance of the election, the Communist Party approached the CCF leaders and proposed cooperation in the campaign so as not to split the labour vote. Earlier that year, party leader Tim Buck and Sam Carr, his assistant and election organizer, wrote Woodsworth that they planned to run candidates in more than a dozen ridings and hoped that some agreement could be reached with the CCF, "making possible an elimination of any possibilities for splits in the working class vote and mutual support on the basis of a minimum program of immediate needs for the toilers of Canada."[5] Woodsworth rejected any talk of cooperation, believing that the goal of the Communist Party was not cooperation but rather a Communist takeover of the CCF. "In tactics at least, there is no agreement whatever between the Communist Party and the C.C.F.," he replied to Buck and Carr. "The overthrow of the C.C.F. rather than that of capitalism would seem to be the main object of the Communist Party of Canada."[6]

As for the Social Credit Party, its victory in Alberta was so recent that it had to scramble to field candidates for the federal campaign. Clearly a regional party, Social Credit saw candidates come forward in all Alberta ridings, including a challenger to Bennett in Calgary West, while the rest ran in ridings in Saskatchewan and British Columbia. In all, Social Credit fielded forty-six candidates, and John H. Blackmore, a former schoolteacher who ran in Lethbridge, emerged as the party leader, although always under the shadow of William Aberhart. He subsequently became Social Credit's parliamentary caucus leader. For many observers, however, Social Credit had no leader on the federal stage, and its platform and campaign lacked the uniformity seen in those of the other parties.[7]

The emergence of Social Credit posed a challenge to all the other parties, but especially to the CCF and Reconstruction, as all three were appealing to the same voters in their condemnation of the capitalist system and their demands for financial reforms. H.H. Stevens met with Aberhart in Vancouver to discuss a formal alliance, but later denied any cooperation between the two parties. What emerged was an unofficial alliance, with few Reconstructionists challenging Social Credit candidates in Alberta (except Calgary and Edmonton) and Saskatchewan. A similar tacit arrangement was worked out between the Reconstructionists and the United Farmers of Ontario, although Agnes Macphail denied any affiliation with the Reconstruction Party (but claimed that the new party had appropriated some her ideas).[8]

The CCF generally opposed cooperation with Social Credit, but there were a few exceptions. In Yorkton, Saskatchewan, for example, Jacob Benson openly ran as a joint CCF–Social Credit candidate. In Weyburn, Saskatchewan, rookie candidate Tommy Douglas was backed by Social Crediters when it was rumoured that local Liberals tried to split the vote by offering $3,000 to a defeated CCF candidate to run against Douglas under the Social Credit banner.[9] Douglas may have run afoul of the provincial CCF executive, but clearly not enough to hinder his long political career. Social Credit supporters also actively campaigned in Prince Albert in an effort to defeat Mackenzie King.[10]

For the most part, nomination of candidates went smoothly and was largely left up to local ridings and regional party leaders, although in a few cases the party leaders chose, or needed, to intervene. Bennett offered a nomination to the economist and popular author Stephen Leacock in Simcoe North, where Leacock had a summer home, but was turned down. Bennett accepted his own nomination in Calgary West in person during his Western campaign swing. Mackenzie King did not travel west in time to accept his nomination in Prince Albert and appeared content with not having to make the trip. The hope was to avoid nasty nomination contests, which could attract unpleasant scrutiny or unwanted publicity. Nevertheless, there were a few problems.

In Quebec, where the Liberals appeared certain of victory, the biggest problems often arose in the selection of candidates and not during the campaign itself. In early September, Mackenzie King, Ernest Lapointe, and Premier Louis-Alexandre Taschereau met publicly at a lunch for Young Liberal leaders and endorsed party unity in the selection of candidates. In those ridings with a Liberal incumbent, the standing MP was allowed to run again, but in ridings with a sitting Conservative MP, major contests arose over the Liberal nomination. An effort to have formal conventions in these ridings so "there would be at least a semblance of popular choice" led to several raucous nomination conventions, with rival factions taunting, threatening, and jeering each other. In the large riding of Saint-Maurice–Laflèche, for example, rival factions representing the riding's two largest towns each put forward a candidate for the Liberal nomination. The two sides almost came to blows before one was selected.[11]

In Trois-Rivières, a heated contest saw P.J.A. Cardin, the former minister of marine, surrounded and prevented from entering a meeting by rival protesters. In the end, Cardin refused to return to preside over the meeting, Philippe Bigué got the Liberal nomination, and two others ran as Independent Liberals, bringing the total number of candidates in the riding to six. In Maisonneuve-Rosemont, Sarto Fournier, a law student, was the unexpected winner, defeating the early favourite, Ubald Fortin. J.O. Cordeau, who expected Fortin to be selected, had dropped out prior to the convention to run for the Reconstruction Party. Fournier apparently fainted when he won the nomination, but went on to become the youngest person elected in 1935.[12]

Deep in southwestern Ontario, rookie politician Paul Martin faced a tough and bitter nomination battle in Essex East against his main opponent, Dr. Percy Gardner, a local resident and popular city councillor. One of the other defeated Liberal candidates, Joseph Gabriel McPharlin, quit the party in protest and ran under the Reconstruction Party banner (he later joined the Tories).[13] The neighbouring riding of Essex West picked Norman McLarty, a senior Liberal and Martin's friend, while farmer Murray Clarke won the Liberal nomination in Essex South. The three Liberal candidates occasionally shared public platforms and found other ways to collaborate. Out west, in the BC riding of Comox-Alberni, many

Liberals threw their support to A.W. Neill, an independent, over Alexander MacNeil, the nominal Liberal candidate, and Neill went on to win the nomination and the riding. In the same riding, the CCF endorsed Colin Cameron, although many local party members backed Malcom Mackinnon, who ran under the Labour banner.[14] In Yukon, Liberal candidate Charles Reid withdrew his nomination at the request of the National Liberal Federation, leaving the field open for J.P. Smith, an Independent Liberal. Such cases were relatively rare, however.

The Conservatives had fewer problems, although in the Montreal riding of Mount Royal there was more than one candidate, with the loser, E.C. Werry, charging that he was defeated by a "hodge-podge of illegally chosen delegates." He withdrew his name from nomination before the first ballot and W. Allen Walsh was nominated. With a Conservative, a Liberal, a Reconstructionist, a CCFer, and two independents, this riding also posted six candidates. A bigger problem was the defection of Conservatives to the Reconstruction Party, and here the new party benefited from dissension within Tory ranks. In London, Ontario, for example, former Conservative MP John White joined the Reconstructionists after losing the Tory nomination to Fred Betts. In Simcoe East, W.M. Cramp left his position as president of the local Conservative Club to accept the Reconstruction nomination.[15] Stevens's message appealed to other Tories, and many former Conservatives were drawn into membership in the Stevens Clubs that appeared across the country.

Getting the Message Out to Voters

Getting the message out to voters was central to all parties. Radio had quickly become an integral part of Canadian elections, and all the parties participated, especially the Liberals and Conservatives. The new medium had been used widely in the 1930 campaign but came into its own in 1935. At the start of the decade, there were more than sixty stations across the country and over one-third of Canadians owned a radio, and the numbers were rising fast. What had been a novelty in the 1920s had evolved into a necessity.[16] In 1932, the Bennett government established the Canadian Radio Broadcasting Commission (CRBC) to oversee and regulate broadcasting in Canada and to set up a national radio system. By 1935, radio had come to dominate family living rooms, to the envy of neighbours and friends without one. "It is impossible to overestimate the power of the radio in the Depression years," wrote popular historian Pierre Berton. "More than railways they stitched the country together; more than the movies they brought solace to the impoverished."[17]

Political broadcasts and campaign advertising were widely used during the election campaign, and millions of Canadians could now hear the voices of those who were asking for their votes. All radio political broadcasts were undertaken on a commercial basis, with each party paying for its airtime. None was provided by the government.[18] In addition to straight studio broadcasts, it was not unusual for campaign speeches to be broadcast simultaneously (sometimes over a national chain of radio stations) to reach a broader audience. Conservative broadcasts were dominated by the prime minister; Liberal broadcasts tended to feature a greater variety of prominent Liberals.

One of the most effective Conservative strategies was the series of "Sage" broadcasts that ran between September 7 and October 11. Produced by the Toronto advertising firm hired to oversee Conservative publicity, it consisted of six broadcasts, each fifteen to thirty-five minutes long. These were dramatized political advertisements with actors portraying average Canadians. Audiences were invited into the home of Mr. and Mrs. Sage to discuss the failings of Mackenzie King and the Liberals. King "doesn't care whether it helps or hinders the people of the country so long as it helps him to be Prime Minister," said Mr. Sage. "Mr. King's so fearful that he does anything at all that he thinks will please his crowd." What particularly angered the Liberals was that at no time during the broadcasts was it mentioned that the skits were produced for the Conservatives and were essentially Conservative propaganda. Complaints were made immediately to the CRBC, and the later broadcasts included a declaration that the Conservatives were involved in the production.[19] The Liberals may have been annoyed about the Sage radio spots but they used radio effectively as well, and also produced a short film about King that was shown in 221 Paramount theatres.

Newspapers remained the central vehicle for publicity and propaganda, and here the Liberals had the decided advantage. They could count on the support of the two major Toronto papers, the *Star* and the *Globe*, as well as the *Winnipeg Free Press*, the *Vancouver Sun*, the *Regina Leader-Post*, the *Ottawa Citizen*, Quebec's *Le Soleil*, and the *Halifax Chronicle*. Apart from the *Montreal Gazette*, the Conservatives had little newspaper support. The Conservative newspaper *La Patrie* had run into financial trouble and was sold to the Liberal (and much bigger and more popular) *La Presse* in 1932, which meant that the Conservatives went into the election without any Quebec newspaper under their control and with the editorial support of only a few dailies, such as *Le Canadien*.[20] Only a handful of papers in the rest of the country backed the Tories. Alberta boasted six daily newspapers, including the *Calgary Herald* and *Edmonton Journal*, both of which supported the Conservatives; the Liberals could count on the *Edmonton Bulletin* and the dailies published in Lethbridge and Medicine Hat. The sixth – the Calgary *Albertan* – was independent. Interestingly, most Alberta dailies (along with the business community) were critical of Aberhart and Social Credit and complained that the premier was unwilling to discuss the controversial tenets of Social Credit, the inconsistencies and contradictions of which they were happy to point out.

Not only did Bennett not attract the support of many newspapers; he actively feuded with journalists and newspapers. For example, John W. Dafoe, the veteran editor of the influential *Winnipeg Free Press*, regarded Bennett "as a rich, aristocratic, intolerant despot; as a man whose views, particularly on the question of Empire, made him the very antithesis of a real Canadian." Bennett didn't help matters by threatening to sue the *Free Press* for libel over its publication of Stevens's speech (discussed in Chapter 1), and when the election was called, the paper launched an anti-Bennett campaign. Material came from a large file of damning reports on Bennett dating back to 1913, which the paper had been sitting on for just such an occasion.[21]

Conversely, King and the Liberals cultivated good relations with the press. In July, before the campaign started, King travelled to Toronto to meet with J.E. Atkinson of the *Star* and William Gladstone Jaffray of the *Globe* to confirm their support for the party in the upcoming election. The *Globe* had long been a Liberal stalwart but its support had waned in recent years. At the end of the day, and thanks to a lengthy meal at the Old Mill Restaurant in Toronto's west end, Jaffray hinted that King could expect full support from the *Globe*.[22] The Liberals also benefited from the free publicity offered by the *Star*, which produced and distributed a pro-Liberal pamphlet free of charge.

Books about the leaders of the two major parties were another source of publicity. Bennett's biography was offered not as a "heavy, detailed history of a dull political figure, but a scintillating picture of the most dominating figure in Canadian life."[23] Six editions had been published by early 1935. An earlier brief biography of King, written by John Lewis, was enlarged and revised by Norman Rogers, a Queen's University political science professor and Liberal candidate in Kingston. King oversaw the revisions, contributed many himself, and involved himself in all the details, down to the illustrations and the texture of the cloth cover. Ten thousand copies of the first edition were printed, reportedly with the help of a subsidy from Liberal coffers to the tune of $6,000, and appeared, under Rogers's name, in early spring, just in time for the campaign. The book's publication also coincided with the new edition of King's earlier work *Industry and Humanity*, revised and re-released during the campaign to highlight his credentials as a reformer.[24]

The Conservative Campaign

For the Conservatives, campaigning really got underway in September. Bennett launched the national campaign with four thirty-minute radio broadcasts from Toronto early in the month, then headed west and was on the road for most of the next six weeks. A major disadvantage was apparent from the start – there were no Tory premiers and few prominent Conservatives to sit with him on stage or accompany him across the country. Senator and former leader Arthur Meighen was reluctant to get out on the hustings to support Bennett or his party, and he remained ensconced in the confines of the Senate chamber. Several cabinet members had retired to private life or gone off to the Senate or some other appointment and were unavailable. Most candidates stayed in their ridings, worried about their own futures. Martha Black, running in Yukon in place of her ill husband, had no radio broadcasts to help with her campaign, and she travelled hundreds of miles in boats with failing motors and in broken-down cars over muddy roads to get to her voters. Like most Conservative candidates, she had little time to support other candidates or to devote to a national campaign.[25]

A little help came from outside the party when Stephen Leacock campaigned for a local Montreal Tory in the riding of Mount Royal. Leacock dismissed the CCF as "little boys blowing soap bubbles," and Stevens as someone who "finds a perfect hornet's nest of iniquity everywhere he goes." As for the Social Credit Party, he quipped: "They will go to Ottawa and babble, babble, babble. You

R.B. Bennett and his sister, Mildred Herridge, on the campaign trail
(no date). | Library and Archives Canada, C-21528

see, section 98 doesn't apply to them."[26] Leacock was the exception,
however. There was cooperation, of course, among Conservative
candidates, and it was not unusual for all the candidates in any city
to gather together or rent a local hall for a joint campaign rally, but
few ventured far beyond their town or region. Among the Tories,
only Robert Manion contributed to any kind of national campaign.
This situation only reinforced the notion that Bennett was a one-
man show, especially compared with the Liberals, who had an em-
barrassment of riches. It was a study in contrast between Bennett
the lone campaigner and King the team leader.

Bennett made his first major campaign stop in Regina on
September 14, then made whistle stops in Lethbridge (September
17) and Calgary (September 19). His private railcar made frequent
stops for impromptu visits and short speeches. In Medicine Hat, he
lingered for forty-five minutes of handshaking and a short talk with
a group of schoolchildren.[27]

In Calgary, Bennett's adopted hometown, he was welcomed by thousands of enthusiastic voters with thundering ovations and local bands. He defended his record and talked of trade and wheat and argued that he needed a second term to complete the job. If economic times had been better, he said, the Empire trade agreements alone "would have ensured the retention of any Government for fifteen years," but new ideas were needed now.[28] Bennett accepted his party's nomination in Calgary West, then later that day met with Frank Holloway, an old friend, for dinner at the Palliser Hotel. They spoke of many things but inevitably talk turned to the election campaign. When Holloway asked him how the campaign was progressing, Bennett dropped his guard and replied: "I wouldn't say this to anyone else, Frank, but I think we've lost. And one man has crucified the Party: Stevens."[29]

Bennett arrived in British Columbia on September 21, and things started to unravel. Giving a speech at Victoria's Royal Theatre, he faced hecklers who attacked him for his government's actions and his personal wealth. "If you would work your mouth less and your other parts more," he responded, "you would be better off."[30] Bruce Hutchison, an upcoming journalist, was in the audience that night and recorded his impressions:

In the wings a large figure slumped on a very small chair, and for a moment I did not recognize him. He was no longer the lusty, vibrant Bennett I had watched so often as he hurled his thunderbolts across the House of Commons. The man on the chair looked ill, almost unconscious, his face as white as the familiar stiff collar, his hands dangling limp beside him. But it was Bennett all right – the Prime Minister of Canada alone in a dark corner, deserted, drained, and friendless at the end of the road. The curtain went up at last. The listless figure sprang to life and strode to the centre of the stage, majestic in tail coat and air of defiance, master of himself and the crowd. Then, as the hecklers began to shout, he shouted them down, the almighty voice booming out like a cannon to hush the clamorous theatre. This triumph of the spirit over the flesh was heroic, unnatural, and, as I supposed, unlikely to be repeated.[31]

Bennett made headlines that night when he claimed that the intent of the On-to-Ottawa trekkers was to kidnap and hold him hostage while a Soviet government was established in Canada. He stood for law and order, he proclaimed, and connected the alleged kidnapping plot to the Liberals and their promise to repeal section 98 of the Criminal Code. "Section 98 stands, and those who violate it must bear the consequences," he said; removing it would only encourage more of the subversive elements in the country. Hearing of Bennett's outlandish charge, Stevens responded that there may have been a communist or two in the ranks of the Regina protesters, but overall they were "a nice bunch who couldn't kidnap a rat."[32]

In Vancouver, Bennett – dressed in formal black attire – waded into an enthusiastic crowd of Conservative supporters on the CPR platform and was met with three cheers and a singalong to "For He's a Jolly Good Fellow." Later, however, at his speech in the Vancouver Arena on September 23, he faced what the *Vancouver Sun* called "an ugly, hostile crowd" and gave as good as he got: "Calling upon all his arrogant, domineering, force of character, hurling at the stormy mob all the biting invective of which his peerless command of language is capable, he fought the unruly multitude savagely for more than 20 minutes. He beat them into submission. Then he made his speech."[33] It was a similar situation as Bennett headed east at the end of the month. In a speech to five thousand supporters crowded into a Hamilton hockey rink, Bennett labelled the hecklers "freaks," and they yelled, "You're through, Bennett!" as they were escorted out by police.[34]

The campaign moved east at the beginning of October, beginning with a series of speeches in Quebec's Eastern Townships. Bennett warned crowds in Sherbrooke, Granby, and Magog against communism; they would lose their possessions, faith, and families if one of the other parties was elected. He accused King of trying to be all things to all people: one day he was for sound money, the next he supported inflation; today he was for free trade, yesterday he advocated protection; he even claimed to be a radical. "If the campaign lasted another month," Bennett declared, King "would probably get around to calling himself a Conservative."[35]

In speeches to an estimated crowd of 3,800 in St. John (October 2) and 1,200 in Fredericton (October 3), where he stopped to offer support for cabinet colleague and future Tory leader Richard Hanson, Bennett defended his government's performance and declared that William Aberhart was a friend. He had no criticism of the Alberta leader, but of H.H. Stevens he said: "The only difficulty, apparently, is that he could not get wealth when he wanted it and consequently anybody who did succeed in getting it must be a criminal."[36] Then it was on to Halifax, then New Glasgow, followed by a stop at the train station in Truro, Nova Scotia, and finally a Saturday night rally in Charlottetown on October 6.

Before a cheering crowd of four thousand in Charlottetown, he denounced communism one more time, and praised the Bank of Canada. Across the region, he responded to questions about out-migration – a serious concern for many Maritimers – by returning to his major campaign theme of trade and tariffs. More trade was the solution, he explained; only the opening up of international and Canadian markets to Maritime products would create the jobs needed to keep people at home. He also talked about how much Canadian taxpayer money had gone into building Maritime railways. "How many of your offspring are helping to pay those taxes?" someone shouted from the audience. "Well, I am frank to say not any so far as I know," Bennett replied.[37]

The Charlottetown speech was the last in the swing through the Maritimes, and the campaign entered the home stretch. Bennett visited with his brother, Captain Ronald Bennett, in Sackville, New

Brunswick, then headed for home. On October 7, a Quebec City crowd of fourteen thousand "vociferous, volatile French Canadians" gave him a rousing welcome, surrounded by placards underlining his major themes: "Contre le Communisme," and "Pour la Maitien de l'Article 98."[38] He had now visited all provinces, and in the six-day eastern tour had made an estimated twelve speeches and three off-the-cuff talks at train stations to 48,700 people, plus thousands more over the radio. Now it was back to Ontario, where he planned to end the campaign.

The Liberal Campaign

In contrast to Bennett's one-man show, Mackenzie King and the Liberals could count on – and actively encouraged – a range of provincial premiers and former cabinet ministers to contribute to the campaign, usually by appearing at King's side at his first rally in each province.[39] Nova Scotia's Angus L. Macdonald campaigned in his province and made a few speeches in Ontario. Saskatchewan premier Jimmy Gardiner campaigned in both the Maritimes and Ontario, and accompanied King during much of the latter's Western campaign swing. In Manitoba, Premier John Bracken backed the Liberals and made several public appearances with King by his side. In Quebec, Premier Taschereau did not actively campaign, but near the end made a few speeches and participated in a national radio broadcast.

Ontario premier Hepburn was the most active of all the premiers. He was keen to rid the country of its last Tory government, and threw himself and the Ontario Liberal Party into the fight. King welcomed the boost Hepburn could bring to the party's chances, and the two men shared a stage in Woodstock on August 13 to launch the Ontario campaign. Hepburn went on to speak in dozens of Ontario ridings.[40]

At the end of August, Hepburn travelled west – contrary to doctor's orders – to take the battle to the Tories and Social Crediters on

Mackenzie King and Mitchell Hepburn in Hepburn's Toronto office (1934). Despite their personal and political differences, the 1935 election brought the two Liberals together in a common cause. | Library and Archives Canada, C-087863

the prairies.[41] He spoke at Winnipeg, Regina, Moose Jaw, Swift Current, Lethbridge, and through British Columbia with stops in Kamloops, Victoria, and Vancouver, where his speech was disrupted by a group of rowdy longshoremen. On the way home, there were more stops, including one at Edmonton and a whistle stop in Yorkton, where he spoke to a crowd of two thousand. At one event, he knocked over a glass, spilling the water, and joked: "I am glad I didn't upset an empty glass because an empty glass always annoys me."[42]

Hepburn hammered away at the need for freer trade with the United States and for markets for Canadian natural products; he called for the expansion of credit and for constitutional reform to give the federal government stronger powers to undertake national action on the great economic and social issues of the day. He told

Westerners that they had the chance to right the wrongs inflicted in 1911, when the West voted in favour of reciprocity with the United States only to have the Conservatives sweep Ontario and destroy the bill.[43]

Hepburn also toured the Maritimes and, at the request of Quebec Liberals Chubby Power and Jean-François Pouliot, he agreed to a speech in Quebec City, where he spoke in French to an estimated crowd of eight thousand. Sharing the stage with more than a dozen Quebec Liberals, including Taschereau, Power, and Cardin, he was introduced by Ernest Lapointe, who called him the "greatest fighter in Canadian politics." After the rally, the crowd spilled into the streets chanting, "Mitch Hepburn, Mitch Hepburn, Mitch Hepburn!"[44]

King welcomed the support but felt it wise to resist the premiers when they called for more dramatic action. Hepburn urged King to come out more forcefully with bold new policies, seeing some kind of action as necessary to take some of the air out of the CCF campaign and to deflect what he saw as growing support in Ontario for Stevens and the Reconstruction Party.[45] From Victoria, activist Premier Duff Pattullo called on King to get on the activist bandwagon; many other Liberals pressed him to come out swinging with a platform to grab the attention of Canadian voters.

King reiterated that oppositions don't win elections, governments lose them. For him this meant saying as little as possible and letting Bennett, the Conservatives, and the Depression win the election for the Liberals. He would stay the course: promise a trade deal with the United States, speak in favour of national unity, do nothing to alienate the regions, and issue vague promises to solve the problems facing the country. Why risk dividing the party – and its support in the country – by discussing policies and actions? "It is only ourselves who can destroy ourselves," he confided to his diary.[46]

In Quebec, the growing split within the provincial Liberal Party was papered over, and both the Taschereau stalwarts and the younger

Action Libérale Nationale (ALN) supporters worked for the federal Liberals. The biggest obstacle for the Liberals in Quebec was the Liberal promise to repeal section 98 of the Criminal Code. Lapointe supported repeal and was attacked in Quebec, where section 98 remained popular. He was accused of being sympathetic to communists and, as he later reported, "my leader and I were described as the friends of the men who want to pull down the steeples, the men who protect those who walk on crucifixes, and so on."[47]

The Quebec Liberal campaign came crashing down – literally – in the village of St-Joseph d'Alma when a large part of a plaster ceiling collapsed on a stage full of Liberal dignitaries. More than a dozen were injured, including Lapointe, who was struck and reportedly lost consciousness for ten minutes. Lapointe's critics may have seen it as celestial retribution for his stand on section 98, but it did not slow down either him or the Liberal campaign.[48]

Mackenzie King began his part in the national Liberal campaign slowly and methodically from home in Ottawa. For much of the first half of August, he focused on preparing speeches and a few radio spots, and wrote his "issues" contribution for *Maclean's*. He gave a speech to the Central Ontario Liberal Association in Kingston on August 7, and followed it with a brief tour of the province.

The campaign picked up steam in September as King left for the Maritimes. On September 3, he gave a speech at Fredericton's Capitol Theatre in support of W.G. Clarke, the Liberal candidate in York-Sunbury, who was challenging Conservative cabinet minister R.B. Hanson. At a major rally at the Halifax hockey rink on September 4, King was accompanied by Premier Angus Macdonald and virtually all the Liberal candidates in Nova Scotia. The event was broadcast on radio stations in Halifax, Sydney, Yarmouth, and even Charlottetown, so most Maritimers could tune in.[49] Other stops included Moncton and Charlottetown on September 5. On his way home through Quebec, King met with Cardinal Villeneuve, who promised him Catholic support when he became prime minister, and after dinner with Premier Taschereau he delivered an outdoor speech – mostly in French – to a large crowd that braved the cool evening and occasional drizzle. Then it was back to Ottawa.

In the middle of September, King embarked on the Western swing of the campaign, in a part of the country where the Liberals were already in trouble. His first stop was Winnipeg (September 19) and he gave a speech in Brandon later that day. It was less successful than he hoped, and he blamed his clothes, which had made him too hot. He met with Saskatchewan premier Jimmy Gardiner, who briefed him on the state of the Western campaign. Reports were good, but King was concerned about Western Liberal leadership, other than Gardiner. "There is no one outstanding," he wrote in his diary. "The people are like sheep without a shepherd. I confess the situation does not look too certain here." Part of his concern was over the rise of Social Credit. "The people seem to forget & seem to want promise. These new theories have bewildered them & they can't see a way out." He was even more critical of his Alberta team leaders, especially when compared with Aberhart. "Here is the whole story in a nut-shell," he complained. "The Liberal Leader a drunken unreliable lawyer of a blustering bull-dozing type, the Social credit Leader, kindly, persuasive, clean living, most presentable etc – is it any wonder he won & the Liberals lost."[50]

King travelled on to Regina and Saskatoon (September 20), where he gave a speech at a local church, accompanied, as usual, by the local Liberal candidates and other party notables. He spoke from the Liberal playbook, talking of tariffs, banking and currency issues, railways, and the Canadian Wheat Board. There were more brief speeches, delivered from the back of his train car, along the route, including at Duck Lake and Prince Albert, his own riding. In Alberta, he quietly predicted a Social Credit victory although he hoped to win a seat or two. He tried to make the argument that a vote for Social Credit would only help the Conservatives, but it is unclear how successful he was.

In Edmonton, King met with Aberhart and the two men got along quite well. King left with a positive view of the new premier, whom he invited to join him on the platform that night. Aberhart considered the offer before declining.[51] A few days later, however, as the Liberal train wound its way back east, King learned that a few Social Crediters had warned some of his supporters to stay away from one of his local rallies, and his tune quickly changed. "My feeling is that Aberhart should be hanged," he wrote in his diary. "His action has been bribery & corruption."[52]

Throughout the Western tour, King was supported by other prominent Liberals. In Vancouver (September 27), he spoke to well-wishers from the train station platform and toured Stanley Park with the help of Ian Mackenzie. In Victoria, he was met by Premier Pattullo and members of his government, and the two shared the stage at a local theatre. In Regina (October 1), he was accompanied by Walter Scott, Saskatchewan's first premier; in Winnipeg (October 2), he was joined on stage by Premier Bracken and T.A. Crerar, who had undertaken his own personal political odyssey as Liberal, Unionist, Progressive, and Liberal once more. King also gave speeches in Calgary, Medicine Hat, and Swift Current, where he spoke from the back of a truck. Everywhere he stressed that Bennett had become the whole Conservative Party and warned Western Canadians of the drift towards dictatorship. Luckily, we were not there yet, he said; there was still time to vote Liberal.[53]

By early October, King and the Liberal train were back in Ontario. The first stop was to support Liberal candidates in Port Arthur and Fort William. In Fort William, the candidate was Dan McIvor, a younger, left-leaning minister whose nomination had been opposed by some old guard Liberals and the provincial party under Mitch Hepburn (who wanted one of their own as candidate).[54] In Port Arthur, it was Clarence Decatur Howe. The American-born Howe graduated from MIT with a civil engineering degree and landed a teaching position at Dalhousie University in 1908. He worked his

Mackenzie King campaigning in Vancouver (September 28, 1935). |
Photographer William B. Shelly, Library and Archives Canada, C-013256

way west and made his fortune building grain elevators before being
drawn into politics despite having no previous political affiliations,
thanks to a friendship with Norman Lambert of the National Liberal
Federation. Howe met King in 1934 and agreed to run in Port Arthur,
where he lived.

Port Arthur was a very large riding comprising hundreds of miles
of territory, with about half the voters living outside of town. The
sitting Conservative MP had chosen not to run, and the communists
put up a strong candidate, Reverend A.E. Smith, a United Church
minister. Communist Party leader Tim Buck visited the riding and
spoke to a crowd of over two thousand; CCF leader Woodsworth
also came to the Lakehead. Howe travelled widely and spoke wherever he could to whomever would listen. The visit of the Liberal
Party leader was a great boost, and King, Howe, and McIvor appeared
together on stage. Howe would go on to serve in Liberal cabinets

until 1957 and gain the nickname of "minister of everything," but that night, October 3, 1935, he was a rookie politician who, King noted, said the right things but did not speak very well.[55]

Like other party leaders, King was occasionally confronted by hecklers or those who wished to disrupt his campaign. While Bennett or Stevens would respond with wit or sarcasm, or at least challenge hecklers, King remained humourless and dour. At one early October rally where he was speaking of social welfare, an unhappy listener called out, "If you add another $10 to it I will vote for you." King responded piously. "Haven't we reached a terrible condition in the affairs of a great party," he asked, "when a man will say to a political leader in front of a great audience 'If you give me a bribe of $10 I will vote for you?' That is the very thing we are fighting against."[56]

The caravan continued east through Sudbury to Toronto, where King again faced calls for a more active campaign. This time it came from the president of the National Liberal Federation, Vincent Massey. Massey was concerned over what he believed was a growing weakness in Liberal ranks – a weakness that was having a negative impact on many local Liberal candidates. He blamed it on the length of the campaign, the lack of money, and – perhaps unexpectedly – the impressive Conservative campaign. He wrote King on October 1 that the campaign "is on the whole going well but we need a more vigorous fighting spirit on the part of the candidates and workers." Massey went on to explain the situation from his vantage point, laying out the state of the Liberal campaign as it headed for the home stretch:

> Our feeling here is that Bennett is very much our major enemy. Stevens seems to be losing ground, although in some constituencies his candidates are formidable. We had a meeting of 30–35 candidates here yesterday and impressed on them the necessity of

concentrating on three subjects in the concluding days of the campaign: 1) the menace of Bennett and the miserable prospect which five more years of his opportunism and one-man rule would mean; 2) the necessity of answering Tory misrepresentations on the subject of trade and fiscal politics. The tariff seems to have become the major issue in the campaign and the most flagrant mis-statements are being made in Tory propaganda about our attitude to the Empire Trade Agreements, Canadian-Japanese trade, etc. The Tories are using $10. to our $1. in their broadcasting and general publicity campaign in the press and elsewhere. This fact in itself might be used against them. 3) We feel that probably the dominant note in the concluding days should be that the alternatives before the electorate are a Liberal Government or a patchwork of insincere alliances between all the other parties and groups with Bennett, the arch-opportunist, controlling the levers. This idea is incorporated in the slogan "King or Chaos" which we are using widely.[57]

On October 5, Massey met with King in the latter's private rail car as it sat in the Toronto train station to discuss the state of the campaign. The meeting started badly, as King was asleep when Massey arrived and was in a foul mood at being woken up to speak once more against the idea of initiating a more dynamic campaign full of promises of action and reform. King had told his private secretary not to let Massey in, but there he was in King's private car. He was annoyed that Massey was trying to tell him what to do, and felt that he had "caused me more pain & concern than anyone or all else in the party besides." The one-sided conversation went downhill from there. King lashed out, blaming Massey for harming his health with these interruptions, and told him that his ideas were all wrong and that he should support the party leader; he accused him of selfish interference and charged that all he was interested in was himself and a future posting to London. "It was a scathing review," King later wrote. "He was quite crushed, – perhaps I went too far but it was 'the last straw.'"[58] King was upset for the rest of the day.

Following the dust-up with Massey, King left Toronto to continue the Liberal tour across southern Ontario. In Chatham (October 7), he visited Dr. James Rutherford, MP and Liberal nominee for Kent, in the hospital. Rutherford was in a very serious auto crash early in September when his car flipped three times and he had to be cut free from the wreck (but not, apparently, before diagnosing his own injuries).[59] They spoke briefly (King assured him he would win), then King posed for photographs with nurses on the hospital lawn and left for Windsor and meetings with local candidates Norman McLarty and Paul Martin. Rutherford campaigned from his hospital bed.

It was local politics in Windsor, which had been formed only earlier in the year from the amalgamation of the border cities of Windsor, East Windsor (Ford City), Sandwich, and Walkerville. Paul Martin attacked Bennett's 1932 imperial preference, which permitted greater competition from South African corn producers and hurt the agricultural producers of the riding; he was also aided by the support of the riding's large francophone population.[60] "Strolling around town," Martin recalled in his memoirs, "I talked to voters in the stores on Ottawa Street or in the market, on church steps (I attended mass at a different church each Sunday), and sometimes at the factory gates early in the morning. Campaigning in the warm summer months was a particular delight."[61] Martin bought his first car to use on the campaign trail, until it was hit by a cow.

Martin's major opponent in Essex East was Dr. Raymond Morand, the sitting Conservative MP, who was not only a friend but also Martin's personal physician. Indeed, during the campaign, Martin was forced by a sore throat to visit him for medical advice. The CCF chose Joseph Levert, the owner of a local greenhouse business, who worked hard to attract the organized labour vote. The Communist Party was small in the Windsor area, but when it endorsed Levert, he became an easy target for red-baiting and general anti-communist rhetoric. Martin refused to debate Levert.[62]

King spoke to a large gathering in the Windsor arena, accompanied on stage by local Liberal candidates. Martin announced that if elected he would take an independent stand in Ottawa, prompting King to later note in his diary: "Martin was going to exercise his independence at Ottawa. I felt like telling him he better get elected first."[63] For his part, King again denounced one-man parties and dictatorships, this time directing his attention at Social Credit. What was Social Credit beyond a promise of $25 a month? he asked rhetorically. What was their policy on the tariff or the railways? "Who is the Social Credit Leader in the Federal campaign?" King also touted the Liberals' reform policies, damned the CCF for damaging national unity with all their talk of class struggle, and dubbed the Reconstruction Party "an outcrop of the Tories." As for the new party's name, King stated, Stevens got it "from a book called 'Industry and Humanity,' which I wrote eighteen years ago."[64]

The campaign almost over, King touched down in a number of other Ontario towns and villages before heading to Toronto and Ottawa for the finale.

The Reconstruction, CCF, and Social Credit Campaigns

The election campaigns of the three new parties were more regional and local in nature than those of the Liberals and Conservatives, with individual candidates left much more on their own in their ridings. As discussed in Chapter 4, the organization and financing of these new parties were less robust and their choice of candidates more limited compared with the older parties. The Reconstruction Party was more focused on its leader than either the CCF or Social Credit, and H.H. Stevens was the only one of the three leaders to mount anything close to a national campaign.

Stevens did not wait for an official announcement and started campaigning immediately after announcing the creation of the Reconstruction Party. Declaring that the choice in the election was between a handful of economic dictators and the people, he made his first speech in Toronto on July 23, then headed west for a campaign swing that took him to all the major cities from Sudbury to Vancouver. At first, the campaign appeared to gain momentum. Talking to the "man on the street," Grant Dexter of the *Winnipeg Free Press* reported in July that Stevens had "made a very deep impression on the general vote."[65] In September, the Toronto *Globe*'s Harry Anderson called Stevens the "real threat" to Liberal chances in Ontario. "Stevens seems to be something new," he wrote Mackenzie King, "something that many who are ready for any experiment are too willing to try."[66] But that newness faded as the campaign progressed.

Stevens toured the interior of British Columbia and ventured into a number of smaller prairie ridings, where he was met by enthusiastic crowds. Landing in Alberta just days before the Social Credit provincial sweep, he was greeted by thousands, even in Prime Minister R.B. Bennett's Calgary West riding. Stevens's message resonated with Social Credit devotees and CCF followers. There was a commonality in the three parties despite their larger critique of Canadian society: all three attacked the concentration of economic power in the hands of a few, and called for measures to protect the "common man." It also meant, however, that these three parties were all chasing the same voters.

In early September, Stevens toured the Maritimes and Quebec, with stops in Sydney, New Glasgow, Charlottetown, and Moncton. In Quebec, he held rallies in Quebec City and Sherbrooke in support of several Reconstruction candidates, confident that his message of credit reform and attacks on the trusts had some appeal among supporters of the Action Libérale Nationale (ALN). In Sherbrooke, the local auditorium was struck by lightning just as Stevens arrived,

"Canada can if Canada will." View of the Reconstruction Party headquarters in the Western Canada building on West Pender Street in Vancouver (1935). | Photographer Leonard Frank, Vancouver Public Library Archives, 7878

and he had to wait in his car for an hour before he could speak. Nevertheless, he was still able to call for the creation of a dominion agriculture board and a similar one for the livestock industry as a way of controlling prices and reining in the power of the "great corporations." He condemned Premier Louis-Alexandre Taschereau for doing nothing to help Quebec's farmers while cozying up to the financiers on St. James Street. "Premier Taschereau is not a Liberal," he concluded. "He is a Tory."[67]

Stevens devoted the last three weeks of the campaign to Ontario, where the majority of Reconstruction candidates were. In the whirlwind campaign, he drove across southern Ontario, with stops in Simcoe, Brantford, Galt, and many other places. His biographer estimates that Stevens travelled over two thousand miles, held up to a dozen daily meetings, and delivered over one hundred speeches.[68]

In Owen Sound, he promised to put unemployed men to work on construction infrastructure projects, building roads and houses, and used the recent discovery of gold deposits in Ontario as a justification for printing more money. In Belleville, when asked about veterans, he proposed the creation of a permanent parliamentary committee to investigate veterans' problems and make recommendations to the government. However vague this proposal was, he promised that a Reconstruction government would heed those recommendations.[69]

Stevens attacked just about everybody: the other major parties, business leaders, corporations, and the large retail stores. He blamed the banks and the larger companies – the "mass buying organizations" – for causing the loss of jobs in smaller towns. In Campbellton, New Brunswick, he promised to break up control of the livestock industry (taking particular aim at Canada Packers) and fix fair prices for livestock and dairy farmers. Bennett was "a great lawyer," he said, "but we've got some horse sense. Mr. Bennett fixed the price of wheat. If he can do that, why can't we fix prices of livestock, dairy products and other farm products?"[70] The next day (September 18), he was in Quebec City charging that the Quebec coal industry was a monopoly, controlled by one man – a friend of the prime minister. In fruit-producing regions like Beamsville, Ontario, he proclaimed that big canning companies should not be able to dictate prices to the local fruit farmers. He also condemned the large textile companies for discriminating against local merchants, and maintained that the powerful agricultural companies must absorb more of their expenses instead of passing them on to the farmers. In all these areas, there should be some kind of "referee," "to hold the scales in equity," and that would be implemented under a Reconstruction government.[71] He never ran out of things to say.

Early in October, Stevens began referring to conspiracies directed against him, and he made some fairly extreme allegations. In a speech at the Windsor Armouries on October 3, he accused the

Liberals of plotting with financial interests to force him out of public life, and again singled out Simpson's president C.L. Burton for attack. Another target was his former cabinet colleague Charles Cahan, and defeating him in Montreal was a clear objective. Throughout the campaign, there were allegations of slander and threats of legal action. Almost always, it was the ubiquitous but illusive "they" who were behind these actions. "They have declared that I shall be crucified and driven out of public life," he said. "Well, ladies and gentlemen, I have never been known as a quitter, and I have not the faintest idea of quitting now."[72]

The CCF and its leader, J.S. Woodsworth, faced an uphill battle attracting votes. Manitoba farmers did not really embrace the new party and stuck with the Liberals, and in Alberta the CCF was completely overshadowed by Social Credit. Only in Saskatchewan did the CCF message appeal to rural voters. Beyond that, the party attracted support in a few urban ridings, primarily in Winnipeg and Vancouver. In Quebec, the party was opposed by the Catholic Church; its brand of mild socialism was condemned as atheism and an attack on private property. It made no headway at all in the Maritimes, with the possible exception of a few areas on Cape Breton Island, and fielded no candidates. It is difficult not to conclude that most voters were unsympathetic to the CCF message; they had no problem with private property and capitalism, especially if it worked well for them.

The party was also hindered, on the one hand, by persistent charges that it was communist-dominated or made up of communist fellow-travellers, and, on the other, by its uneasy relationship with the Communist Party. Some similarities in goals – advocacy of the end of capitalism, support for the introduction of socialism, and the fact that many in the party were or had been connected to the Communist Party or were members of various communist groups – made it easy for the Liberals and Conservatives to paint the whole party with the communist brush. For example, at a rally in the Hotel Vancouver, Gerry McGeer, the Liberal candidate in Vancouver-Burrard, drew a direct connection between the CCF and the communists. "Make no mistake about it," he declared, "the C.C.F. can only achieve their ends by civil war or revolution." McGeer went on to talk about what had happened in Russia at the time of the Bolshevik Revolution and about the millions of people who had been executed and starved. "Maybe that explains why the C.C.F. and the Communists sneer at the name of God whenever it is spoken."[73]

The CCF tried to distance itself from the Communist Party, reminding Canadians that it offered a form of democratic socialism and was opposed to violence of any kind. The great fear was that any cooperation with the Communist Party would, at best, damage the CCF's claim to speak for the progressive left in Canada, or, at worst, lead to a communist takeover of the CCF itself. It was therefore a delicate balancing act – dealing with the communists on one side and fending off red-baiting accusations on the other.

When its calls for cooperation were rejected, the Communist Party came out as a rival of the CCF in a number of ridings. In Winnipeg North, Communist leader Tim Buck opposed the CCF incumbent, A.A. Heaps. Mackenzie King got on well with Heaps and considered staying out of his constituency as a way of preventing Buck from winning, but ultimately the Liberals nominated lawyer and military veteran C.S. Booth.[74] Heaps was helped by sympathetic coverage from two Winnipeg papers, the *Free Press* and the *Winnipeg Tribune*, but had to deal with charges of communist sympathies despite being very critical of Buck. Booth immediately condemned Heaps and the CCF for their plans to establish a Soviet dictatorship in Canada, while on the left, Buck and the communists attacked Heaps in the newspapers and at his rallies. Heaps reportedly even attended some Communist Party rallies, taking to the platform to answer questions and respond to accusations. In Vancouver East, Communist candidate Malcolm Bruce, who was originally from

Prince Edward Island and had been jailed in 1931 under section 98 and spent two years in prison (with Tim Buck), competed against leading CCFer Angus MacInnis. Another CCF candidate who faced tough communist attacks was Olive Jane Whyte in Essex West, Ontario. At one of her meetings, responding to questions from the communists in attendance, she stated that if the Ford Motor Company would not "play the game" in the aftermath of a CCF victory, there was nothing to stop a CCF government from starting its own auto company to compete against Ford. Such comments likely did little to boost her popularity in Windsor.[75]

Woodsworth undertook a fairly modest national campaign, avoiding the Maritimes and Quebec altogether. He visited Alberta, British Columbia, and Saskatchewan through September before moving into Ontario near the end of the month and speaking in fourteen cities there, including Toronto, Orillia, Midland, and Penetanguishene. In Sudbury on October 1, he again attacked the concentration of wealth in Canada and condemned the banks and corporations, which, he claimed, for all intents and purposes controlled the government. At the same rally, he announced his opposition to further immigration, stating that "not one more man should be brought in to complicate an already complicated situation."[76] Following his stop at Orillia on October 6, he left for the West, and his own riding, to finish the campaign.

In the West, Woodsworth maintained his focus on the social and economic conditions prevailing in the country. In Winnipeg on October 8, he compared economic conditions in Canada and the United States, and concluded that the situation in Canada was only slightly better than that under slavery, deep in the American South, before the Civil War. The next night, in Brooklands, Manitoba, he spoke more positively about the CCF and explained how the young party had already made an impact by raising issues and focusing attention on them in the House of Commons. Sometimes, he argued, attention led to action.[77] If nothing else, this reflected a little

"Work and Wages NOT Relief," states one placard. CCF leader J.S. Woodsworth at work (1935). | Library and Archives Canada, C-055451

optimism that the CCF could hold the balance of power in the new Parliament.

In Alberta, the August 1935 Social Credit provincial sweep left a huge hole for the Liberals and Conservatives, and the Social Credit Party was somewhat of an unknown quantity in the federal election campaign. Social Credit rallies were already half political campaign and half Sunday revival meeting, with campaign speeches reflecting a mixture of the Social Credit manifesto and the Bible. It was hard to resist the promise of a social credit dividend if the party was elected, while the strains of "What a Friend We Have in Jesus" wafted in the air.

The Social Credit campaign was limited to the Western provinces, and nobody really knew how well the evangelical tinge of Aberhart's passion would spill over into federal politics. For the most part, the provincial leader remained on the sidelines, although he did campaign briefly in Saskatchewan. Early in October, Aberhart spoke in Regina in support of the Social Credit candidates and, even though a federal victory was unattainable, at least in 1935, he did believe that a strong federal campaign in Saskatchewan might spark the creation of a *provincial* Social Credit party that would have a real chance at victory in the upcoming provincial election.[78]

Social Credit "has taken Alberta almost entirely out of the picture so far as other parties are concerned," explained one journalist. The question was how far it could spread in the short period before the federal vote.[79] If nothing else, it had shown the Liberals and Conservatives that many people were willing to reject the traditional parties and vote for something unknown, and that, out of desperation, they were willing to turn to more populist and dynamic leaders – or demagogues – on either the right or the left who offered simple solutions to enormously complicated problems. Liberal hopes dimmed quickly, and King's only hope was that this new "weird business" would be kept to the one province and not infect any others.[80]

Social Credit posed an even more serious challenge in Alberta and Saskatchewan to the CCF and the Reconstruction Party, both of whose only strategy was to accuse each other of secret deals or cooperation with Social Credit and to argue that a vote for Social Credit would only split the vote and allow one's opponent (from whichever party) to win. This strategy might have had some effect in a couple of ridings in Saskatchewan and British Columbia, but it did not carry much weight in Alberta.

Throughout the entire campaign, there was an ongoing and long-range debate between the two leading contenders, and between them and the other party leaders, with each leader responding to recent speeches, claims, and accusations by the others. Topics included old age pensions, the report of the Price Spreads Royal Commission, and the Bank of Canada, among others, but the biggest of all was the tariff issue, with various calls for new trade agreements mixed with criticism of opponents' failings. Bennett claimed that the 1932 imperial trade agreements were a great accomplishment; King called for revisions. Bennett warned that King would destroy those agreements (and much of the Empire in the process) and lower the tariff so much that it would destroy Canadian industry by opening up the country to unfair competition from other countries, such as Japan. "Mr. King takes sides with Japan," Bennett proclaimed in Hamilton. "I take Canada. Our laws are made in Ottawa not Tokio [sic]."[81] King countered that freer trade would bring prosperity, not hinder it. Bennett charged that although King claimed to want a trade deal, he had done nothing during nine years in office; as for the new "destructive party," it would do no better.

Stevens attacked both leaders for focusing on the wrong issues (trade and tariffs) and not on the real issues as spelled out in the recommendations of the Price Spreads Royal Commission. In London, Ontario, he said: "There they are like two witches on broomsticks cavorting across the skies hoping the people will be bewitched."[82] For its part, the CCF put little faith in using the tariff to alleviate the Depression. In fact, it argued, it was economic nationalism and the competition for markets that led to the First World War and now threatened to bring the country into war again. If war broke out, Woodsworth said, the first thing he would do as prime minister would be to conscript wealth, not humans. "Do that," he said, "and I have a suspicion we won't get into the war."[83]

The Final Days of the Campaign

An outsider might be forgiven for thinking that Toronto's Maple Leaf Gardens was the focus of the last week of the 1935 election campaign. Three national leaders – Bennett, King, and Stevens – held their largest campaign rallies there in the final days before the vote. It was there that each candidate made one last pitch to sway Canadian voters.

The first and largest rally was staged by the Liberals on October 7, in what was dubbed a "monster rally" (the other parties used the same word for their rallies). With 17,500 in attendance, it was called the biggest political meeting ever held in Canada. "The vast floor was packed," wrote a *Globe* journalist, "galleries thronged on all four sides, tier upon tier, fifty rows of seats and every chair occupied." The crowd was entertained by a Highlanders Band and a male quartet. King and his procession were led to the stage to the skirl of bagpipes. In an exciting and novel turn, the eight Liberal premiers were for the first time connected from their provincial domains in a single national radio broadcast, where they could all emphasize – and anticipate – national unity under a newly elected Liberal government. "'Tory Toronto' was anything but Tory last night," proclaimed the *Globe*. "From the wide-open spaces of the West, from far-off British Columbia, from French-Canada and from the Provinces down by the sea came the voices of Liberal statesmen like Gardiner and Pattullo, Taschereau and Macdonald, all confidently predicting a Liberal sweep in the Federal election next Monday."[84]

As King was speaking at Maple Leaf Gardens, Bennett's campaign was gaining momentum as it wound its way into Ontario. In Montreal on October 8, he appeared before a crowd of twelve thousand at the Montreal Forum, sharing the stage with local Conservative candidates Sir George Perley, Charles Cahan, and Lucien Gendron, and attacking the Liberals on the issue of repeal of section 98. "Looking physically fit, jaunty and at times full of fire," Bennett claimed that the Liberals would wreck trade within the Empire.

Following events in Cornwall and Lindsay, Ontario, on October 9, Bennett took the stage at Maple Leaf Gardens that evening before a crowd estimated at fifteen thousand. He returned to a more traditional Conservative message. Gone were the radical ideas of the New Deal. Law and order was a major theme, as Bennett pledged to stand strong for Canada in the face of subversion at home and abroad. The huge crowd was mostly friendly, but he was interrupted by hecklers. "We have great problems still unsolved," he concluded. "And you're one of them!" called out someone from the crowd. Bennett blamed the communists for the interruption and gave it as another reason to maintain section 98.[85]

With time running out, Bennett once again raised the possibility of forming a national unity government but this time he used the words "Union Government." It was time to put the country above politics, he announced on October 10. Critics called it a desperate move to remain in power when he knew he could not win. Bennett's statement was quickly condemned by King, who went on to say that a national unity government had been Bennett's goal all along.[86] That was the last reference to national unity government during the campaign.

Stevens arrived in Toronto from Woodstock, Ontario, where, on October 10, he had challenged Bennett to debate "who is the traitor to the people of Canada."[87] He walked to the stage at Maple Leaf Gardens on October 11 to the "thundering cheers of 10,000 voices." It was by far the Reconstruction Party's largest campaign rally, and a *Globe* reporter described how the crowd "cheered him with all the fire and spirit with which they greeted Mr. King and Conservative Leader Bennett."[88] Stevens repeated his attacks on the large department stores, on Canada Packers, and on both Mackenzie King and R.B. Bennett, the "servants" of St. James Street. As for the banks, he proclaimed that they were not "the God-authorized owners of Canada and must serve business, not sneer at men who seek money for legitimate enterprises." Interrupted by a heckler, he didn't miss a beat and retorted: "It doesn't matter what you think of me. If you can do the job better come and do it."[89]

Bennett left Toronto the morning after his rally at Maple Leaf Gardens and drove first to Brantford in the afternoon and then London in the evening. The following day, he had a brief visit in Kincardine in the afternoon and an evening meeting in Owen Sound, where he renewed his 1930 pledge to finish construction of

King or Chaos?   179

a trans-Canada highway. He concluded his campaign on Saturday, October 12, with speeches in Smith Falls in the morning and Belleville at night, then returned to Ottawa to rest, vote, and await his fate.

King remained in Toronto after his rally at the Gardens and tried to patch things up with Vincent Massey during a meeting at the King George Hotel. Both men apologized for their earlier behaviour and promised to talk again, but this turned out to be their last meeting before the election.[90] King made his final Ontario stops in Niagara Falls and Brockville, then headed to Montreal for another "monster meeting" at an east end arena on Friday, October 11. He returned to Ottawa for one last speech on Saturday night.

Woodsworth concluded the CCF campaign in Winnipeg with a couple of last-minute speeches in his riding. It was one of the few times any leader addressed foreign policy and the looming international crisis, and he repeated his call for the conscription of wealth should war erupt.[91]

Stevens, the first to begin campaigning, kept on until the very end. He spoke in Burlington on the last day, October 12, and finished in Hamilton that evening with the one national radio broadcast his party could afford. He spoke right up to midnight and the speech was broadcast to his riding in Kootenay East, British Columbia, where his campaign was overseen by his son and where hundreds of party workers were waiting to celebrate in a local hotel. In Quebec that same day, all the Reconstruction Party candidates on the island of Montreal staged a rally at the Atwater Market, attacking the old traditional parties that had done little for Quebecers. Louis Francoeur, the candidate in St. James, pledged that Stevens and the new party would fight for the rights of French Canadians. As it stood, he complained, "if you talk French in any of the Ottawa ministries, you might as well be talking Chinese." Another candidate, R.L. Calder in Chambly-Rouville, predicted Reconstruction victories in ten Quebec ridings.[92]

And so the campaign came to an end. "For over a month the three major parties have been waging a bitter and intensive campaign, with the organizations exerting every effort to bring the respective platforms before the public," wrote one Ottawa journalist. "Local party organizations have spent considerable effort in lining up the electors. On Monday hundreds of automobiles will be placed in commission to get out the vote, and scores of workers will sit at telephones throughout the day ringing up electors who they believe may be partial to the party cause."[93] The ballots had been printed and ballot boxes distributed across the scores of constituencies. Civil servants and many other workers were given a half-holiday to enable them to vote; bars and liquor stores were closed in anticipation of the vote. Sunday was a day of rest for all the leaders. The following day, Monday, October 14, hundreds of hopeful candidates would learn just how effective their campaigns had been.

6

And in the End

If the choice was between King and chaos, more than half
the voters had preferred chaos.

– H. Blair Neatby[1]

MONDAY, OCTOBER 14, 1935, turned out to be a fine autumn day
in most of the country, although there were showers in parts of the
prairies and in Vancouver and across British Columbia. There would
be no excuses that weather conditions in any way prevented a large
voter turnout. Most voters could walk to the nearest polling station,
and in Ottawa it was reported that one voter arrived in a wheelchair.
Others drove, and for those who could not, the parties usually
provided transportation. If a parent had children whom they could
not leave, some form of daycare might be provided. "If a woman
voter tells me she cannot come to vote because of the young children," one "motherly and enthusiastic" woman explained to a *Globe*
reporter, "I am going to offer to take care of the family while she
goes with the driver."[2]

Everything seemed to go smoothly. The most serious incident
occurred near Windsor, Nova Scotia, when an offer of a drive to the

polling station led to a fight between two men. One was shot and killed, the other suffered a knife wound. In Winnipeg, a man was arrested for attempting to vote in another's place, and some skirmishes occurred at a few polling stations in Montreal. Eighteen men and women were arrested in that city for impersonating dead people in order to vote. In general, however, it was fairly quiet in Quebec, and one municipal detective was reported as saying that it was the quietest election he had ever seen.[3]

Three party leaders (R.B. Bennett, Mackenzie King, and H.H. Stevens) voted in Ottawa, even though they were running in the Western ridings of Calgary West, Prince Albert, and Kootenay East, respectively. Only J.S. Woodsworth cast a vote for himself, in his Winnipeg riding. The prime minister spent most of the day between his hotel room and his office in the East Block on Parliament Hill, where, in the end, he delivered his concession speech. Stevens went to the polls with his daughter Patricia, who was voting for the first time, and then spent much of the day at his party's Ottawa headquarters. King walked to his polling station, along Laurier Avenue, with his dog, Pat. He took Pat with him into the polling booth, claiming that the dog seemed to think he should have the right to vote. He returned to Laurier House confident of victory, and listened to the results with his friends Joan and Godfrey Patteson. Once victory seemed assured, he began writing messages to successful candidates, happy when Liberals won, satisfied when Conservatives lost.

All across the country, results were broadcast on the radio and newspapers tried to keep up as best they could, often by posting returns as they came in. In Toronto, for example, the *Globe* advertised seven telephone numbers for people to call for information on the vote, and broadcast the results on a local radio station and posted them on a large screen outside its downtown building. In Vancouver, the *Sun* began flashing results on a screen and announcing them over loudspeakers set up outside its offices; several local theatres also posted results throughout the evening. Conservative Martha Black listened to the results in Winnipeg on her way to Ottawa, but the broadcast ended before the final results for Yukon were announced. She did not find out until the next day that she had won by 134 votes and would be one of only two female MPs (along with Agnes Macphail) in the new House of Commons. When she called the offices of the *Winnipeg Free Press* to find out who won her Yukon riding, the response was, "Oh, that other dame!" (Macphail being the first).[4] For her part, Macphàil announced that she was "glad I'm no longer the only woman in the House of Commons."[5]

The first results on election night came in from Halifax's two-member riding, where Liberals R.E. Finn and Gordon B. Isnor were elected in what had been a Tory stronghold. It was a portent of what was to come over the rest of the evening. Moments later, it was announced that two Conservatives who had held seats in Cape Breton had gone down to defeat. The Liberal sweep of the Maritimes had begun. In Quebec, Fernand Rinfret, the former secretary of state, was re-elected, defeating, among several others, Emma Gendron, an Independent candidate and the only woman running in the province. Rinfret was the first of several former Liberal cabinet members to be re-elected in Quebec; others included P.J.A. Cardin and Ernest Lapointe.[6]

Conservative cabinet members were less fortunate. Many had already retired and chosen not to run; others, including Robert Manion (Fort William) and G.R. Geary (Toronto-Trinity), lost their seats. For the first time since 1900, Wellington South, Ontario, was won by someone other than a Guthrie, as former justice minister Hugh Guthrie had retired from politics and his son could not hold the seat for the Conservatives. On the brighter side, Conservative R.S. White, the "snowy-haired and whiskered politician" who had first won election in 1888, was elected in Montreal's St. Antoine–Westmount riding.[7]

Agnes Macphail hung on in Grey-Bruce, Ontario, where she had run under the United Farmers of Ontario–Labour banner. In addition to being only one of two women elected, she was also one of only a handful of independent, farmer, or labour candidates to secure a victory. She would find herself alone in the new Parliament, as many of her former colleagues – Progressives, United Farmers of Alberta (UFA), and United Farmers of Ontario (UFO) – had all but disappeared. "There was a prediction made by skeptics in 1921 that the U.F.O. would soon peter out, until its Ontario representation would be able to ride to Ottawa on a bicycle," the Walkerton *Herald Times* editorialized three days after the vote. "In fourteen years that prediction has come true, and Agnes Macphail rides the bicycle ... Her victory at the polls is a personal triumph."[8]

Out West, in Winnipeg North, A.A. Heaps held his seat with a four-thousand-vote majority over Liberal C.S. Booth, and five thousand over Tim Buck, the Communist Party leader. In Wetaski-win, Alberta, Co-operative Commonwealth Federation (CCF) member William Irvine was less fortunate, coming in third behind both the Liberal and the victorious Social Credit candidate, Norman Jaques. In Quebec, Independent Henri Bourassa lost to a somewhat obscure Liberal challenger, and the House of Commons lost one of its foremost parliamentarians and longest-serving members. In Ontario, Paul Martin, who won his riding along with the two other Windsor Liberals, embarked on a spontaneous parade through town to the office of the *Windsor Daily Star*. Others were not so lucky – over one-third of the candidates lost their deposits. The greatest number of losers was in Ontario, and hardest hit was the Reconstruction Party, more than 130 of whose candidates failed to win enough votes to get back their deposits.[9]

All the major party leaders won their seats, some more comfortably than others. Prime Minister Bennett proved to be the one Conservative holdout in what was now a Social Credit fortress in Alberta. In Winnipeg, J.S. Woodsworth won a solid victory but likely benefited from the splintering of the vote between his Liberal, Reconstruction, and Social Credit rivals. In Ottawa, after listening to concession speeches from Bennett, Woodsworth, and Stevens, Mackenzie King did little celebrating and soon went to bed, where he dreamt of asking the victorious Agnes Macphail to join the Liberals instead of "wasting the rest of her life on extreme groups, or being part of the Opposition." H.H. Stevens secured his seat in Kootenay East, but when he saw the dismal returns despite all the hard work he and thousands of supporters had invested in the campaign, he was overheard saying, "Why did they do it? Why did they do it?"[10] It was a question that many others were asking as well.

The Winners and Losers

Some 4,406,854 Canadians voted in 1935, close to 75 percent of the eligible voting population.[11] By any measurement, the Liberals came out ahead, winning 173 seats compared with the Conservatives, who came in a distant second with 40 seats (this figure includes Martha Black, who ran and won as an Independent-Conservative in Yukon). It was a reversal of 1930, when the Liberals won only 91 compared with the Conservatives' 137, and, in terms of seats, the greatest victory for one party in Canadian history to that time. See Tables 1 and 2.

The Liberals won almost everywhere. They swept the Maritimes, winning twenty-five of a possible twenty-six seats; the lone holdout was the riding of Royal, New Brunswick, which was won – by less than 150 votes – by Conservative Alfred Brooks. In Quebec, the Liberals took fifty-five of sixty-five seats, and they could count on the support of the five Independent-Liberals who also won. The Conservatives were reduced to five mainly anglophone seats in Montreal, and were effectively wiped out in francophone ridings, the lone exception being Sir George Perley in Argenteuil, who held on to his riding with fewer than 200 votes over the Liberal challenger.[12]

TABLE 1

Results of the 1930 Canadian general election

	Conservative		Liberal		United Farmers of Alberta		Progressive		Other	
	Seats	%	Seats	%	Seats	%	Seats	%	Seats	%
Nova Scotia	10	71.4	4	28.6						
New Brunswick	10	90.9	1	9.1						
Prince Edward Island	3	75.0	1	25.0						
Quebec	24	36.9	40	61.5					1	1.5
Ontario	59	72.0	22	26.8			1	1.2		
Manitoba	11	64.7	4	23.5					2	11.8
Saskatchewan	8	38.1	11	52.4			2	9.5		
Alberta	4	25.0	3	18.8	9	56.3				
British Columbia	7	50.0	5	35.7					2	14.3
Yukon and NWT	1	100.0								
Total	137	55.9	91	37.1	9	3.7	3	1.2	5	2.0

TABLE 2

Results of the 1935 Canadian general election

	Conservative		Liberal		Reconstruction		CCF		Social Credit		Other	
	Seats	%	Seats	%	Seats	%	Seats	%	Seats	%	Seats	%
Nova Scotia			12	100.0								
New Brunswick	1	10.0	9	90.0								
Prince Edward Island			4	100.0								
Quebec	5	7.7	55	84.6							5	7.7
Ontario	25	30.5	56	68.3							1	1.2
Manitoba	1	5.9	14	82.4			2	11.8				
Saskatchewan	1	4.8	16	76.2			2	9.5	2	9.5		
Alberta	1	5.9	1	5.9					15	88.2		
British Columbia	5	31.3	6	37.5	1	6.3	3	18.8			1	6.3
Yukon and NWT	1	100.00										
Total	40	15.9	173	70.6	1	0.4	7	2.9	17	6.9	7	2.9

Note: The Liberal column includes two Liberal-Progressives in Manitoba. The Conservative column includes one Independent Conservative candidate in Yukon and NWT.

In Ontario, the Liberals won an impressive fifty-six seats (up from twenty-two in 1930) out of a possible eighty-two, giving them their largest win in that province since 1874. They were equally successful further west. In Manitoba, where the party was traditionally strong, they won fourteen of seventeen seats; in Saskatchewan, they took sixteen of a possible twenty-one. Only in Alberta, British Columbia, and the one riding in Yukon did the Liberals fail to win a majority of seats. In Alberta, they were reduced to one seat – Edmonton West, won by James Mackinnon – out of seventeen; in British Columbia, they won the largest number of seats of any party, but only six out of a possible sixteen seats; and in Yukon, the Independent-Liberal lost to Independent-Conservative Martha Black.

There were few bright spots for the Conservatives. They were reduced to a single seat in all of the Maritimes and only five in Quebec. The base of the party was now squarely in Ontario, but even there, the twenty-five Tory victories were concentrated in the greater Toronto-Hamilton area. Things were equally bleak west of Ontario, where the Tories could manage only one victory in each of the Prairie provinces (including Bennett's own seat in Calgary West) and Yukon, and five more in British Columbia. The forty-seat Conservative total was even lower than the catastrophe of 1921; indeed, it was the worst Tory showing since Confederation. Most of the sitting cabinet ministers were defeated (only six of seventeen survived), including all of those from Quebec. It was a major disaster even if one assumes that a majority of Reconstruction Party voters would have otherwise voted Tory. Political scientist J. Murray Beck estimated that if the Reconstruction vote had stayed with the Tories, it would have made a difference in perhaps only five or six seats (two in Nova Scotia and Ontario and one each in New Brunswick and Manitoba). Historian Larry Glassford is a little more optimistic, suggesting that the Conservatives might have won as many as fifteen more seats if not for the Reconstruction Party's presence.[13] In neither case would it have made a difference to the outcome of the election. Clearly there were other factors contributing to the Conservative debacle.

With the exception of the Social Credit Party, the other parties' hopes or expectations were dashed. H.H. Stevens and the Reconstruction Party had little to show for all their efforts before and during the campaign, winning no seats other than Stevens's riding of Kootenay East. The CCF began 1935 with roughly fifteen MPs in its caucus, but, despite fielding candidates in 118 ridings, when the dust settled after the election, it held only 7 (8 if we include Agnes Macphail, the UFO-Labour MP for Grey-Bruce, Ontario, who usually voted with the party). East of Ontario, where the CCF ran very few candidates, it won nothing, as might be expected, but it also fared very badly in Ontario despite fielding fifty candidates. It was a little better in the West, where the CCF garnered two victories each in Manitoba and Saskatchewan. From those four seats came three present and future party leaders, including J.S. Woodsworth (Winnipeg North Centre) in Manitoba, and M.J. Coldwell (Rosetown-Biggar) and Tommy Douglas (Weyburn) in Saskatchewan. The fourth was A.A. Heaps, who held his seat in Winnipeg. Another future CCF notable, Stanley Knowles, was less fortunate, losing in Winnipeg South Centre to Liberal Ralph Maybank by a considerable majority. In Alberta, the party met complete disaster: it had nine Alberta MPs when the election was called in August, but all were defeated in October. The CCF was increasingly becoming an urban-based party, but in 1935, with seats only in Manitoba, Saskatchewan, and British Columbia, it had little claim to being a national party. The Communist Party ran fourteen candidates, won no seats, and garnered only 0.74 percent of the popular vote, and party leader Tim Buck lost to Heaps in Winnipeg. Only Social Credit accomplished what it set out to do by winning fifteen of Alberta's seventeen seats and picking up two others in Saskatchewan, including Joseph Needham's in The Battlefords.

The Maritimes, Quebec, Ontario, Manitoba, and Saskatchewan were solidly Liberal, and Alberta was almost swept by Social Credit, leaving British Columbia as the only province where the vote was more evenly divided between the various parties. British Columbia was the site of the only victory for the Reconstruction Party (H.H. Stevens in Kootenay East), and the CCF captured three ridings, two in Vancouver, as might have been expected, and one in Nanaimo. The Liberals won not only in Vancouver but also in Kamloops, Skeena, and Cariboo. The Conservative wins were equally dispersed across the province, from Vancouver South to Kootenay West to Fraser Valley. In addition, many of the contests were very close. Liberal Thomas Reid won in New Westminster, defeating the CCF candidate by only 250 votes; two other ridings were won by less than 300 votes by men who would go on to have long, if not distinguished, political careers: Liberal Ian Mackenzie in Vancouver Centre and Conservative Howard Green in Vancouver South. British Columbia was the outlier province in 1935.

The new Parliament would feature a new majority Liberal government with a much-weakened opposition consisting of the Conservative rump and several regionally based parties. And even then, the opposition would be further divided, with the Conservatives to the right and the CCF (and perhaps H.H. Stevens) to the left of the new government. Only the Liberals had any kind of nationwide support, and only they could boast of support from both English and French Canada. Mackenzie King, the unimpressive, less divisive but more conciliatory party leader, was hardly the popular choice. He was the leader Canadians might not want, but perhaps the one they deserved. And, given the regional anger, the depths of the Depression, and the rise of the new parties, the Liberals did manage to win votes all across the country except in Alberta, and they were the only party that could claim to be a national party.

The popular vote tells a different story, however. Across the country, the Liberals won 1,975,841 votes, or 44.8 percent of the total. More surprisingly, given the great number of seats they won, the Liberal vote percentage dropped from 45.2 percent in 1930 (even as the total number of Liberal votes rose by approximately 200,000). About 6 percent of the 1930 vote had gone to the now-defunct Progressives and a few other smaller parties. See Tables 3 and 4.

The Liberal vote generally rose in the east and fell in the West. In the Maritimes, Liberal support shifted from approximately 50 percent in 1930 to well above 50 percent in 1935. Quebec remained largely the same in terms of percentage: whereas the Liberals took 53.2 percent of the vote in 1930, they rose to 54.4 percent in 1935. It was in Ontario that the Liberals made their biggest gain, with their support jumping significantly from 26.8 percent in 1930 to 42.4 percent in 1935. On the prairies, the Liberals gained seats but their percentage of the vote actually declined. In Manitoba, the Liberal vote rose slightly from 37 to 40 percent, but in Saskatchewan it fell from 45 percent in 1930 to 40 percent in 1935. In British Columbia, the drop was even more pronounced, with Liberal support going from 40.9 percent in 1930 to 31.8 percent in 1935. It was a similar story in Alberta, but in this province Liberal support was already slipping, and with the advent of the Social Credit Party, their share of the vote fell further, from around 30 percent in 1930 to just over 20 percent in 1935.

The Conservatives did not fare well. They received 1,305,565 votes in 1935, or 29.6 percent, a significant drop of almost 20 percentage points from their 48.8 percent share in 1930. They lost just about everywhere, and in their traditional stronghold of Ontario, it was a particularly devastating loss, with their share of the vote falling from 72 percent and fifty-nine seats in 1930 to 35.3 percent and twenty-five seats in 1935. In no province did the party win over 40 percent of the vote; in Quebec, Manitoba, Saskatchewan, and Alberta, they drew less than 30 percent. In three provinces – Saskatchewan, Alberta, and British Columbia – the party finished third.

TABLE 3

Popular vote in the 1930 Canadian general election

	Conservative		Liberal		United Farmers of Alberta		Progressive		Other		Total votes
	Votes	%	Votes	%	Votes	%	Votes	%	Votes	%	
Nova Scotia	140,503	52.5	127,179	47.5							267,682
New Brunswick	109,716	59.3	75,342	40.7							185,058
Prince Edward Island	29,692	50.0	29,698	50.0							59,390
Quebec	455,452	44.7	542,357	53.2					22,109	2.2	1,019,918
Ontario	745,406	54.8	590,079	43.4			12,815	0.9	11,274	0.8	1,359,574
Manitoba	111,294	47.7	86,840	37.2			9,228	4.0	26,027	11.2	233,389
Saskatchewan	124,000	37.6	150,241	45.5			26,854	8.1	29,083	8.8	330,178
Alberta	67,832	33.9	60,126	30.0	60,848	30.4			11,496	5.7	200,302
British Columbia	119,074	49.3	98,933	40.9					23,626	9.8	241,633
Yukon and NWT	846	60.3	557	39.7							1,403
Total	1,903,815	48.8	1,761,352	45.2	60,848	1.6	48,897	1.3	123,615		3,898,527

TABLE 4

Popular vote in the 1935 Canadian general election

	Conservative		Liberal		Reconstruction		CCF		Social Credit		Other		Total
	Votes	%	Votes	%	Votes	%	Votes	%	Votes	%	Votes	%	
Nova Scotia	87,893	32.1	142,334	52.0	38,175	13.9					5,365	2.0	273,767
New Brunswick	56,145	31.9	100,537	57.2	18,408	10.5					672	0.4	175,762
Prince Edward Island	23,602	38.4	35,757	58.2	2,089	3.4							61,448
Quebec	322,794	28.2	623,579	54.4	100,119	8.7	7,326	0.6			92,703	8.1	1,146,521
Ontario	562,513	35.3	675,803	42.4	183,511	11.5	127,927	8.0			44,493	2.8	1,594,247
Manitoba	75,574	26.9	113,887	40.5	16,439	5.9	54,491	19.4	5,751	2.0	14,850	5.3	280,992
Saskatchewan	65,078	18.8	141,121	40.8	4,361	1.3	69,376	20.1	61,505	17.8	4,129	1.2	345,570
Alberta	40,236	16.9	50,539	21.2	1,785	0.7	30,921	13.0	111,249	46.6	3,783	1.6	238,513
British Columbia	71,034	24.6	91,729	31.8	19,208	6.7	97,015	33.6	1,796	0.6	8,001	2.8	288,783
Yukon and NWT	696	55.6	555	44.4									1,251
Total	1,305,565	29.6	1,975,841	44.8	384,095	8.7	387,056	8.8	180,301	4.1	173,996	3.9	4,406,854

Note: The Liberal column includes two Liberal-Progressives in Manitoba. The Conservative column includes one Independent Conservative candidate in Yukon and NWT.

Looking at just the popular vote, the 1935 election was not so much a big win for Liberals as it was a disaster for the Conservatives. Taken together, the drop in percentage of popular support for both the Liberals and Conservatives suggests that Canadians had voted for the new parties in large numbers. Alberta was the obvious case, of course, but in neighbouring Saskatchewan, where well over 80 percent of the vote had gone to the two traditional parties in 1930, their share of the total vote fell below 60 percent in 1935. This vote shift was one of the key long-term developments arising from the 1935 election.

The Reconstruction Party did surprisingly well in terms of the popular vote – at least in Eastern Canada – collecting 384,095 votes, or 8.7 percent of the total. Although its vote share languished in the single digits in most provinces, Stevens did win significant support in Nova Scotia (13.9 percent), New Brunswick (10.5 percent), and Ontario (11.5 percent). In these provinces, Stevens won 17 percent of the vote in Montreal, 14 percent in Toronto, and 13 percent in Halifax.[14] These votes did not translate into many seats, but they really ate into Conservative support in these provinces.

The CCF received 387,056 votes, or 8.8 percent of the total, and this vote was concentrated to the west of the Ontario-Quebec border (the party won 0.6 percent of the vote in Quebec and zero votes in the Maritimes). In Ontario, the party earned 8 percent of the vote, but this was concentrated in Toronto (15 percent), Hamilton, and London; outside these urban areas the party won only 4.6 percent of the vote.[15] The CCF's real gains were in the West, where it won around 20 percent of the vote in Manitoba and Saskatchewan, and 13 percent in Alberta. In British Columbia, it drew an impressive 33.6 percent of the vote, meaning that although the CCF won fewer seats than the Liberals, it won the popular vote in that province (the Liberals came in at 31.8 percent).

The anomalies of the Canadian electoral system were on full display in 1935. While the Liberals won close to 45 percent of the votes, they won over 70 percent of the seats. The Conservatives held on to almost 30 percent of the vote, but won only 16.3 percent of the seats in the new Parliament. The Reconstruction Party attracted almost the same number of votes as the CCF but won only one seat to the CCF's seven. The Social Credit Party won far fewer votes (180,301) than either of the two other new parties, and only 4.7 percent of the total, but because these votes were concentrated in Alberta and Saskatchewan, they translated into seventeen seats. Under a proportional representation system, the new Canadian Parliament would have looked very different. As it stood, 1935 was less a triumphant victory for the Mackenzie King Liberals than an expression of a greatly divided electorate that, thanks to the first-past-the-post system, gave the Liberals a huge majority.

Assessing the Vote

Analysis of the election began immediately. The *New York Times* proclaimed a big Liberal victory but cautioned that it could not be said that Canada had rejected "the third-party idea." King would now take office with "the great advantage of having made fewer promises and thus fewer commitments than any of his rivals." From London, the *Times* reported that the Liberal victory was "more complete than Mr. King's most ardent supporters dared to anticipate," and speculated that support for the third parties had diminished at the end because voters wanted a stronger and more stable government. More international support came from a somewhat unexpected source: Marcus Garvey, the Jamaican American civil rights leader and founder of the Black nationalist and anti-colonial Universal Negro Improvement Association (UNIA). Garvey was no stranger to Canada, where there were several UNIA branches. King was a "man of vision" who won a "wonderful victory," and after "studying him at close range," Garvey concluded that "he is a good friend of the coloured people."[16]

For many Conservatives, the obvious explanation for their poor showing was the defection of H.H. Stevens and the split in the party that it provoked. Certainly, Bennett blamed Stevens for the loss and could never forgive him for his actions. A young Conservative, John Diefenbaker, who watched from the sidelines, also considered Stevens's defection as the major cause of the Conservatives' bad showing, estimating (rather unrealistically) that it cost the party at least forty seats. Diefenbaker was quite critical of Stevens, and later argued that had Stevens stayed in the party, most of what he demanded for the "common man" was to be found in Bennett's New Deal, which, given half a chance, might have worked.[17]

Howard Ferguson analyzed the Conservative defeat for Lord Beaverbrook, watching from London. Bennett's team in Quebec "was no good and had no influence." In the Maritimes, the "fishermen were sore and felt they had not had sufficient assistance. The Liberals bribed them with generous promises." In the West, the "failure is easily accounted for – five years failure of crops, lonely Prairie isolation"; in British Columbia, "there was no effort made to recover it [the province]." Ferguson pointed to a number of problems with the Tory campaign, including weak party organization, the mood of the country, and how Bennett's one-man show compared unfavourably with King's team approach. But it was Stevens who was the real culprit: "Bennett's defeat is a case of being assassinated in the house of his friends," Ferguson concluded. The only bright spot was the failure of both the Reconstruction Party and the CCF to gain any traction. Outside Alberta, "we have got back to the Party system, and have declared against modern nostrums."[18]

Robert Manion, one of the defeated cabinet ministers, was equally sharp in his critique of the 1935 electoral debacle. He listed three reasons for his – and his party's – defeat: the weak Conservative organization, "seen by everyone for years except R.B. [Bennett]," the Depression, and H.H. Stevens. For his own defeat in Fort William, Ontario, he placed the blame squarely on Stevens, along with his own "absence from the constituency" while he campaigned on behalf of other candidates.[19]

Another observer, journalist Bruce Hutchison, shifted the blame for the Conservative defeat to the Depression itself. "Depression, not Liberalism, had ruined him [Bennett]," Hutchison wrote. Others looked to the winners rather than the losers, concluding that the election "merely demonstrated the wisdom of the Liberal party's policy of having no policy."[20] Still others pointed to the system itself, which seemed to favour the traditional parties. "The old two-party system turned out to be much stronger in the affections of the voters than I had expected," wrote Frank Underhill a few days after the election. But then, noting that a quarter of voters did not vote for the old parties, he pointed to the first-past-the-post system (and the lack of funds) to explain why the CCF failed to do better than expected. "There is never a landslide in the voting in Canada but only in the distribution of seats," he wrote George Ferguson of the *Winnipeg Free Press* soon after the election. "Since the Liberals have profited by the system this time I take it for granted that any radical ideas which Mr. King may have about changing the system will remain deep down in his heart where apparently he has stored away quite a collection of radical opinions."[21]

The easiest explanation for what happened in 1935 is that disgruntled Conservative voters turned to the new parties, especially the Reconstruction Party, while the Liberals, by maintaining their support roughly at 1930 levels, were able to take advantage of the vote splitting to gain an enormous victory in terms of seats, even though not in popular support. But that is only part of a much more complex story. All the parties had reason to claim afterwards that had it not been for another party, their share of the popular vote would have been much higher. The Conservatives claimed that they would have done much better save for the appearance of the Reconstruction Party; the Liberals would have attracted more votes had there been no CCF; the CCF would have done much better except for the appearance of the Social Credit Party, which hammered the CCF in Alberta and Saskatchewan, and of Stevens's new party, which cut into CCF support in Ontario; the Reconstruction Party lost because it had to fight both Social Credit and the CCF for the vote of working men and women all across the country. And on it went.

It is impossible to be precise, but clearly all the new parties did eat into each other's support, and together they drew votes away from the traditional parties. The Reconstructionists did attract small business people who otherwise might have been drawn away from the Conservative Party by the CCF; the CCF appealed to farmers and workers who otherwise might have voted Reconstruction; and Social Credit appealed to both farmers and workers and pulled the rug out from under the two other new parties in Alberta and parts of Saskatchewan close to the Alberta border. The CCF appealed to many Liberals on the left of the party, but some Conservatives may have switched to the Liberals as a way of keeping the socialists out of office. Reconstructionists clearly appealed to many Conservatives, but also appealed to some disenchanted Liberals, including some in Quebec who were looking for a non-socialist alternative to tackle the economic troubles facing the country. Perhaps the only certainty was that they all fed on the corpse of the Conservatives, the only party that failed to attract new voters.

Explaining that failure leads us back to Prime Minister R.B. Bennett, who must bear much of the burden of the defeat. The list of his missteps and errors in judgment is a long one. Bennett had allowed his party's organization to atrophy, and when he tried to turn it around, it was already too late. Even as he dominated in the House of Commons, he allowed his party, which was dependent on his leadership as well as his cash, to languish. He took on too much personally and left his cabinet in the dark far too often; by the time the election was called, the already weakened cabinet was in disarray, neglected, and unprepared for a fight, as ministers jumped ship or retired. An autocrat who was inflexible and ignored advice he did not like, Bennett alienated too many of his colleagues. The split with Stevens was the biggest personality clash, but it was also a symptom of a more basic problem in the party. "In times like these," observed one writer of this Depression-era contest, "a well-groomed prosperous-looking millionaire, who has an autocratic habit of speech, is not a good vote-getter."[22] To make matters worse, Conservatives were on the run all across the country as one Conservative provincial government after another was tossed out in favour of the Liberals (and Social Credit in Alberta). It did not augur well for Conservative chances anywhere; it also meant that Bennett went into the campaign without either regional ministers or provincial parties to help organize and campaign, and hopefully save the party from disaster.[23]

The biggest problem, not surprisingly, is that Bennett had to shoulder the responsibility for his government's lack of success in solving the relentless and intractable problems of the Depression. He had made bold promises before the election of 1930 but failed to deliver on them. As he faced re-election in 1935, the Canadian economy was still in recession, unemployment remained very high, much of the country was on relief, and recovery was nowhere in sight. Canadians knew all of this as they went to the polls, and they held Bennett and his government accountable. Writer John Cripps put the blame squarely on Bennett even as the prime minister rose to the challenge. "No one can fail to admire," Cripps wrote, with a backhanded compliment, in *Political Quarterly*, "the courage of a man who decides, despite a recent illness that almost proved fatal, to lead his party to the polls and to inevitable disaster."[24]

Bennett's response to the Depression – his New Deal – came late and failed to last the night. He was never able to convince Canadians of the seriousness of his desire for radical reform; it is not at all clear that he had convinced himself either. There were too many questions about the New Deal. Was it a serious attempt to raise Canadian spirits and confidence as President Roosevelt had done in the United States, and to introduce far-reaching reform policies that would actually alleviate the worst of the Depression? Was Bennett positioning himself as the godfather of the Canadian social welfare system? Or was it all a sham, an ill-conceived and haphazard package of reform proposals that were not to be taken seriously and that served only to rally the Conservative troops and give them something to fight for in the approaching election? Another question was asked about Bennett personally: did he really mean it? It was difficult for many Canadians to take Bennett seriously; after all, he personified the modern wealthy capitalist who had shown little concern for the average working-class Canadian in the past; now, in 1935, he emerged from the wilderness transformed into a left-wing crusader.

One critic posed the question as "Bennett: Convert or Realist?" and suggested that the "truth is that Bennett's transformation, or what seems like his transformation, is not a transformation at all. It is a characteristic impulse, an instinct of his nature." Bennett was "the child of a puritanical environment, with a nonconformist conscience; a natural revivalist." At the end of the day, he was neither convert nor realist: he was "a preacher."[25] Bennett may have read the writing on the wall and turned to the New Deal as a way of responding to the challenges that the Depression posed for Canadian conservatism. But he came a little too late and under-prepared, and in the end was responsible for the failure to capitalize on the boost in popular support that came with the New Deal. On the one hand, he alienated many Conservatives who did not like his shift towards radicalism; on the other, he failed to deliver on the promised reforms and lost support from those who liked what they saw in the New Deal. His serious health problems might not have been foreseeable, but the responsibility for the whole affair was his.

There is also room for speculation on the might-have-beens of Canadian electoral politics. Perhaps Bennett's biggest mistake was in not dissolving Parliament and calling the election right after his

New Deal broadcasts. With new ideas and restored energy, he and his team might have been able to shift the national focus from their past failures to their bold new policies and the new direction for the country. Instead, by waiting several months, he let any advantage he may have gained slip away. In addition, would a re-elected Bennett government have quickly introduced the New Deal reforms, directly challenging the Supreme Court to respond? Had that been the case, the Bennett Conservatives might have been remembered as a much more activist government than the one Canadians elected in October 1935. This could have been a turning point election of a very different kind.

For their part, the Mackenzie King Liberals essentially held fast and let the Conservatives deliver the win to them. King assessed the political mood of the country better than most others in his party, and he knew which way the political winds were blowing. Province after province turned Liberal, his party won most of the by-elections in advance of the election, the divisions within the Conservative Party would only favour his party, and he realized that the advent of the Reconstruction Party would harm the Tories far more than the Liberals.

Perhaps most surprising is that, given the economic disaster, the social turmoil, and the suffering and privation of the early 1930s, Canadians re-elected Mackenzie King and the Liberals on a platform that offered surprisingly little that was new. People in other countries were turning to fascist dictators, populists, demagogues, and New Dealers, but Canadians rested with the familiar and the ordinary, even the boring. There is not a little irony in the fact that, at a time when Canadian provincial voters elected the likes of Duff Pattullo, William Aberhart, Mitch Hepburn, and Maurice Duplessis, at the national level they put their trust once again in Mackenzie King, the most genteel Victorian of them all. They appeared to have chosen complacency over change: when the decade of the 1930s began,

Canadians had Mackenzie King as their prime minister; now, in 1935, after five years of the worst depression in Canadian history, they had him once again.

The Liberals Take Over

King's first action after the election was to consummate the trade agreement with the United States that everyone seemed to want, and he offered to go to Washington himself to seal the deal. The negotiations had stalled just days before the election. "The obstacle," one observer wrote, had been in Washington, not Ottawa. "Washington clearly preferred to sign an agreement with a Government fresh from the polls, rather than with one just at the end of its legal tenure of life."

Trade negotiations resumed on November 4, a deal was reached five days later, and the agreement was formally signed on November 15, one month after the election. The two countries exchanged Most Favoured Nation status and reduced a few individual tariff rates on a list of other goods, primarily natural products. Roosevelt praised the agreement as "another act of cementing our historic friendship," but critics then and now have been quick to assess the agreement as more favourable to the United States than Canada, arguing that the Americans took advantage of King's eagerness to sign any kind of agreement.[26] In any event, 1935 has come to be seen as a turning point with respect to tariff policy, as trade between the two countries rose significantly in subsequent years, and this agreement was followed by further negotiations in 1937 and 1938, first with Britain and then trilateral negotiations with the Americans and British, that produced new trade agreements. Bennett's election warning that King would scuttle the 1932 imperial trade agreements had not exactly come to pass, but the new pacts largely superseded the earlier ones.[27]

King and Bennett met the day after the election to discuss the transition. King had little time to relax and enjoy the moment of

Fulfilling a campaign promise: Signing of the Canada–United States Trade Agreement in Washington, DC (November 1935). Seated, left to right: Secretary of State Cordell Hull, Prime Minister Mackenzie King, President Franklin D. Roosevelt. | Library and Archives Canada, C-031017

victory, as his thoughts quickly turned to forming a cabinet. The new government's agenda was already full. One pundit wrote in *Maclean's*:

> There is unemployment. Mr. King, avoiding historic precedent, didn't promise to end it or perish, but its spectre is with him, nevertheless. Also relief. Also the provinces. It will be an interesting Parliament. New Ministers under fire; new reputations to be made; new policies to be tested. Mr. King will take his seat to thunderous cheers, but when these die down there will be shadows – unemployment, relief, finances, the spectre of sanctions, clouds in Europe.[28]

King had an abundance of talent to choose from, but the new cabinet was inevitably shaped by the outcome of the election.

Visitors, colleagues, and friends descended on Ottawa with advice for the new prime minister as he attempted to balance region, language, and group to shape his new team. First, King summoned Ernest Lapointe to consult on the new cabinet. Lapointe, re-elected in Quebec East, planned to return as King's French lieutenant, and asked for the external affairs portfolio. King refused, confiding to his diary that "English speaking Canada would not welcome his [Lapointe's] having control of External Affairs, during a European war that increasingly seemed imminent."[29] Lapointe would have to be content with justice, and he remained very influential when it came to the selection of other cabinet ministers from Quebec. He insisted on bringing in other victorious Quebecers, including P.J.A. Cardin (Richelieu-Verchères), Fernand Rinfret (St. James), and Chubby Power (Quebec South).

Although he always kept the final decision for himself, King often asked those around him for their advice and suggestions for cabinet positions. *Ottawa Citizen* editor Charles Bowman, who had travelled with King on one of his Western campaign trips, was asked a few days after the election for his thoughts on the new cabinet, in particular, whom he saw as a potential minister of finance. Bowman's first choice was William Euler, the veteran MP who had won re-election in Kitchener, Ontario. When King made no comment (Euler was ultimately given trade), Bowman then suggested asking Mitch Hepburn. King responded by paraphrasing something Sir Wilfrid Laurier – King's political mentor – had told him years before: "Mr. King, you are a young man in politics, but you may some day be called upon to form a government. Never in your cabinet include a man – no matter how able – who is addicted to over-indulgence in liquor."[30] It was advice that King would not always heed, but for the moment it meant no position for the mercurial Hepburn.

King also approached *Winnipeg Free Press* editor J.W. Dafoe, another staunch Liberal supporter, for advice and, at one point, offered him his choice of either a cabinet position or appointment as Canada's minister in the United States. Dafoe dismissed the first as a "courtesy offer" and refused at once, but he did consider the diplomatic appointment. Ultimately, however, he refused both, choosing to remain where he always wanted to be, at the editor's desk of one of Canada's most influential newspapers.[31]

In the end, the new cabinet consisted of sixteen men. Nine of them, including King, had previous cabinet experience, so it was a veteran and experienced government (albeit with an average age of fifty-two) suggesting a return to old ways rather than a push in new directions. Still, the mixture of veterans and rookies led one observer to dub this new collection of cabinet colleagues as a mixture of "both firebrands and fire extinguishers."[32] Charles Dunning, a former Saskatchewan premier, was persuaded by King to re-enter politics (he had not run in the election but soon won a by-election in Prince Edward Island) and was given the important finance portfolio, a post he had held in the previous Liberal government. T.A. Crerar, who had returned to the Liberal fold and won re-election in Churchill, Manitoba, was given natural resources. King turned to some newcomers to fill out the ranks, including Norman Rogers (labour and health). Rogers – Queen's University professor, author of King's biography, and an increasingly close confidant (and former private secretary) of the prime minister – entered politics in 1935 and won a seat in Kingston, Ontario. He was seen as a politician of great promise but died tragically, in an airplane crash, in 1940.

Another rookie brought into the cabinet – "out of the blue" – was C.D. Howe.[33] Howe had scored an impressive win in Port Arthur, Ontario, and was given the railways and canals and marine portfolio. During the campaign, he had rashly announced that he would not move to Ottawa if elected, but he could hardly have meant it. In his mind, at least, accepting the Liberal nomination and entering politics meant a cabinet position if he won, and he fully expected to receive an offer from the prime minister. He left Port Arthur for Ottawa by train just days after the election.[34] What could not have been known was that Howe and a few others not yet in cabinet, including Lionel Chevrier in Stormont and Paul Martin in Essex East, both in Ontario, were just at the beginning of what would become long and remarkable political careers.

In other ways, the new cabinet reflected the new dynamics in Canadian politics in the wake of the election. The contingent from Quebec was strong, as one would expect given the overwhelming support the province gave to the incoming government, and it included Lapointe (justice), Cardin (public works), Rinfret (secretary of state), Power (pensions and health), and Raoul Dandurand (Senate leader). Joseph Michaud (fisheries) could be added to the list as he was a francophone Quebecer, although he represented Edmundston, New Brunswick. In fact, readers of *Canadian Forum* were warned that the new government would be controlled by Quebec, and that meant by "Taschereau's machine." It made no difference that Taschereau would be out of office in a matter of months; it still meant that "our business interests are once more in control of our affairs."[35]

In a sense, this was a testament to "French power" in Ottawa, but even though the Liberals swept Quebec, the province's percentage of seats in the Liberal caucus declined, from almost half following the 1930 election (40 out of 91) to less than a third in 1935 (55 out of 173).[36] King was in a much stronger position in 1935; he had much more room to manoeuvre and a larger caucus to call on for support. Ironically, French Canada may have returned to the Liberals en masse, and King would continue to rely on Lapointe for political advice on most important issues, especially those dealing with Quebec, but King was now technically less dependent on the Quebec wing, and it was likely to have less influence in the new government.

Western Canada was well represented in the new cabinet as well, with veterans Dunning and Crerar, and the addition of British Columbia's Ian Mackenzie in national defence. Perhaps the most

Mackenzie King's government held a comfortable majority in Parliament, but the new cabinet reflected the outcome of the 1935 election. Prime Minister Mackenzie King and members of the cabinet broadcasting messages to the Canadian people after the special emergency cabinet meeting following Great Britain's declaration of war on Germany on September 3, 1939. Left to right: Chubby Power, Ernest Lapointe, King, Norman Rogers. | National Film Board of Canada, Library and Archives Canada, C-016770

important appointment was Jimmy Gardiner, the Saskatchewan premier who had played such an important role in the Liberal election campaign. Gardiner likely knew before the election that he would be invited to join the federal cabinet should the Liberals win, and two weeks after the election, he left for Ottawa to become minister of agriculture. He would stay on for the next twenty-two years.[37] W.J. Patterson succeeded Gardiner as premier of Saskatchewan.

There were concerns about the West, despite the many seats won there. Alberta, in particular, was left out of the Liberal sweep, and the party's problems in Alberta, and in the West in general, were only just beginning. The election demonstrated that Liberal support was dropping in the West, and the feelings were reciprocated as King – and future Liberal leaders – increasingly turned their focus to Central Canada. King may have once seen the West as a land of promise but, concluded historian Robert Wardhaugh, after 1935 he "saw an area stricken by drought and depression, unable even to pay its debts, and constantly begging the federal government ... for relief."[38]

The West might have been losing faith in the Liberals, but the Liberals now knew they could win without the West. And Western troubles were likely only compounded by King's decision not to appoint a cabinet minister from Alberta, leaving things up to Gardiner as the Western regional leader. Albertans had not behaved well during the recent election – or in any election since 1921 – and now they were getting their just deserts. "After sixteen years, he was fed up"; Mackenzie King "had given up on Alberta."[39]

The Return to Politics

Federally and provincially, the Liberal Party had struck a fine balance in the early 1930s, and this balance was sustained through the 1935 campaign and helped deliver electoral victory. But the magic did not last. Whereas the federal and provincial wings of the party once stood as allies in their effort to bring down the ruling Conservative government, politics soon remerged in the federal-provincial relationship and the unity of 1935 slowly faded.

Duff Pattullo's hopes for a more activist federal government and for more relief for his home province of British Columbia were dashed weeks after the election, at the first Dominion-Provincial Conference under the new federal government. Any thoughts that the Liberals were about to open the federal purse had already been dashed with the appointment of Charles Dunning as minister of finance, and King's views on support for the provinces proved to be only slightly more liberal than Bennett's had been. Another area of disagreement emerged from Pattullo's provincial spending program, which had come to be called the "Little New Deal." Only with the outbreak of war in 1939 did these problems resolve themselves.

In Quebec, the entire federal-provincial landscape altered within a few weeks of the election. The Quebec Liberals had offered significant help to their federal counterparts during the campaign, and Premier Taschereau may have had reason to believe that he had emerged from it stronger than ever. But it was not be. The Liberals were reduced to a minority government in the November 1935 provincial election, and went down to defeat at the hands of the Union Nationale in 1936 as Quebec entered the era of Maurice Duplessis. Over subsequent years, the power of the provincial Liberal Party declined significantly, making the party's federal wing – and those who led it, from Ernest Lapointe to Louis St-Laurent – more important than ever. Relations between Ottawa and Quebec City declined as well, especially as war loomed.

In Ontario, Mitch Hepburn believed that he had personally delivered his province for Mackenzie King and the Liberals, and that this achievement earned him a say in the selection of Ontario members of King's cabinet. He had a few names to suggest, and there was even talk of Hepburn himself returning to Ottawa in a senior portfolio. King disagreed and, as noted above, quickly rejected any thought of it, claiming that since he had not interfered in Hepburn's cabinet selection process, Hepburn should not do so now for the new federal cabinet. And, King claimed, somewhat disingenuously, that if he discussed cabinet making with Hepburn, he would have to discuss it with the other seven Liberal premiers as well.[40] There was nothing Hepburn could do about it, but it was the beginning of a prolonged deterioration in the relationship. The two leaders disagreed on number of subsequent issues, particularly how to respond to the 1937 General Motors strike in Oshawa, and by 1939 they were barely on speaking terms.

Whereas all the Liberal cards had aligned prior to the 1935 election, they began scattering in all directions soon after, and the Liberal coalition lost any sense of cohesion it may have had. The harmony of 1935 had turned to discord by the outbreak of war in 1939, when King's policy of cautious engagement in the war was attacked from opposite sides – by Hepburn for being too timid in Britain's hour of need, and by Duplessis for being too reckless and leading inevitably to another conscription crisis. These divisions formed the crux of the 1940 federal election, but that is another story.

Not surprisingly, there were other changes in Ottawa in the wake of the election, beyond changes in federal-provincial relations. William Herridge, Bennett's brother-in-law, minister in Washington, and architect of much of Bennett's New Deal, resigned his post almost immediately, as did Conservative Howard Ferguson, Canada's High Commissioner in London. Waiting in the wings was Vincent Massey. Despite the bitterness that emerged late in the campaign and the mutual dislike and suspicion between the two men, King immediately appointed Massey to replace Ferguson as High Commissioner. It was a fitting post for an important Liberal supporter, and distant enough to temper the personal differences. Massey travelled in the prime minister's private rail car just days after the election, and was sworn in as the train rocked its way to Quebec City.[41] Norman Lambert, who had worked tirelessly to secure the funding to maintain the Liberal campaign, stayed on as president of the National Liberal Federation, and was appointed to the Senate in 1938.

As the only Reconstruction Party MP, H.H. Stevens found himself all alone and isolated on the opposition benches in Parliament. He was now a "general without an army," one observer wrote. "In politics, as in a State, to the rebel who fails, woe betide." Had he come back with a group of MPs at his side, it might have been different; as it stood, however, "he is the Samson who pulled down the pillars of the temple, with catastrophe for all; and the word is wrath."[42] His party went down to defeat because his "candidates were unknown mediocrities,"[43] and he was now spurned by his former colleagues. In 1938, once Bennett, the former prime minister and his former friend, retired, Stevens returned from the political wilderness, rejoined the Conservative Party, and remained a Conservative for the rest of his political career. He retired in 1942 never knowing what might have been had he stayed in the party long enough to succeed Bennett. If the party had turned to him, could a dynamic call for his brand of change – his support for the "little guy" – have found enough support in working-class and rural Canada to succeed where Bennett had failed?

The memory of Stevens's role in the 1930s and as the brief leader of the Reconstruction Party largely faded with time. His years as a storming Methodist MP who was fighting the good fight for the average Canadian worker and small business owner were soon overshadowed by his earlier career in British Columbia, when he had strongly advocated blocking the *Komagata Maru*. Today, if he is remembered at all, it is as a racist British Columbia politician who refused entry to those immigrants and then worked tirelessly to prevent all Asian immigration into Canada. In 2019, his name was removed from a federal building in Vancouver's Mount Pleasant neighbourhood.

J.S. Woodsworth lived to fight another day, even though his party was disappointed by the election results. One lesson learned was that stronger party organization was necessary for future success. Woodsworth had not been the biggest proponent for centralized control of the party, preferring instead to rely on the different regions. "I feel very strongly that we have to unify our national efforts," fellow MP M.J. Coldwell wrote to him, just days after the election. Coldwell later added his concern regarding the "lack of cohesion in the national movement."[44] Others in the party shared similar views about the CCF's poor organization and financing.[45] Nevertheless, thanks to Woodsworth's dedication and parliamentary skills, the small CCF cohort was able to punch well above its weight in the new House of Commons, and these efforts helped maintain and sustain the fledgling party over the next long decade of Depression and war. Woodsworth did not see it through; he resigned as party leader due to his opposition to participating in the war, and died not long after, in 1942.

To the surprise of some, and despite his earlier health problems, R.B. Bennett stayed on as leader of the opposition and, by all accounts, performed well. "Greyer, graver and older-looking than five years ago, he has been the soul of graciousness, good-humoured and whimsical to friends and foes," was how one reporter put it. Bennett retired in 1938 and was off to the United Kingdom, where he became Viscount Bennett of Mickleham, Calgary, and Hopewell, and, for the first time, bought a home in southern England (Surrey), next door to his boyhood friend Lord Beaverbrook. "'Look at me well,' he said to his staff when bidding them good-by. 'You will never see my like again. I'm a combination of Stalin, Mussolini and Hitler.'"[46] Bennett died in England, in relative obscurity, in 1947.

With Bennett gone, a leadership convention was held to choose a successor, someone who could rebuild the party from the bottom up. A number of candidates came forward, others thought about it and then declined, but in the end the party decided on Robert Manion. Manion had lost his seat in the election, but he remained popular in the party and had been one of the few Tories who had undertaken anything close to a national campaign in 1935. He was also a Catholic and had a francophone spouse, which was considered a plus, or at least some way to attract Quebecers back to the party.[47] But the election had exposed a serious Conservative weakness in Quebec, and French Canada generally, and the roots of this weakness were deep and endured well beyond 1935. The election loss that year sent the Conservatives into the political wilderness for a generation, and it was left to Manion and a few other veteran MPs like R.B. Hanson, once he was back in the House of

Commons, to outsiders like Manitoba's John Bracken, and to a new generation of Conservatives such as British Columbia's Howard Green and, in a few years, Saskatchewan's John Diefenbaker to rebuild the Conservative Party.

In 1936, the Liberals repealed section 98 of the Criminal Code. Most of Bennett's New Deal was ruled *ultra vires* by the Judicial Committee of the Privy Council (JCPC) on January 27, 1937. If nothing else, the court decision underlined how much the Constitution was a factor in any effort by governments to intervene in the lives of Canadians, and how, as some Canadians believed, national action on major social problems was hindered by the Constitution itself. Clearly it exposed some of the constitutional roadblocks to reform, with Bennett, at the federal level, calling for radical reforms that impinged on provincial jurisdiction, while at the provincial level, Aberhart in Alberta advocated radical provincial actions that clearly fell under federal jurisdiction. Any talk of social change, new government programs, and so on would also necessitate a constitutional discussion, regardless of where governments, provinces, or individuals stood on the issues. There was a problem in the Constitution and it led to decades of debate; it also sparked calls for an end to appeals to the JCPC.

Even though the New Deal was found unconstitutional, the 1935 election can be seen, in hindsight, as a turning point in that it foreshadowed the end of inactive government and the beginning of a new age where governments were directly involved in overseeing social welfare, economic planning, and Keynesian pump priming of the economy. Finance Minister Charles Dunning was conservative in thought and likely palatable to the Canadian business community, but the genie was out of the bottle. The Liberals were on record as favouring unemployment insurance and soon found themselves shifting to the left, not to socialism but to a more progressive, interventionist government. King "proceeded cautiously, inching his way into social reconstruction," journalist Grattan

O'Leary wrote. "He borrowed much of his social program from the Progressives and the C.C.F. and calmly took the credit for reforms which he instituted as a measure of self-preservation."[48] A key step was the establishment of the Rowell-Sirois Royal Commission in 1937 to investigate all aspects of dominion-provincial relations. The 1935 election set the stage, but the real change began following the outbreak of the Second World War in 1939. The war greatly accelerated the growth in government intervention, planning, and regulation, and by the end of the new decade Mackenzie King's Liberals were well on their way to implementing – apparently without any sense of irony – many of the policies of Bennett's New Deal.

THE FEDERAL ELECTION OF 1935 marked a turning point, with the breaking once and for all of the old two-party system. It was the first election where there were five major parties competing and in which a significant percentage of the voting public turned in new directions. The election results also reflected the growing regional divisions in the country, especially in terms of Western alienation, and Western Canada emerged as an important bloc in Canadian politics. The West could no longer be ignored, and Westerners showed themselves willing to turn their backs on the traditional party system in favour of new parties of a variety of political stripes, from the left to the right. Thanks largely to the Depression, Canadian politics was reinventing itself.

The Reconstruction Party did not long survive this one election campaign, and most Reconstructionists (including Stevens) returned to the safer and broader ambit of the Conservative Party. But internal tensions remained between those who spoke for big business and the corporate elites and those who represented the smaller independent business wing of the party. In addition, Canadian Conservatism began to shift from its old reliance on the National Policy of tariff protection, balanced budgets, and the Empire into a more modern party forced to confront the pressing issues facing modern, industrial Canada. The transformation continued well past the 1935 election, but in 1942 a new Progressive Conservative Party became a reality.

Social Credit lived on in Alberta, where it dominated politics until the 1960s. It also appeared in various other iterations – in British Columbia, in a distinct Quebec version, and in a federal presence that lasted several decades before finally fading away.

The CCF survived, both provincially and federally, evolving from its Western agricultural roots into a more viable urban progressive party and transforming into the modern New Democratic Party. Along the way, it introduced a social democratic alternative to the traditional parties and helped include more working-class issues directly in the political process. This compelled the traditional parties to broaden their base of support in response, and to turn themselves into more "national" parties in order to meet the challenge of the CCF. The Conservatives clearly lost the 1935 election, but their defeat no longer automatically meant a Liberal victory.

Nevertheless, the Liberal Party survived the challenges from the new parties, holding on to its vote in 1935, and this accomplishment must not be underestimated. The greatest turning point resulting from the 1935 election can perhaps be found here, with the return to office of the Liberal Party, even though it was no stranger to political power. This was no longer the party of Sir Wilfrid Laurier, as the experience of the Great Depression appeared to strongly call into question his pronouncement that the twentieth century would "belong to Canada." The Liberals were confronted with the same shifting forces in Canadian society as the Conservatives, and the old Liberal policies of reciprocity and national autonomy were equally called into question. The 1935 election demonstrated that their old base of support in the West was evaporating, and that the Liberalism of the future would be focused more on Central Canada and the Maritimes. After 1935, with the Conservatives on the right and the rise of the CCF on the left, the Liberals found themselves in the middle – the "mushy middle," some people called it – and they were quick to turn it to advantage. Social welfare, a growing international profile, international collaboration on trade, and, above all, a focus on Quebec and national unity came to represent twentieth-century Liberalism in Canada.

In 1935, Mackenzie King assembled a strong cast of candidates, regional lieutenants, and provincial premiers; he built and maintained a national coalition comprising the two major linguistic groups; and the Liberal organization coalesced into an effective electoral machine. Its continued success for the next two decades – through the Depression, the Second World War, and into the Cold War – was a testament to that machine. In the process, the Liberal Party became, to borrow political scientist Reg Whitaker's term, the Government Party. It all began with the election of 1935.

Appendix 1
List of Key Players

Aberhart, William (1878–1943): Ontario-born high school principal turned fundamentalist Baptist preacher and head of the Prophetic Bible Institute in Calgary. A popular radio broadcaster in the 1920s, he entered politics after being introduced to the ideas of Social Credit. As founding member and leader of the Alberta Social Credit Party, he was elected premier (1935–43). Social Credit was never introduced but Aberhart's party remained in office until 1971.

Bennett, Richard Bedford (1870–1947): Born in New Brunswick and trained as a lawyer, he achieved success in business in Calgary before entering politics, first as a member of the Alberta Legislative Assembly and then federally as a Conservative in the riding for Calgary in 1911. He served in various capacities in Sir Robert Borden's cabinet during the First World War and in both of Arthur Meighen's short-lived governments in the 1920s. Selected leader of the Conservative Party in 1927, he became prime minister in 1930 and served until 1935. Often criticized for being unable to solve the economic crisis in the Depression, he retired and moved to England in 1939, and died there in 1947.

Black, Martha (1866–1957): American-born politician and wife of MP George Black. When her husband became seriously ill, she ran as an Independent Conservative, winning the Yukon riding and becoming one of only two women to win a seat in the 1935 election.

Blackmore, John H. (1890–1971): An American-born former Alberta schoolteacher, he was elected MP in Lethbridge in 1935 and subsequently became parliamentary caucus leader of the Social Credit Party of Canada (1935–68).

Bourassa, Henri (1868–1952): A French Canadian nationalist politician and newspaper editor, he served as MP 1896–1907 and again 1925–35. He ran as an Independent in 1935 and was defeated.

Bracken, John (1883–1969): An Ontario-born professor at the University of Saskatchewan, he entered politics and served as Progressive Party premier of Manitoba (1922–43), oversaw the merger with the Manitoba Liberals in 1931, and later served as leader of the new federal Progressive Conservative Party (1942–48).

Buck, Tim (1891–1973): A leader and founding member of the Communist Party of Canada, he was jailed under section 98 of the Criminal Code in the early 1930s. He ran and lost in the 1935 election.

Cahan, Charles H. (1861–1944): A Nova Scotia lawyer, newspaper editor, and member of the Nova Scotia legislature, he entered federal politics as a Conservative in a Montreal riding in 1925 and served until 1940. He served as secretary of state in R.B. Bennett's government (1930–35).

Coldwell, M.J. (1888–1974): A British-born Saskatchewan schoolteacher, he entered politics first as president of the Saskatchewan Labour Party and then as a leading Co-operative Commonwealth Federation (CCF) MP (1935–58). He served as the second CCF leader (1942–60).

Crerar, Thomas Alexander "T.A." (1876–1975): Western business-man, schoolteacher, and former Liberal. He served as minister of agriculture in the Union Government (1917–19) before re-signing, then became founder and leader of the Progressive Party (1920). He returned to the Liberal Party, was defeated in 1930 and re-elected in 1935, and served as minister of mines and re-sources (1935–45) before being appointed to the Senate (1945).

Dafoe, John Wesley (1866–1944): Influential editor of the *Winnipeg Free Press* (1901–44). A long-time champion of Western Canada and supporter of lower tariffs and freer trade, he had close rela-tions with two Liberal prime ministers (Sir Wilfrid Laurier and Mackenzie King). He declined King's offer of the position of minister in the Canadian legation in Washington (1935).

Dexter, Grant (1896–1961): Leading journalist who spent his entire career with the *Winnipeg Free Press* as a reporter from 1912, Ottawa correspondent (1938–48), and editor (1948–54). Very much an Ottawa insider, he had a first-hand look at Bennett's New Deal.

Douglas, Thomas Clement "Tommy" (1904–86): A Scottish-born Canadian Baptist minister, he entered politics in 1935 and won a seat for the CCF in Weyburn, Saskatchewan. He went on to become CCF premier of Saskatchewan (1944–61) and leader of the New Democratic Party (1961–71).

Dunning, Charles (1885–1958): Immigrated from England to Sas-katchewan, where he became a successful farmer and business-man. He entered politics in 1912, becoming Liberal premier (1922–26), joined the King Liberals in 1926, and served as min-ister of railways and canals and finance minister until he was defeated in 1930. He did not run in the 1935 election but won a by-election soon after and joined the King government as finance minister (1936–39).

Duplessis, Maurice (1890–1959): A French Canadian lawyer turned politician, he was first elected in Trois-Rivières as a Conservative in 1927, becoming leader of the provincial party in 1933. He joined forces with a group of disgruntled provincial Liberals to form the Union Nationale (1935), and won a majority in 1936 to become premier of Quebec (1936–39, 1944–59).

Dupré, Maurice (1888–1941): Quebec Conservative politician. First elected in 1930, he served as solicitor general in Bennett's government but was defeated in 1935.

Duranleau, Arthur (1871–1951): Montreal lawyer and Conservative politician. He was minister of marine (1930–35) and acting minister of fisheries (1932–34) in the Bennett government.

Dysart, Allison (1880–1962): A Liberal lawyer, he entered provincial politics in 1917 and became leader of the opposition in 1926. He led the Liberals to a sweeping victory in New Brunswick in 1935 and served as premier (1935–40).

Ferguson, Howard (1870–1946): A Conservative premier of Ontario (1923–30), he left to become Canada's High Commissioner in London (1930–35).

Gardiner, James G. (1883–1962): An Ontario-born farmer and teacher in Saskatchewan, he entered provincial politics in 1914 and served in the Liberal government, succeeding Charles Dunning as premier from 1926 to 1929. He was re-elected as premier (1934–35) but left for Ottawa to serve as minister of agriculture (1935–57).

Guthrie, Hugh (1866–1939): Ontario politician. He entered the House of Commons as a Liberal in 1900, joined the Unionists in 1917, and stayed as a Conservative until 1935. He served briefly as leader of the opposition in the 1920s, and as Bennett's minister of justice (1930–35).

Hanson, Richard B. (1879–1948): A New Brunswick–born lawyer and former mayor of Fredericton, he entered federal politics as a Conservative (1921–35), replaced H.H. Stevens in cabinet as minister of trade and commerce (1934–35), but was defeated in the 1935 election. Re-elected in 1940, he served briefly as interim Conservative leader (1940–41).

Heaps, Abraham Albert "A.A." (1885–1954): A politician and labour leader, he served as Labour MP for Winnipeg North (1925–40). An early supporter of the CCF, he won one of the few CCF seats in the 1935 election.

Hepburn, Mitch (1896–1953): A colourful Ontario politician, he was elected to the House of Commons in 1926 but left for provincial politics in 1934. He swept to victory in the 1934 Ontario election and served as Liberal premier (1934–42). He was a great help to King and the Liberals in the 1935 election, but the relationship deteriorated over subsequent years.

Herridge, William (1888–1961): Ottawa lawyer, R.B. Bennett's brother-in-law, and Canada's minister to Washington (1931–35). He wrote speeches for Bennett and was influential in initiating Bennett's New Deal broadcasts.

Howe, Clarence Decatur "C.D." (1886–1960): An American-born engineer and businessman, he earned a reputation building grain elevators. He entered politics as a Liberal in 1935 and served in various ministries until he left politics in 1957.

Hutchison, Bruce (1901–92): A British Columbia journalist and author, he worked at various times for the *Winnipeg Free Press*, *Victoria Times*, and *Vancouver Sun*. He was a long-time observer of Canadian politics and international affairs.

Irvine, William (1885–1962): A Scottish-born Methodist minister and political activist in Alberta, he entered the House of Commons as a Labour MP in 1921 and was a founding member of the CCF in 1932. He ran for the CCF in the 1935 election but lost.

King, William Lyon Mackenzie (1874–1950): An Ontario-born Liberal politician, he entered the House of Commons in 1908 and served as minister of labour in the Laurier government. He was defeated in 1911 and 1917, was selected Liberal leader in 1919, and served as prime minister at different periods (1921–25, 1926–30, and 1935–48). He was the dominant politician of his era.

Lambert, Norman (1885–1965): A journalist and businessman, he became general secretary of the National Liberal Federation in 1932 and later served as president of the Liberal Party (1936–41). He was appointed to the Senate in 1938.

Lapointe, Ernest (1876–1941): Quebec Liberal first elected to the House of Commons in 1904. He served as justice minister before 1930 and after 1935, becoming very influential as Mackenzie King's Quebec lieutenant.

Lewis, David (1909–81): A Russian-born labour lawyer, Rhodes scholar, CCF member, and CCF national secretary (1936–50), he went on the become an MP (1962–75) and New Democratic Party (NDP) leader (1971–75).

Macdonald, Angus L. (1890–1954): A one-time Dalhousie law professor and the Liberal premier of Nova Scotia from 1933 to 1940, he subsequently entered federal politics as minister of defence for naval services (1940–45).

MacInnis, Angus (1884–1964): Born in Prince Edward Island, he became a municipal politician in Vancouver and entered the House of Commons (1930–53) as independent labour MP. He was a founding member of the CCF.

Mackenzie, Ian Alistair (1890–1949): A Scottish-born Liberal politician, he served in BC provincial politics (1920–30) before joining the federal Liberals in opposition (1930–35). He was re-elected (1935–47) and served in several portfolios before being appointed to the Senate (1948–49).

Macphail, Agnes (1890–1954): A journalist and author, she was the first woman elected to the House of Commons (1921–40) with the United Farmers of Ontario. She was a founding member of the CCF and later entered Ontario provincial politics.

Manion, Robert (1881–1943): A former Ontario Liberal, he was first elected to the House of Commons as a Unionist (1917) and served until 1935. He was minister of railways and canals in the Bennett government (1930–35), and succeeded Bennett as Conservative leader (1938–40).

Martin, Paul Sr. (1903–92): Ontario lawyer and long-time Liberal politician and MP (1935–68) and Senator (1968–74). He held several cabinet portfolios, beginning in 1945.

Massey, Vincent (1887–1967): Wealthy Toronto Liberal, former politician, and patron of the arts; first Canadian minister to the United States (1926–30); president of the National Liberal Federation (1932). He became High Commissioner in London (1935–48), and was the first Canadian-born Governor General (1952–59).

O'Leary, Grattan (1888–1976): Quebec-born journalist and author; one-time editor for the *Ottawa Journal*. Although an unsuccessful Conservative candidate in the 1925 federal election, he maintained close relations with several Conservative leaders.

Pattullo, Thomas Dufferin "Duff" (1873–1956): An Ontario-born journalist and local politician in Yukon and British Columbia, he was first elected to the BC legislature in 1916 and served as leader of the opposition (1928) and Liberal premier (1933–41). He was the architect of the "Little New Deal."

Perley, Sir George (1857–1938): American-born Conservative politician and MP (1904–17 and 1925–38). He served in the Borden and Meighen governments, and was minister without portfolio in the Bennett government. One of the few Quebec Conservatives to win re-election in 1935, he died in office in 1938.

Power, Charles Gavan "Chubby" (1888–1968): Anglo-Quebec Liberal politician and MP (1917–55) and Senator (1955–68). A partisan Quebec organizer and Liberal stalwart, he served as Mackenzie King's minister of pensions and health after winning in the 1935 election.

Rhodes, E.N. (1877–1942): A Nova Scotia Conservative MP (1908–21) and premier of Nova Scotia (1925–30), he served as Bennett's minister of finance (1932–35) before being appointed to the Senate (1935–42).

Rinfret, Fernand (1883–1939): Quebec Liberal politician; mayor of Montreal (1932–34); MP (1920–39) and secretary of state in the King government (1935–39).

Rogers, Norman McLeod (1894–1940): A Nova Scotia-born Liberal politician, Queen's University professor, and private secretary and biographer of Mackenzie King, he served as minister of labour in the King government (1935–39).

Sauvé, Arthur (1874–1944): Member of the Quebec National Assembly (1908–30), federal Conservative MP (1930–35), and Senator (1935–44). He served as R.B. Bennett's postmaster general.

Stevens, Henry Herbert "Harry" (1878–1973): British-born businessman, journalist, Vancouver municipal politician, and Conservative MP (1911–30, 1930–35, and 1938–42). He served briefly in the Meighen cabinet in 1921 and 1926, and was minister of trade and commerce in the Bennett government. He formed the Reconstruction Party of Canada in 1935.

Taschereau, Louis-Alexandre (1867–1952): Lawyer and French Canadian Liberal politician; member of the Quebec National Assembly (1900–36) and Liberal premier of Quebec (1920–36). He was defeated by Maurice Duplessis and the Union Nationale in 1936.

Towers, Graham (1897–1975): Montreal-born bank executive; first governor of the Bank of Canada (1934–54).

Underhill, Frank (1889–1971): Author and history professor at the University of Saskatchewan (1914–27) and the University of Toronto (1927–55). A member of the League for Social Reconstruction, he was credited with being one of the authors of the CCF's Regina Manifesto in 1933.

Wilson, Cairine (1885–1962): Born to a wealthy Montreal Liberal family, she was one of the founders of the National Federation of Liberal Women of Canada and served as its president from 1938 to 1948. Appointed as Canada's first female senator (1930), she later served as president of League of Nations Society in Canada (1936–42).

Woodsworth, James Shaver (1874–1942): Ontario-born pacifist and Methodist minister turned socialist and labour activist. He was MP for Winnipeg (1921–42), worked with the "Ginger Group" in Parliament, and was the founding leader of the CCF (1932–38).

Appendix 2
Timeline of Events

1911

September 21   Conservatives win federal election, defeating the Liberals and reciprocity.

1919

October 20   United Farmers of Ontario win provincial election.

1920

March 3   The National Progressive Party holds first formal meeting.

1921

July 18   United Farmers of Alberta win provincial election.

1922

July 18   United Farmers of Manitoba win provincial election.

1928

April   The National Federation of Liberal Women of Canada is created.

1930

July 28   R.B. Bennett and the Conservative Party win the
                 federal election.

1931

August 1   Leaders of the Communist Party are arrested
                 under section 98 of the Criminal Code.

December 11   The Statute of Westminster is enacted.

1932

February 9   The Judicial Committee of the Privy Council
                 rules in favour of the federal government in a
                 case dealing with radio broadcasting.

May 26   Labour and independent MPs meet in William
                 Irvine's parliamentary office to discuss the
                 creation of a new political party.

July 21 –   The Imperial Economic Conference takes place
  August 20   in Ottawa.

August 1   The Co-operative Commonwealth Federation
                 (CCF) is created at its Calgary convention.

October   An order-in-council is issued to establish work
                 camps, run by the Department of National
                 Defence.

November   The National Liberal Federation is created.

1933

February 27   Mackenzie King sets out Liberal policy in a
                 parliamentary speech.

April   Bennett visits Washington to encourage trade
                 talks.

June 12 –   Bennett attends the World Economic Conference
  July 27   in London.

July   The CCF adopts the Regina Manifesto at its
                 Regina convention.

| August 22 | Angus Macdonald's Liberals win a majority in the Nova Scotia provincial election. |
| November 2 | Duff Pattullo's Liberals sweep the BC provincial election. |

1934

January 15	H.H. Stevens delivers speech on "price spreads" to the Retail Shoe Merchants and Shoe Manufacturers Association in Toronto, then offers to resign from cabinet.
January 17	Dominion-provincial conference on unemployment and relief begins.
February 16	The Special Committee on Price Spreads and Mass Buying (Stevens Committee) is established.
June 19	James Gardiner's Liberals sweep the Saskatchewan provincial election.
June 19	Mitch Hepburn's Liberals sweep the Ontario provincial election.
June 27	Stevens delivers speech to Conservative MPs at the Conservative Study Club.
July 7	The Royal Commission on Price Spreads and Mass Buying is launched.
August 27	Hepburn auctions forty-seven Tory automobiles in Toronto's Varsity Stadium.
September	Bennett attends the General Assembly of the League of Nations in Geneva.
October 25	The first cabinet meeting after Bennett's return from England is followed by Stevens's resignation from cabinet.
November 1	The first hearing of the Royal Commission on Price Spreads and Mass Buying takes place.
December 5	Bennett announces his intention to stay on as leader to fight the next election.

1935

January 2–11	Bennett's New Deal broadcasts take place.
January 17	The last parliamentary session before the election opens.
February 2	Sittings of the Royal Commission on Price Spreads and Mass Buying end.
February 23	Bennett falls ill with a serious respiratory infection.
March 7	Bennett suffers heart attack.
March 11	Bank of Canada begins operations.
April 4	The Social Credit Party inaugural convention is held; William Aberhart becomes leader.
April 12	The report of the Royal Commission on Price Spreads and Mass Buying is released.
April 18	Bennett leaves for England for King George V's Silver Jubilee.
May 6	King George V's Silver Jubilee is celebrated.
May 17	Bennett returns from England.
June 3	The On-to-Ottawa Trek leaves Vancouver.
June 5	Stevens attacks Bennett's bill to create a trade and industry commission under control of the Tariff Board.
June 6	The Action Libérale Nationale in Quebec is created, led by Liberal Paul Gouin.
June 10	Bennett rebuts Stevens's speech in the House of Commons.
June 22	Eleven Trek leaders meet with Bennett on Parliament Hill.
June 26	The Liberals sweep the New Brunswick provincial election.
July 1	The Regina Riot takes place.
July 5	Bennett officially informs his caucus that he will be staying on as leader.

July 7	Stevens formally leaves the Conservative Party and announces formation of the Reconstruction Party of Canada.
July 23	Stevens begins the Reconstruction Party election campaign.
July 23	The Liberals win all thirty seats in the PEI provincial election.
August 15	Parliament is dissolved and the federal election is set for Monday, October 14.
August 22	Aberhart's Social Credit Party sweeps the Alberta provincial election.
August 26	Official trade negotiations with United States begin in Washington.
September 3–6	King campaigns in the Maritimes and Quebec.
September 7 – October 11	The Conservatives run the "Sage" political broadcasts.
September 14–23	Bennett campaigns in the West.
September 15	*Maclean's* publishes four "The Issues as I See Them" articles.
September 19 – October 2	King campaigns in the West.
October 2–7	Bennett campaigns in Quebec and the Maritimes.
October 3	Italy invades Ethiopia.
October 3–12	King campaigns in Ontario.
October 7	The Liberal Party holds a rally at Toronto's Maple Leaf Gardens.
October 9	The Conservative Party holds a rally at Toronto's Maple Leaf Gardens.
October 11	The Reconstruction Party holds a rally at Toronto's Maple Leaf Gardens.
October 14	Election day.
October 15	King and Bennett meet to discuss transition.

November 4   Canada-US trade negotiations resume.

November 15   Canada and the United States sign a trade
                 agreement.

November 25   Louis-Alexandre Taschereau's Liberals are
                 reduced to a minority in the Quebec provincial
                 election.

1936

June   Government work camps are closed.

June   The Liberals repeal section 98 of the Criminal
                 Code.

August 17   Maurice Duplessis's Union Nationale wins a
                 majority government in the Quebec provincial
                 election.

1937

January 27   The Judicial Committee of the Privy Council
                 rules most of Bennett's New Deal *ultra vires*.

1939

January 11   Stevens rejoins the Conservative Party caucus.

January 28   Bennett resigns his Calgary seat and leaves for
                 England.

Notes

Introduction

1 H. Blair Neatby, *The Politics of Chaos: Canada in the Thirties* (Toronto: Macmillan, 1972), 35–36.

2 James Struthers, *No Fault of Their Own: Unemployment and the Canadian Welfare State, 1914–1941* (Toronto: University of Toronto Press, 1983), 4–5.

3 Walter D. Young, *Democracy and Discontent: Progressivism, Socialism and Social Credit in the Canadian West* (Toronto: McGraw-Hill Ryerson, 1969), 45.

4 Michiel Horn, ed., *The Dirty Thirties: Canadians in the Great Depression* (Toronto: Copp Clark, 1972), 355.

5 James H. Gray, *The Winter Years: The Depression on the Prairies* (Toronto: Macmillan, 1966), 110.

6 This paragraph and the next rely on Gerald Friesen, *The Canadian Prairies: A History* (Toronto: University of Toronto Press, 1984), 388–92.

7 Friesen, *The Canadian Prairies*, 416.

8 See Ramsay Cook, *The Politics of John W. Dafoe and the Free Press* (Toronto: University of Toronto Press, 1963), 205.

Chapter 1: Depression Politics

1 "Capitalism under Fire," *The Round Table* 25, 98 (March 1935): 389.

2 Margaret Stewart and Doris French, *Ask No Quarter: A Biography of Agnes Macphail* (Toronto: Longmans, Green, 1959), 156. For the automobile

incident, see John Boyko, *Bennett: The Rebel Who Challenged and Changed a Nation* (Fredericton: Goose Lanes Editions, 2012), 99.

3 Grattan O'Leary, *Recollections of People, Press, and Politics* (Toronto: Macmillan, 1977), 79.

4 Cited in Patrice Dutil and David MacKenzie, *Embattled Nation: Canada's Wartime Election of 1917* (Toronto: Dundurn, 2017), 114.

5 "Manion Resents Bennett Roasting, Retorts in Kind," *The Globe*, June 5, 1935, 1.

6 Norman Ward, ed., *A Party Politician: The Memoirs of Chubby Power* (Toronto: Macmillan 1966), 265 and 281.

7 O'Leary, *Recollections of People, Press, and Politics*, 69.

8 For an overview of the 1930 election, see J. Murray Beck, ed., *Pendulum of Power: Canada's Federal Elections* (Toronto: Prentice-Hall, 1968), 191–205.

9 On the Commonwealth talks, see "The End of Mr. Bennett," *The Economist*, October 19, 1935, 742.

10 James Struthers, *No Fault of Their Own: Unemployment and the Canadian Welfare State, 1914–1941* (Toronto: University of Toronto Press, 1983), 109–11.

11 Larry A. Glassford, *Reaction and Reform: The Politics of the Conservative Party under R.B. Bennett, 1927–1938* (Toronto: University of Toronto Press, 1992), 144–46; Boyko, *Bennett*, 388–90.

12 Lita-Rose Betcherman, *Ernest Lapointe: Mackenzie King's Great Quebec Lieutenant* (Toronto: University of Toronto Press, 2002), 194.

13 Diary entry of William Lyon Mackenzie King, January 1, 1935, Library and Archives Canada, MG26-J13.

14 See H. Blair Neatby, *William Lyon Mackenzie King, Volume 3: 1932–1939, The Prism of Unity* (Toronto: University of Toronto Press, 1976), 6–7.

15 Mackenzie King diary, February 9, 1935.

16 Quoted in Ward, *A Party Politician*, 281–82.

17 J.R.H. Wilbur, "H.H. Stevens and R.B. Bennett, 1930–34," *Canadian Historical Review* 43, 1 (March 1962): 2–3.

18 Wilbur, "H.H. Stevens and R.B. Bennett," 7.

19 Hector Charlesworth, *I'm Telling You: Being the Further Candid Chronicles of Hector Charlesworth* (Toronto: Macmillan, 1937), 172.

20 Vincent Massey, *What's Past Is Prologue: The Memoirs of the Right Honourable Vincent Massey, C.H.* (Toronto: Macmillan, 1963), 220.

21 "Capitalism under Fire," 390.

22 Memo, "A Brief History of the Break Between Hon. H.H. Stevens and Hon. R.B. Bennett and his Conservative Government," n.d., Library and Archives Canada (LAC), H.H. Stevens Papers, MG 27 III B9, vol. 126, file "Corres. 1935–36, British Columbia (20A) Election Literature"; Wilbur, "H.H. Stevens and R.B. Bennett," 12.

23 Murray Donnelly, *Dafoe of the Free Press* (Toronto: Macmillan, 1968), 150–51.

24 Ross Harkness, *J.E. Atkinson of the Star* (Toronto: University of Toronto Press, 1963), 259. See also P.B. Waite, *In Search of R.B. Bennett* (Montreal and Kingston: McGill-Queen's University Press, 2012), 203.

25 For all the details, see Wilbur, "H.H. Stevens and R.B. Bennett," 13–14; Memo, "A Brief History of the Break Between Hon. H.H. Stevens and Hon. R.B. Bennett and his Conservative Government."

26 Lord Beaverbrook, *Friends: Sixty Years of Intimate Personal Relations with Richard Bedford Bennett* (London: Heinemann, 1959), 89.

27 Quoted in Neatby, *William Lyon Mackenzie King, Volume 3*, 85.

Chapter 2: What's Left and Who's Right?

1 Bruce Hutchison, "Storm over the Pacific," *Canadian Forum* 15, 176 (July 1935): 291.

2 Walter D. Young, *Democracy and Discontent: Progressivism, Socialism and Social Credit in the Canadian West* (Toronto: McGraw-Hill Ryerson, 1969), 37.

3 Anthony Mardiros, *William Irvine: The Life of a Prairie Radical* (Toronto: Lorimer, 1979), 182; John Herd Thompson, with Allen Seager, *Canada 1922–1939: Decades of Discord* (Toronto: McClelland and Stewart, 1985), 233.

4 David Lewis, *The Good Fight: Political Memoirs, 1909–1958* (Toronto: Macmillan, 1981), 81.

5 Walter D. Young, *The Anatomy of a Party: The National CCF, 1932–61* (Toronto: University of Toronto Press, 1969), 45.

6 The Regina Manifesto can be found in Young, *Anatomy of a Party,* app. A.

7 Thompson and Seager, *Canada 1922–1939,* 234. Woodworth is quoted on page 235.

8 Leo Heaps, *The Rebel in the House: The Life and Times of A.A. Heaps MP* (London: Niccolo Publishing, 1970), 146–47.

9 Mason Wade, *The French Canadians, 1760–1967* (Toronto: Macmillan, 1968), 827.

10 Alvin Finkel, *The Social Credit Phenomenon in Alberta* (Toronto: University of Toronto Press, 1989), 28–29.

11 David E. Smith, *Prairie Liberalism: The Liberal Party in Saskatchewan, 1905–71* (Toronto: University of Toronto Press,1975), 225.

12 John A. Irving, *The Social Credit Movement in Alberta* (Toronto: University of Toronto Press, 1959), 110–11.

13 The platform can be found in Irving, *The Social Credit Movement in Alberta,* app. A, 349–51.

14 David R. Elliott, "Antithetical Elements in William Aberhart's Theology and Political Ideology," *Canadian Historical Review* 54, 1 (March 1978): 49.

15 C.B. Macpherson, *Democracy in Alberta: Social Credit and the Party System* (Toronto: University of Toronto Press, 1953), 152.

16 Robin Fisher, *Duff Pattullo of British Columbia* (Toronto: University of Toronto Press, 1991), 248.

17 Fisher, *Duff Pattullo,* 245, 249.

18 Margaret A. Ormsby, "T. Dufferin Pattullo and the Little New Deal," *Canadian Historical Review* 43, 4 (December 1962): 277, 278.

19 Fisher, *Duff Pattullo,* 284.

20 Neil McKenty, *Mitch Hepburn* (Toronto: McClelland and Stewart, 1967), 34.

21 John T. Saywell, *"Just Call Me Mitch": The Life and Times of Mitchell F. Hepburn* (Toronto: University of Toronto Press, 1991), 4.

22 Saywell, *"Just Call Me Mitch,"* 211.

23 Lita-Rose Betcherman, *Ernest Lapointe: Mackenzie King's Great Quebec Lieutenant* (Toronto: University of Toronto Press, 2002), 197.

24 Bernard L. Vigod, *Quebec before Duplessis: The Political Career of Louis-Alexandre Taschereau* (Montreal and Kingston: McGill-Queen's University Press, 1986), 210.

25 See E.R. Forbes and D.A. Muise, eds., *The Atlantic Provinces in Confederation* (Toronto: University of Toronto Press, 1993), 277.

26 Diary entry of William Lyon Mackenzie King, June 27, 1935, Library and Archives Canada, MG26-J13.

27 It was the CCF. See Young, *The Anatomy of a Party,* 88.

Chapter 3: It's Time for a New Deal

1 "Backstage at Ottawa," *Maclean's,* July 1, 1935, 16.

2 The broadcasts are reprinted in J.R.H. Wilbur, ed., *The Bennett New Deal: Fraud or Portent?* (Toronto: Copp Clark, 1968), 70–80; see also Ernest

Watkins, *R.B. Bennett: A Biography* (Toronto: Kingswood House, 1963), 220.

3 Diary entry of William Lyon Mackenzie King, January 4 and 5, 1935, Library and Archives Canada, MG26-J13.

4 Mackenzie King diary, January 8, 1935.

5 See also "Canada's 'New Deal' Programme," *The Round Table* 25, 99 (June 1935): 585–86.

6 Donald Forster and Colin Read, "The Politics of Opportunism: The New Deal Broadcasts," *Canadian Historical Review* 60, 3 (September 1979): 336–37.

7 W.H. McConnell, "The Genesis of the Canadian 'New Deal,'" *Journal of Canadian Studies* 4, 2 (May 1969): 37.

8 Forster and Read, "Politics of Opportunism," 337. For reaction to the speeches, see 327–29, and McConnell, "Genesis," 36.

9 Forster and Read, "Politics of Opportunism," 329.

10 "Economic Reform Bennett's Slogan," *Montreal Gazette,* January 3, 1935, 1.

11 Margaret Stewart and Doris French, *Ask No Quarter: A Biography of Agnes Macphail* (Toronto: Longmans, Green, 1959), 215.

12 Mackenzie King diary, January 18, 1935.

13 "Backstage at Ottawa," *Maclean's,* March 1, 1935, 13; Underhill, quoted in Wilbur, *Bennett New Deal,* 109.

14 Donald J. Horton, *André Laurendeau: French-Canadian Nationalist, 1912–1968* (Toronto: Oxford University Press, 1992), 75.

15 For the February 22, 1935, letter, see Vincent Massey, *What's Past Is Prologue: The Memoirs of the Right Honourable Vincent Massey, C.H.* (Toronto: Macmillan, 1963), 220. The poem can be found in Claude Bissell, *The Young Vincent Massey* (Toronto: University of Toronto Press, 1981), 230.

16 Mackenzie King diary, January 9, 1935.

17 Wilbur, *Bennett New Deal,* 94–96.

18 Mackenzie King diary, January 14, 1935.

19 See Wilbur, *Bennett New Deal,* 149.

20 Mackenzie King diary, January 15 and 17, 1935.

21 Mackenzie King diary, January 18 and 25, 1935.

22 Letter, Bennett to Howard Ferguson, March 7, 1935, Archives of Ontario (AO), Howard Ferguson Papers, F8-2 MU 10919 (box 3), container B299693, file "Jan. To Dec. 1935." For King's condolences to Bennett, see his letter to the prime minister, March 5, 1935, Library and Archives Canada (LAC), Mackenzie King Papers, MG 26 J, reel C-3678.

23 Mackenzie King diary, February 3 and March 7, 1935.

24 "Memorandum," March 13, 1935, LAC, Robert J. Manion Papers, MG 27 III B7, vol. 84, file "Memorandum – Political (Personal), 1931–1935, 1938–1941."

25 P.B. Waite, *In Search of R.B. Bennett* (Montreal and Kingston: McGill-Queen's University Press, 2012), 206.

26 McConnell, "Genesis," 37 (emphasis in original).

27 "Memorandum," March 2, 1935, LAC, Manion Papers, MG 27 III B7, vol. 84, file "Memorandum – Political (Personal), 1931–1935, 1938–1941."

28 "Canada: The Parties and the Election," *The Round Table* 25, 100 (September 1935): 820.

29 Mackenzie King diary, April 3, 1935.

30 Watkins, *R.B. Bennett*, 223.

31 Larry A. Glassford, *Reaction and Reform: The Politics of the Conservative Party under R.B. Bennett, 1927–1938* (Toronto: University of Toronto Press, 1992), 169; John Boyko, *Bennett: The Rebel Who Challenged and Changed a Nation* (Fredericton: Goose Lanes Editions, 2012), 358–60.

32 Wilbur, *Bennett New Deal*, 163–64.

33 Mackenzie King diary, May 21 and June 20, 1935.

34 Mackenzie King diary, March 15 and May 27, 1935.

35 Watkins, *R.B. Bennett*, 224.

36 H. Blair Neatby, *William Lyon Mackenzie King, Volume 3: 1932–1939, The Prism of Unity* (Toronto: University of Toronto Press, 1976), 104.

37 Letter, Stevens to A.J. Anderson, July 11, 1935, LAC, H.H. Stevens Papers, MG 27 III B9, vol. 58, file "Corres. 1935–36, A-1."

38 Mackenzie King diary, June 19, 1935.

39 Richard Wilbur, *H.H. Stevens, 1878–1973* (Toronto: University of Toronto Press, 1977), 172–76; Glassford, *Reaction and Reform*, 169; Boyko, *Bennett*, 358–60.

40 Watkins, *R.B. Bennett*, 224.

41 Letter, Stevens to Anderson, July 11, 1935, LAC, Stevens Papers, MG 27 III B9, vol. 58, file "Corres. 1935–36, A-1.

42 Letter, Stevens to D.M. Duggan, July 4, 1935, LAC, Stevens Papers, MG 27 III B9, vol. 125, file "Corres. 1935–36 (1) Bennett, Hon. R.B."

43 Memo, "A Brief History of the Break between Hon. H.H. Stevens and Hon. R.B. Bennett and his Conservative Government," n.d., LAC, Stevens Papers, MG 27 III B9, vol. 126, file "Corres. 1935–36, British Columbia (20A) Election Literature."

44 "Ex-Minister to Battle for Reform," Calgary *Daily Herald,* July 8, 1935, 13.

45 "Feds Sure His Program to Be Supported Here," *Ottawa Citizen,* July 10, 1935, 1.

46 Wilbur, *Bennett New Deal,* 3; "Backstage at Ottawa," *Maclean's,* April 1, 1935, 57.

47 Mackenzie King diary, May 18 and July 11, 1935.

48 Norman Ward and David Smith, *Jimmy Gardiner: Relentless Liberal* (Toronto: University of Toronto Press, 1990), 174; Mackenzie King diary, June 19 and 26, 1935.

49 Marc T. Boucher, "The Politics of Economic Depression: Canadian-American Relations in the Mid-1930s," *International Journal* 41, 1 (Winter 1985–86): 20–21; Mackenzie King diary, June 4, 1935.

50 See Robert Bothwell and John English, "'Dirty Work at the Crossroads': New Perspective on the Riddell Incident," *Historical Papers/Communications historiques* 7, 1 (1972): 263–85, https://doi.org/10.7202/030752ar 263-86.

51 For more on the On-to-Ottawa Trek, see the collection of documents in Michael Horn, ed., *The Dirty Thirties: Canadians in the Great Depression* (Toronto: Copp Clark, 1972), 340–87; and Pierre Berton, *The Great Depression 1929–1939* (Toronto: Penguin, 1990), 373–406.

52 Boyko, *Bennett,* 338–40.

53 Waite, *In Search of R.B. Bennett,* 220.

54 "Wheat Bill and Social Measures Outstanding in Parliament Session," *Calgary Daily Herald,* July 6, 1935, 1.

55 For a complete list, see "October 14 Date Set for Federal Election," *Montreal Gazette,* August 15, 1935, 1–2.

56 "Backstage at Ottawa," *Maclean's,* August 15, 1935, 11.

57 Graham Spry, "Politics," *Canadian Forum* 15, 177 (August 1935): 324.

58 Murray Donnelly, *Dafoe of the Free Press* (Toronto: Macmillan, 1968), 152.

Chapter 4: The Campaign Begins

1 "Canada: The Parties and the Election," *The Round Table* 25, 100 (September 1935): 820.

2 R.B. Bennett, "The Issues as I See Them," *Maclean's,* September 15, 1935, 10. The *Vancouver Sun* reprinted the *Maclean's* "The Issues as I See Them" series: September 16, 1935, 7.

3 "Canada Is Willing, but U.S. Hesitant, to Sign Trade Pact," *The Globe,* September 9, 1935, 1.

4 "Bennett Again Warns of Peril of Revolution," *The Globe,* September 24, 1935, 1.

5 "Protégez la patrie Canadienne contre le communisme!" *Le Canadien,* September 12, 1935, 6.

6 Bennett, "The Issues as I See Them," 28.

7 Bernard Vigod, *Quebec before Duplessis: The Political Career of Louis-Alexandre Taschereau* (Montreal and Kingston: McGill-Queen's University Press, 1986), 212.

8 "Un choix facile à faire," *Le Canadien,* October 10, 1935, 6.

9 Norman Ward, ed., *A Party Politician: The Memoirs of Chubby Power* (Toronto: Macmillan, 1966), 267.

10 "Bertrand Charges Bennett Dictator," *Montreal Gazette,* October 7, 1935, 2.

11 Mackenzie King, "The Issues as I See Them," *Maclean's,* September 15, 1935, 30.

12 King, "The Issues as I See Them," 29.

13 King, "The Issues as I See Them," 31; "King Sounds Note of Hope," *The Globe,* September 6, 1935, 1.

14 Memo, J.B. Maclean to Napier Moore, May 31, 1937, and E.C. Calder to J.B. Maclean, June 14, 1937, Archives of Ontario (AO), Maclean-Hunter Limited Papers, F138-8, container B213980, file "William Lyon Mackenzie King, 1930–1937"; Floyd Chalmers, *A Gentleman of the Press* (Toronto: Doubleday, 1969), 286.

15 John A. Irving, *The Social Credit Movement in Alberta* (Toronto: University of Toronto Press, 1959), 139.

16 "The Social Credit Movement in Alberta," *The Round Table* 26, 101 (December 1935): 158–59.

17 Alvin Finkel, *The Social Credit Phenomenon in Alberta* (Toronto: University of Toronto Press, 1989), 32–40.

18 J.S. Woodsworth, "The Issues as I See Them," *Maclean's,* September 15, 1935, 32.

19 Walter D. Young, *Democracy and Discontent: Progressivism, Socialism and Social Credit in the Canadian West* (Toronto: McGraw-Hill Ryerson, 1969), 63.

20 "C.C.F. and the Orientals," *Vancouver Sun,* October 8, 1935, 5.

21 H.F. Angus, "Liberalism Stoops to Conquer," *Canadian Forum* 15, 179 (December 1935): 389.

22 "How Will B.C. Go? Figure It from This," *Vancouver Sun,* October 10, 1935, 2; "Oriental Better than Some Whites," *Vancouver Sun,* October 12, 1935, 4.

23 H.H. Stevens, "The Issues as I See Them," *Maclean's,* September 15, 1935, 11.

24 Richard Wilbur, *H.H. Stevens, 1878–1973* (Toronto: University of Toronto Press, 1977), 183.

25 C.P. Stacey, *Canada and the Age of Conflict: A History of Canadian External Policies, Volume 2: 1921–1948: The Mackenzie King Era* (Toronto: University of Toronto Press, 1981), 180; Norman Hillmer, *O.D. Skelton: A Portrait of Canadian Ambition* (Toronto: University of Toronto Press, 2015), 180–81.

26 Wilbur, *Stevens,* 195; Kenneth McNaught, *A Prophet in Politics: A Biography of J.S. Woodsworth* (Toronto: University of Toronto Press, 1959), 272.

27 Lester Pearson, *Mike: The Memoirs of the Right Honourable Lester B. Pearson, Volume 1: 1897–1948* (Toronto: University of Toronto Press, 1972), 95. Reflecting on this brief conversation almost four decades later, Pearson found Bennett's confidence amusing, considering that he was about to face the greatest electoral defeat in a Canadian federal election – that is, until Pearson's own defeat in 1958.

28 Valerie Knowles, *Strangers at Our Gates: Canadian Immigration Policy, 1540–1990* (Toronto: Dundurn, 1992), 108; other statistics taken from M.C. Urquhart, ed., *Historical Statistics of Canada* (Toronto: Macmillan, 1965).

29 John E. Zucchi, *Italians in Toronto: Development of a National Identity, 1875–1935* (Kingston and Montreal: McGill-Queen's University Press, 1988), 166–88; O.W. Gerus and J.E. Rea, *The Ukrainians in Canada* (St. John, NB: Canadian Historical Association, 1985), 14–15; Peter D. Chimbos, *The Canadian Odyssey: The Greek Experience in Canada* (Toronto: McClelland and Stewart, 1980), 119.

30 Jack Jedwab, "Uniting Uptowners and Downtowners: The Jewish Electorate and Quebec Provincial Politics: 1927–1939," *Canadian Ethnic Studies* 18, 2 (1986): 7–19; George Hoffman, "The New Party and the Old Issues: The Saskatchewan Farmer-Labour Party and the Ethnic Vote, 1934," *Canadian Ethnic Studies* 14, 2 (1982): 1–19.

31 Alison Prentice et al., *Canadian Women: A History* (Toronto: Harcourt Brace Jovanovich, 1988), 282–83.

32 Veronica Strong-Boag, *The New Day Recalled: Lives of Girls and Women in English Canada, 1919–1939* (Toronto: Penguin, 1988), 196.

33 Sylvia B. Bashevkin, "Independence versus Partisanship: Dilemmas in the Political History of Women in English Canada," in *Rethinking Canada: The Promise of Women's History,* ed. Veronica Strong-Boag and Anita Clair Fellman (Toronto: Copp Clark, 1986), 255.

34 Prentice et al., *Canadian Women,* 277–78. See Patricia A. Myers, "'A Noble Effort': The National Federation of Liberal Women of Canada, 1928–1973," in *Beyond the Vote: Canadian Women and Politics,* ed. Linda Kealey and Joan Sangster (Toronto: University of Toronto Press, 1989), 39–62.

35 Diary entry of William Lyon Mackenzie King, March 14 and 21, 1935, Library and Archives Canada, MG26-J13.

36 Joan Sangster, "The Role of Women in the Early CCF," in Kealey and Sangster, *Beyond the Vote,* 127.

37 Joan Sangster, *Dreams of Equality: Women on the Canadian Left, 1920–1950* (Toronto: McClelland and Stewart, 1989), 98.

38 Strong-Boag, *The New Day Recalled,* 258.

39 Margaret Stewart and Doris French, *Ask No Quarter: A Biography of Agnes Macphail* (Toronto: Longmans, Green, 1959), 219–20.

40 Mrs. George Black, *My Seventy Years* (Toronto: Thomas Nelson and Sons, 1938), 310.

41 "15 Women Seek Seats in House," *Windsor Daily Star,* October 12, 1935, 1.

42 "Women's Vote Is Expected to Break Record," *The Globe,* October 14, 1935, 5.

43 Allan Levine, *Scrum Wars: The Prime Ministers and the Media* (Toronto: Dundurn, 1993), 157–58; John Boyko, *Bennett: The Rebel Who Challenged and Changed a Nation* (Fredericton: Goose Lane Editions, 2012), 392–94.

44 Larry A. Glassford, *Reaction and Reform: The Politics of the Conservative Party under R.B. Bennett, 1927–1938* (Toronto: University of Toronto Press, 1992), 188.

45 Glassford, *Reaction and Reform,* 281n53.

46 Boyko, *Bennett,* 392–94; Glassford, *Reaction and Reform,* 195.

47 Mackenzie King diary, February 4 and May 10, 1935.

48 Norman Ward and David Smith, *Jimmy Gardiner: Relentless Liberal* (Toronto: University of Toronto Press, 1990), 193.

49 Letter, Grant Dexter to John Dafoe, September 3, 1935, Library and Archives Canada (LAC) John W. Dafoe Papers, MG 30 D45, reel M-77.

50 Reginald Whitaker, *The Government Party: Organizing and Financing the Liberal Party of Canada, 1930–58* (Toronto: University of Toronto Press, 1977), 24–25.

51 Claude Bissell, *The Young Vincent Massey* (Toronto: University of Toronto Press, 1981), 226–27.

52 Whitaker, *The Government Party,* 36.

53 Paul Martin, *A Very Public Life, Volume 1: Far from Home* (Toronto: Deneau Publishers,1983), 150.

54 Ward, *A Party Politician,* 335.

55 Letter, George McLeod to Mackenzie King, August 7, 1935, LAC, Mackenzie King Papers, MG 26 J, reel C-3682.

56 Letter, Gardiner to Mackenzie King, May 14, 1935, LAC, King Papers, MG 26 J, reel C-3680.

57 John T. Saywell, *"Just Call Me Mitch": The Life and Times of Mitchell F. Hepburn* (Toronto: University of Toronto Press, 1991), 183–84, 222.

58 Saywell, *"Just Call Me Mitch,"* 225.

59 J.L. Granatstein, "Financing the Liberal Party, 1935–1945," in *Policy by Other Means: Essays in Honour of C.P. Stacey,* ed. Michael Cross and Robert Bothwell (Toronto: Clarke, Irwin, 1972), 185–86.

60 Granatstein, "Financing the Liberal Party," 183; Whitaker *The Government Party,* 72 and 74; Neil McKenty, *Mitch Hepburn* (Toronto: McClelland and Stewart, 1967), 73.

61 Wilbur, *Stevens,* 188.

62 J.R.H. Wilbur, "H.H. Stevens and the Reconstruction Party," *Canadian Historical Review* 45, 1 (March 1964): 26; Glassford, *Reaction and Reform,* 196; Wilbur, *Stevens,* 193.

63 Harold J. Schultz, "Portrait of a Premier: William Aberhart," *Canadian Historical Review* 45, 3 (September 1964): 187.

64 Schultz, "Portrait of a Premier," 195–98.

65 Finkel, *Social Credit Phenomenon,* 258n193.

66 Walter D. Young, *The Anatomy of a Party: The National CCF, 1932–61* (Toronto: University of Toronto Press, 1969), 145.

67 Young, *Anatomy of a Party,* 151.

68 Letter, J.S. Woodsworth to F. Underhill, February 27, 1934, LAC, J.S. Woodsworth Papers, MG 27 III C7, reel C-9160.

69 David Lewis, *The Good Fight: Political Memoirs, 1909–1958* (Toronto: Macmillan, 1981), 80.

70 Letter, F. Underhill to J.S. Woodsworth, May 2, 1933, LAC, Frank Underhill Papers, MG 30 D 204, vol. 16, file "J.S. Woodsworth – Correspondence 1926–1943." See also R. Douglas Francis, *Frank H. Underhill: Intellectual Provocateur* (Toronto: University of Toronto Press, 1986), 98.

71 Grace MacInnis, *J.S. Woodsworth: A Man to Remember* (Toronto: Macmillan, 1953), 282.

72 Letter, J.S. Woodsworth to R. Lambert, February 5, 1935, LAC, Woodsworth Papers, MG 27 III C7, reel C-9160.

73 Letter, J.S. Woodsworth to John Mitchell, May 14, 1935, LAC, Woodsworth Papers, MG 27 III C7, reel C-9160; see also Allen Mills, *Fool for Christ: The Political Thought of JS Woodsworth* (Toronto: University of Toronto Press, 1991), 104.

74 Young, *Anatomy of a Party*, 179.

75 J.S. Thomson, "Topics of the Day," *Dalhousie Review* 15 (January 1936): 495.

Chapter 5: King or Chaos?

1 Letter, Howard Ferguson to W.H. Ireland, August 14, 1935, Archives of Ontario (AO), Howard Ferguson Papers, F8-2 MU 10919, box 3, container B299693, file "Jan. To Dec. 1935."

2 "900 Expected to Run In Federal Election," *The Globe*, August 29, 1935, 1; "Nearly 90,000 in Capital Eligible to Vote in General Election," *Ottawa Citizen*, October 9, 1935, 3/10; "135,000 Voters Go to Polls Monday, in Vancouver," *Vancouver Sun*, October 12, 1935, 1.

3 J.E. Rea, *T.A. Crerar: A Political Life* (Montreal and Kingston: McGill-Queen's University Press, 1997), 169.

4 "Three Parties Bid for Power," *The Globe*, October 8, 1935, 1. For a list of all the ridings and names, see "Number of Voters in Constituencies," *Montreal Gazette*, October 11, 1935, 2.

5 Walter D. Young, *The Anatomy of a Party: The National CCF, 1932–61* (Toronto: University of Toronto Press, 1969), 262–63.

6 Kenneth McNaught, *A Prophet in Politics: A Biography of J.S. Woodsworth* (Toronto: University of Toronto Press, 1959), 270.

7 See, for example, the letter from John Dafoe to Escott Reid, November 15, 1935, Library and Archives Canada (LAC), John W. Dafoe Papers, MG 30 D45, reel M-77.

8 "Not Stevens Candidate, States Miss Macphail," *The Globe*, September 21, 1935, 10; see also Janine M. Brodie, *Crisis, Challenge and Change: Party*

and Class in Canada Revisited (Ottawa: Carleton University Press, 1988), 172.

9 Norman Ward and David Smith, *Jimmy Gardiner: Relentless Liberal* (Toronto: University of Toronto Press, 1990), 191–92; David E. Smith, *Prairie Liberalism: The Liberal Party in Saskatchewan, 1905–71* (Toronto: University of Toronto Press,1975), 226.

10 Robert A. Wardhaugh, *Mackenzie King and the Prairie West* (Toronto: University of Toronto Press, 2000), 189.

11 Norman Ward, ed., *A Party Politician: The Memoirs of Chubby Power* (Toronto: Macmillan, 1966), 336–38.

12 "Cardin Halted by Factionalism at Convention," *Montreal Gazette*, September 17, 1935, 1; "Liberals Planning Attack on Stevens," *Montreal Gazette*, September 19, 1935, 1; "Montreal Sending Youngest and Oldest," *The Globe*, October 17, 1935, 3.

13 Paul Martin, *A Very Public Life, Volume 1: Far from Home* (Toronto: Deneau Publishers, 1983), 147.

14 "290 Candidates Named for Election," *Vancouver Sun*, October 1, 1935, 1.

15 "Convention for Mount Royal Is Called Illegal," *Montreal Gazette*, September 18, 1935, 1; "Liberal Split Loses London," *The Globe*, October 15, 1935, 1; Richard Wilbur, *H.H. Stevens, 1878–1973* (Toronto: University of Toronto Press, 1977), 188.

16 Mary Vipond, *The Mass Media in Canada*, 3rd ed. (Toronto: Lorimer, 2000), 38.

17 Pierre Berton, *The Great Depression 1929–1939* (Toronto: Penguin, 1990), 266.

18 Frank W. Peers, *The Politics of Canadian Broadcasting 1920–1951* (Toronto: University of Toronto Press, 1971), 165.

19 Larry A. Glassford, *Reaction and Reform: The Politics of the Conservative Party under R.B. Bennett, 1927–1938* (Toronto: University of Toronto Press, 1992), 192; Allan Levine, *Scrum Wars: The Prime Ministers and the Media* (Toronto: Dundurn, 1993), 173–74. Soon after the Liberals returned to office, they outlawed such dramatized broadcasts and made it mandatory to identify political broadcasts.

20 Levine, *Scrum Wars*, 156.

21 Murray Donnelly, *Dafoe of the Free Press* (Toronto: Macmillan, 1968), 149.

22 Claude Bissell, *The Young Vincent Massey* (Toronto: University of Toronto Press, 1981), 231; Diary entry of William Lyon Mackenzie King, July 19–20, 1935, Library and Archives Canada, MG26-J13.

23 Dust jacket, Andrew D. MacLean, *R.B. Bennett: Prime Minster of Canada* (Toronto: Excelsior Publishing, 1935).

24 Norman McLeod Rogers, *Mackenzie King* (Toronto: George Morang and Nelson and Sons, 1935). On the King book, see "The 'Biography' in Politics: Mackenzie King in 1935," *Canadian Historical Review* 55, 2 (June 1974): 239–48; Reginald Whitaker, *The Government Party: Organizing and Financing the Liberal Party of Canada, 1930–58* (Toronto: University of Toronto Press, 1977), 82.

25 Mrs. George Black, *My Seventy Years* (Toronto: Thomas Nelson and Sons, 1938), 310.

26 "Stephen Leacock Speaks for Walsh," *Montreal Gazette,* October 14, 1935, 17.

27 "Coal Industry Greatly Aided, Bennett Says," *The Globe,* September 18, 1935, 1.

28 "Grain Policy Is Defended by Bennett," *The Globe,* September 17, 1935, 2.

29 Ernest Watkins, *R.B. Bennett: A Biography* (Toronto: Kingswood House, 1963), 227.

30 "Moscow Planned to Seize Bennett," *The Globe,* September 23, 1935, 1; "Prime Minister's Hopes High," *Vancouver Sun,* September 21, 1935, 1.

31 Bruce Hutchison, *The Far Side of the Street* (Toronto: Macmillan, 1976), 101.

32 "Red Plan to Hold Him Hostage Told by Prime Minister," *Montreal Gazette,* September 23, 1935, 1; "Gendron Supports Section 98 Stand," *Montreal Gazette,* September 23, 1935, 2; Wilbur, *H.H. Stevens,* 96.

33 "Bennett Beats Booers: 'No Quarter' Fight with Roaring Arena Crowd," *Vancouver Sun,* September 24, 1935, 1.

34 "Bennett Meets with Cheering and Boos, Too," *The Globe,* October 1, 1935, 1.

35 "Bennett Out to Give Work, Quebec Hears," *The Globe,* October 3, 1935, 2.

36 "Mr. Bennett Storms Turrets of Liberalism in Maritimes," *Ottawa Citizen,* October 4, 1935, 1/3.

37 "Premier Showing Weariness under Strain of Campaign," *Ottawa Citizen,* October 7, 1935, 1–2.

38 "Premier Showing Weariness," 1–2.

39 Letter, Mackenzie King to Mitch Hepburn, August 6, 1935, AO, Mitch Hepburn Papers, F10-4 MU 4935, container B294118, file "King, W.L.M., 1935."

40 Neil McHenty, *Mitch Hepburn* (Toronto: McClelland and Stewart, 1967), 70; "King or Chaos, Hepburn States," *The Globe,* October 10, 1935, 2.

41 On Hepburn's health, see letter from Hepburn to King, August 31, 1935, AO, Hepburn Papers, F10-4 MU 4935, container B294118, file "King, W.L.M., 1935."

42 John T. Saywell, *"Just Call Me Mitch": The Life and Times of Mitchell F. Hepburn* (Toronto: University of Toronto Press, 1991), 233.

43 Saywell, *"Just Call Me Mitch,"* 230; "Trade Is Need, Says Hepburn," *The Globe,* September 27, 1935, 1.

44 "Hepburn Gives French Speech," *Windsor Daily Star,* October 2, 1935, 2; Saywell, *"Just Call Me Mitch,"* 235.

45 Saywell, *"Just Call Me Mitch,"* 227.

46 King Diary, September 21, 1935.

47 Lita-Rose Betcherman, *Ernest Lapointe: Mackenzie King's Great Quebec Lieutenant* (Toronto: University of Toronto Press, 2002), 199.

48 "Lapointe Hurt, with Thirteen Others," *The Globe,* September 23, 1935, 1; Betcherman, *Ernest Lapointe,* 199.

49 For the details of planning for the Halifax event, see the letter from M.B. Archibald to Mackenzie King, August 27, 1935, LAC, Mackenzie King Papers, MG 26 J, reel 3678.

50 King Diary, September 19, 1935.

51 Wardhaugh, *Mackenzie King and the Prairie West,* 189.

52 King Diary, October 1, 1935.

53 "Tories under One-Man Rule, King Asserts," *The Globe,* October 2, 1935, 1.

54 Robert Bothwell and William Kilbourn, *C.D. Howe: A Biography* (Toronto: McClelland and Stewart, 1979), 58–59.

55 King Diary, October 3, 1935; Bothwell and Kilbourn, *C.D. Howe,* 60.

56 "Bennett Promises as 'Bribes,'" *Vancouver Sun,* October 3, 1935, 5.

57 Vincent Massey, *What's Past Is Prologue: The Memoirs of the Right Honourable Vincent Massey, C.H.* (Toronto: Macmillan, 1963), 221–22.

58 King Diary, October 5, 1935; Bissell, *The Young Vincent Massey,* 233; Massey, *What's Past Is Prologue,* 222.

59 "M.P. for Kent Near Death after Crash," *The Globe,* September 5, 1935, 1.

60 Greg Donaghy, *Grit: The Life and Politics of Paul Martin Sr.* (Vancouver: UBC Press, 2015), 35.

61 Martin, *A Very Public Life,* 149.

62 Martin, *A Very Public Life,* 151; Donaghy, *Grit,* 34.

63 King Diary, October 7, 1935.

64 "Liberal Party Canada's Hope, King Asserts," *The Globe*, October 8, 1935, 2; Martin, *A Very Public Life*, 163.

65 Letter, Grant Dexter to John Dafoe, July 19, 1935, LAC, Dafoe Papers, MG 30 D45, reel M-77.

66 Letter, Harry Anderson to Mackenzie King, September 14, 1935, LAC, King Papers, MG 26 J, reel C-3678.

67 "Taschereau Is Dubbed Tory in Stevens Blast," *Montreal Gazette*, September 20, 1935, 1.

68 Wilbur, *H.H. Stevens*, 196.

69 "Stevens Plans to Issue Notes," *Montreal Gazette*, October 2, 1935, 1; "Stevens Aims at Veterans," *The Globe*, September 26, 1935, 1.

70 "Stevens after Packer Scalps," *Montreal Gazette*, September 17, 1935, 1.

71 "Stevens Warns Textile Firms," *The Globe*, October 11, 1935, 2; "Stevens Turns His Heavy Guns on Coal Barons," *Montreal Gazette*, September 18, 1935, 1; "Women Interrupt Stevens' Address in Brantford Hall," *Ottawa Citizen*, October 7, 1935, 3.

72 "Move by Financiers to Wreck His Career Seen behind Charges," *Windsor Daily Star*, October 4, 1935, 2; King Diary, July 22, 1935.

73 "Reds Would Scrap Empire and Make Canada a Soviet," *Vancouver Sun*, September 28, 1935, 1; "Woodsworth Assails R.C.M.P. Chief," *Windsor Daily Star*, October 11, 1935, 2.

74 King Diary, May 23, 1935.

75 Leo Heaps, *The Rebel in the House: The Life and Times of A.A. Heaps MP* (London: Niccolo Publishing, 1970), 149; "B.C.'s Only Communist Candidate," *Vancouver Sun*, October 2, 1935, 1; "Sees Power behind C.C.F.," *Windsor Daily Star*, October 1, 1935, 2.

76 "C.C.F. Leader Hits Monopoly," *The Globe*, October 2, 1935, 2; "Bennett Reforms for Election," *Vancouver Sun*, October 2, 1935, 4.

77 "On the Hustings," *Ottawa Citizen*, October 8, 1935, 3; "On the Hustings," *Ottawa Citizen*, October 9, 1935, 3.

78 "Social Credit Advance Seen," *Windsor Daily Star*, October 12, 1935, 14.

79 "Social Credit Party in West Upsets Political Apple Cart," *Ottawa Citizen*, September 30, 1935, 1–2.

80 Wardhaugh, *Mackenzie King and the Prairie West*, 185.

81 "Empire Pacts Are Real Issue," *Montreal Gazette*, October 1, 1935, 1.

82 "On the Hustings," *Ottawa Citizen*, October 9, 1935, 3.

83 "Woodsworth Hies for West," *The Globe*, October 7, 1935, 3.

84 "Heralds United Efforts by Nine Liberal Cabinets to Restore Prosperity," *The Globe*, October 9, 1935, 2.

85 "Expect Premier Will Clarify Remarks on House Support," *Ottawa Citizen*, October 10, 1935, 1/4; "Bennett Centres Attack on King's 'Doctrine of Hate,'" *Montreal Gazette*, October 2, 1935, 1.

86 "Bennett 'Feelers' for 'Union Gov't,'" *Vancouver Sun*, October 10, 1935, 2; "'Bennett Confesses Defeat; Now Out for Union Gov't' – Mackenzie King," *Vancouver Sun*, October 11, 1935, 2.

87 "Stevens Invites Bennett to Debate," *Windsor Daily Star*, October 10, 1935, 2.

88 "Meeting Enthusiasm Equals That of King-Bennett Gatherings," *The Globe*, October 12, 1935, 1.

89 "Stevens Holds Greed Must Go," *Montreal Gazette*, October 12, 1935, 1.

90 King Diary, October 8, 1935.

91 "C.C.F. Proposal to End Chaos," *The Globe*, October 14, 1935, 1.

92 "Stevens Raps King 'Combine,'" *Montreal Gazette*, October 12, 1935, 1; "Final Rally Staged by Stevens Forces," *Montreal Gazette*, October 14, 1935, 17.

93 "Nearly 90,000 in Capital Eligible to Vote," 3/10.

Chapter 6: And in the End

1 H. Blair Neatby, *William Lyon Mackenzie King, Volume 3: 1932–1939, The Prism of Unity* (Toronto: University of Toronto Press, 1976), 123.

2 "Women's Vote Is Expected to Break Record," *The Globe*, October 14, 1935, 5.

3 "Fight in Polls Chief Incident in Voting Here," *Montreal Gazette*, October 15, 1935, 1; "Election Fight in Nova Scotia Ends Fatally," *The Globe*, October 16, 1935, 1; "Six Arrests at Polling Booths," *Vancouver Sun*, October 14, 1935, 1.

4 "Election Returns over Special Telephone Lines, by Broadcast and Stereopticon," *The Globe*, October 12, 1935, 1; "135,000 Voters Go to Polls Monday, in Vancouver," *Vancouver Sun*, October 12, 1935, 1; Mrs. George Black, *My Seventy Years* (Toronto: Thomas Nelson and Sons, 1938), 311.

5 "Miss Macphail Glad to Have Another Woman in Commons," *The Globe*, October 29, 1935, 5. See also "Company for Miss Macphail," *The Globe*, October 21, 1935, 4.

6 "Election Flashes," *The Globe,* October 15, 1935, 1.

7 "Liberal Breaks Guthrie Charm," *The Globe,* October 15, 1935, 1; "Montreal Is Sending Youngest and Oldest," *The Globe,* October 17, 1935, 3.

8 Margaret Stewart and Doris French, *Ask No Quarter: A Biography of Agnes Macphail* (Toronto: Longmans, Green, 1959), 220; "Tories Hold Third of Ontario Seats," *The Globe,* October 15, 1935, 1.

9 "Over One-Third Lose Deposits," *The Globe,* October 16, 1935, 1; Anthony Mardiros, *William Irvine: The Life of a Prairie Radical* (Toronto: Lorimer, 1979), 196.

10 Richard Wilbur, *H.H. Stevens, 1878–1973* (Toronto: University of Toronto Press, 1977), 201; Diary entry of William Lyon Mackenzie King, October 15, 1935, Library and Archives Canada, MG26-J13.

11 Unless stated otherwise, the following statistics and numbers were taken from J. Murray Beck, *Pendulum of Power: Canada's Federal Elections* (Toronto: Prentice-Hall, 1968), and Canadian Elections Database, https://canadianelectionsdatabase.ca/PHASE5/?p=0&type=election&ID=305.

12 On the French-English vote split, see Escott Reid, "The Canadian General Election of 1935 – and After," *American Political Science Review* 30, 1 (February 1936): 113–15.

13 Beck, *Pendulum of Power,* 215; Larry A. Glassford, *Reaction and Reform: The Politics of the Conservative Party under R.B. Bennett, 1927–1938* (Toronto: University of Toronto Press, 1992), 198.

14 Reid, "The Canadian General Election of 1935," 115.

15 Reid, "The Canadian General Election of 1935," 115.

16 "Canada Is Swept by the Liberals in Decisive Vote," *New York Times,* October 15, 1935, 1; "Canada Goes Liberal," *The Times,* October 16, 1935, 15; Marcus Garvey, "Canada's Election," *The Black Man: A Monthly Magazine of Negro Thought and Opinion,* October 1935, 2. On the UNIA in Canada, see Carla Marano, "'Rising Strongly and Rapidly': The Universal Negro Improvement Association in Canada, 1919–1940," *Canadian Historical Review* 91, 2 (June 2010): 233–59.

17 John G. Diefenbaker, *One Canada: Memoirs of the Right Honourable John G. Diefenbaker. The Crusading Years 1895–1956* (Toronto: Macmillan, 1975), 163–64.

18 Letter, Howard Ferguson to Lord Beaverbrook, November 2, 1935, Archives of Ontario (AO), Howard Ferguson Papers, F8-2, MU 1019 (box 3), container B299693, file "Jan. To Dec. 1935."

19 Letter, Robert Manion to John J. Gibbons, December 27, 1935, Library and Archives Canada (LAC), Robert J. Manion Papers, MG 27 III B7, vol. 8, file "Personal Correspondence – G – 1930, 1932–1933, 1935–1943."

20 Bruce Hutchison, *The Far Side of the Street* (Toronto: Macmillan, 1976), 102; Reid, "The Canadian General Election of 1935," 116.

21 Letter, Frank Underhill to George Ferguson, November 2, 1935, LAC, Frank Underhill Papers, MG 30 D 204, vol. 16, file "J.W. Dafoe – Correspondence 1925–1943"; H.R. Douglas Francis, *Frank H. Underhill: Intellectual Provocateur* (Toronto: University of Toronto Press, 1986), 99.

22 "The Social Credit Movement in Alberta," *The Round Table* 26, 101 (December 1935): 168.

23 Glassford, *Reaction and Reform*, 200–1.

24 John Cripps, "The Canadian Elections," *Political Quarterly* 6 (Winter 1935): 567.

25 Grattan O'Leary, "Mr. Bennett: Convert or Realist?" *Maclean's*, February 15, 1935, 10.

26 "The Canadian-American Trade Agreement," *The Round Table* 26, 102 (January 1936): 387.

27 C.P. Stacey, *Canada and the Age of Conflict: A History of Canadian External Policies, Volume 2: 1921–1948: The Mackenzie King Era* (Toronto: University of Toronto Press, 1981), 174.

28 "Backstage at Ottawa," *Maclean's*, December 1, 1935, 19/34.

29 John MacFarlane, *Ernest Lapointe and Quebec's Influence on Canadian Foreign Policy* (Toronto: University of Toronto Press, 1999), 79.

30 Charles Bowman, *Ottawa Editor: The Memoirs of Charles A. Bowman* (Sidney, BC: Gray's Publishing, 1966), 201. King made a similar statement to Lapointe, that he would not have someone in the cabinet who drank, to which Lapointe replied: "You will have a pretty difficult time." King Diary, October 17, 1935.

31 Frederick W. Gibson, ed., *Cabinet Formation and Bicultural Relations: Seven Case Studies* (Ottawa: Studies of the Royal Commission on Bilingualism and Biculturalism, 1970), 120–21; Ramsay Cook, *The Politics of John W. Dafoe and the Free Press* (Toronto: University of Toronto Press, 1963), 211.

32 Grant Dexter, "Cabinet Portraits," *Maclean's*, December 15, 1935, 14.

33 "Backstage at Ottawa," *Maclean's*, December 1, 1935, 19.

34 Robert Bothwell and William Kilbourn, *C.D. Howe: A Biography* (Toronto: McClelland and Stewart, 1979), 63.

35 "Back to Big Business Normalcy," *Canadian Forum* 15, 178 (November 1935): 351.

36 MacFarlane, *Ernest Lapointe*, 79.

37 Norman Ward and David Smith, *Jimmy Gardiner: Relentless Liberal* (Toronto: University of Toronto Press, 1990), 190; David E. Smith, *Prairie Liberalism: The Liberal Party in Saskatchewan, 1905–71* (Toronto: University of Toronto Press, 1975), 83.

38 Robert A. Wardhaugh, *Mackenzie King and the Prairie West* (Toronto: University of Toronto Press, 2000), 199.

39 Wardhaugh, *Mackenzie King and the Prairie West*, 191. See also 263–64.

40 Letter, Mackenzie King to Mitchell Hepburn, October 22, 1935, AO, Mitch Hepburn Papers, F10-4 MU 4935, container B294118, file "King, W.L.M., 1935"; Reginald Whitaker, *The Government Party: Organizing and Financing the Liberal Party of Canada, 1930–58* (Toronto: University of Toronto Press, 1977), 314–15.

41 Vincent Massey, *What's Past Is Prologue: The Memoirs of the Right Honourable Vincent Massey, C.H.* (Toronto: Macmillan, 1963), 223.

42 "Backstage at Ottawa," *Maclean's*, December 1, 1935, 34.

43 Grattan O'Leary, *Recollections of People, Press, and Politics* (Toronto: Macmillan, 1977), 78.

44 Walter D. Young, *The Anatomy of a Party: The National CCF, 1932–61* (Toronto: University of Toronto Press, 1969), 147.

45 Letter, Frank Underhill to J.S. Woodsworth, November 26, 1935, LAC, J.S. Woodsworth Papers, MG 27 III C7, reel C-9160.

46 "Backstage at Ottawa," *Maclean's*, December 1, 1935, 34.

47 Glassford, *Reaction and Reform*, 222–29.

48 O'Leary, *Recollections of People, Press, and Politics*, 79.

Suggestions
for Further Reading

The primary sources used for this study can be followed through the notes in the text, and most of the personal papers of the Canadian political class of the 1930s, at least at the federal level, are stored at Library and Archives Canada in Ottawa. The major collections are the obvious ones, including the papers of R.B. Bennett, Mackenzie King, J.S. Woodsworth, H.H. Stevens, John Dafoe, and Robert Manion. A few other collections were consulted, such as the personal papers of Mitch Hepburn and Howard Ferguson in the Archives of Ontario in Toronto. In addition, contemporary published sources – including *Canadian Forum, Maclean's, Dalhousie Review,* and *The Round Table* – proved valuable and added an immediacy to the account of unfolding events. Much of the daily events of the actual campaign were drawn from newspapers, including the *Vancouver Sun,* Toronto *Globe, Ottawa Citizen, Montreal Gazette, Le Canadien,* and an assortment of other local papers across the country. And, of course, the Mackenzie King diaries – available online – were an important source, especially for their detailed day-by-day observations and accounts of the months leading up to the vote.

It is a little surprising, given the wealth of Canadian political history, that so few books have been written about the 1935 federal election and, in general, about Canadian elections that took place before the Second World War. J. Murray Beck's *Pendulum of Power: Canada's Federal Elections* (Toronto: Prentice-Hall, 1968) remains one of the most cited collections. There are a few other sources focused specifically on 1935, but these are contemporary articles written in the aftermath of the election in those journals and magazines mentioned above. Two of the best are Escott Reid's "The Canadian General Election of 1935 – and After," *American Political Science Review* 30, 1 (February 1936): 111–21, and John Cripps's "The Canadian Elections," *Political Quarterly* 6 (Winter 1935): 566–70. For how the election framed the choices for Mackenzie King in selecting his post-election cabinet, see Frederick W. Gibson, ed., *Cabinet Formation and Bicultural Relations: Seven Case Studies* (Ottawa: Studies of the Royal Commission on Bilingualism and Biculturalism, 1970).

There are many works – old and new – that examine the Depression, including the standard A.E. Safarian, *The Canadian Economy in the Great Depression* (Toronto: University of Toronto Press, 1959), and Michiel Horn, ed., *The Dirty Thirties: Canadians in the Great Depression* (Toronto: Copp Clark, 1972); the briefer Michiel Horn, *The Great Depression of the 1930s in Canada* (Ottawa: Canadian Historical Association, 1984), and H. Blair Neatby, *The Politics of Chaos: Canada in the Thirties* (Toronto: Macmillan, 1972); and the more popular Pierre Berton, *The Great Depression 1929–1939* (Toronto: Penguin, 1990), and James H. Gray, *The Winter Years: The Depression on the Prairies* (Toronto: Macmillan, 1966). Broader academic works include James Struthers, *No Fault of Their Own: Unemployment and the Canadian Welfare State, 1914–1941* (Toronto: University of Toronto Press, 1983), and Gerald Friesen, *The Canadian Prairies: A History* (Toronto: University of Toronto Press, 1984). Federal-provincial issues are covered in Robert Wardhaugh and Barry Ferguson, *The Rowell-Sirois Commission and the Remaking of Canadian Federalism* (Vancouver: UBC Press, 2021).

Bennett's New Deal, which really kick-started the 1935 election campaign, has received a little more attention, with J.R.H. Wilbur's edited collection of articles and primary documents, *The Bennett New Deal: Fraud or Portent?* (Toronto: Copp Clark, 1968). Other articles that focus on Bennett's last gasp at reform include Donald Forster and Colin Read's "The Politics of Opportunism: The New Deal Broadcasts," *Canadian Historical Review* 60, 3 (September 1979): 324–49, and W.H. McConnell's "The Genesis of the Canadian 'New Deal,'" *Journal of Canadian Studies* 4, 2 (May 1969): 31–41.

There are relatively few memoirs left by the participants in these events, fewer from the major participants, and even fewer that focus any amount of attention on the 1935 election. The rare exceptions include Vincent Massey, *What's Past Is Prologue: The Memoirs of the Right Honourable Vincent Massey, C.H.* (Toronto: Macmillan, 1963); Mrs. George Black, *My Seventy Years* (Toronto: Thomas Nelson and Sons, 1938); and Norman Ward's edited book, *A Party Politician: The Memoirs of Chubby Power* (Toronto: Macmillan, 1966).

Two younger politicians who went on to lengthy careers also left their remin-
iscences of 1935: Paul Martin, *A Very Public Life, Volume I: Far from Home*
(Toronto: Deneau Publishers, 1983), and David Lewis, *The Good Fight: Political
Memoirs, 1909–1958* (Toronto: Macmillan, 1981). Two journalists of the era
also left memoirs: Grattan O'Leary, *Recollections of People, Press, and Politics*
(Toronto: Macmillan, 1977), and Bruce Hutchison, *The Far Side of the Street*
(Toronto: Macmillan, 1976).

We have been much better served by political biographers, and each of the
major players has received considerable academic scrutiny, although in several
of them the researcher will be hard-pressed to find lengthy examinations of
the 1935 election. R.B. Bennett had once been the forgotten prime minister,
but in the last decade he has been the subject of two new biographical treatments. John Boyko's *Bennett: The Rebel Who Challenged and Changed a Nation*
(Fredericton: Goose Lanes Editions, 2012) was the first and most thorough,
while P.B. Waite produced a very thoughtful examination in *In Search of R.B.
Bennett* (Montreal and Kingston: McGill-Queen's University Press, 2012).
These two books have completely replaced the older treatments found in Ernest
Watkins, *R.B. Bennett: A Biography* (Toronto: Kingswood House, 1963), Lord
Beaverbrook, *Friends: Sixty Years of Intimate Personal Relations with Richard
Bedford Bennett* (London: Heinemann, 1959), and the hagiographical Andrew
D. MacLean, *R.B. Bennett: Prime Minster of Canada* (Toronto: Excelsior
Publishing, 1935).

Mackenzie King has received even greater scrutiny, but the most thorough
treatment of King's 1935 election remains H. Blair Neatby's *William Lyon
Mackenzie King, Volume 3: 1932–1939, The Prism of Unity* (Toronto: University
of Toronto Press, 1976). Robert Wardhaugh adds some depth to the man and
the growing problems facing the Liberals in the West in his *Mackenzie King
and the Prairie West* (Toronto: University of Toronto Press, 2000). Of interest
only because of the effort that King put into it is Norman McLeod Rogers's
Mackenzie King (Toronto: George Morang and Nelson and Sons, 1935). Allan
Levine has produced two helpful books that deal with aspects of 1935: *King:
William Lyon Mackenzie King: A Life Guided by the Hand of Destiny* (Vancouver and Toronto: Douglas and McIntyre, 2011) and *Scrum Wars: The Prime
Ministers and the Media* (Toronto: Dundurn Press, 1993).

J.S. Woodsworth has also attracted considerable attention over the years, at
least through the end of the twentieth century, including Allen Mills, *Fool for
Christ: The Political Thought of JS Woodsworth* (Toronto: University of Toronto
Press, 1991), but the standard biography remains Kenneth McNaught, *A*

Prophet in Politics: A Biography of J.S. Woodsworth (Toronto: University of Toronto Press, 1959), which was reissued with a new introduction by Allen Mills in 2017. The McNaught book largely replaced the earlier Grace MacInnis, *J.S. Woodsworth: A Man to Remember* (Toronto: Macmillan, 1953). The life of H.H. Stevens has largely been preserved by the work of Richard Wilbur, particularly in his *H.H. Stevens, 1878–1973* (Toronto: University of Toronto Press, 1977). William Aberhart has attracted less scrutiny and far less attention than the political party that he led, but two good examinations of the man can be found in Harold J. Schultz, "Portrait of a Premier: William Aberhart," *Canadian Historical Review* 45, 3 (September 1964): 185–211, and David R. Elliott, "Antithetical Elements in William Aberhart's Theology and Political Ideology," *Canadian Historical Review* 54, 1 (March 1978): 38–58.

A few other politicians who played a role in the 1935 election have attracted biographies, including Margaret Stewart and Doris French, *Ask No Quarter: A Biography of Agnes Macphail* (Toronto: Longmans, Green, 1959), and Leo Heaps, *The Rebel in the House: The Life and Times of A.A. Heaps MP* (London: Niccolo Publishing, 1970). For prominent Liberals, see Lita-Rose Betcherman, *Ernest Lapointe: Mackenzie King's Great Quebec Lieutenant* (Toronto: University of Toronto Press, 2002); Greg Donaghy, *Grit: The Life and Politics of Paul Martin Sr.* (Vancouver: UBC Press, 2015); and Robert Bothwell and William Kilbourn, *C.D. Howe: A Biography* (Toronto: McClelland and Stewart, 1979). For a more Western perspective, see J.E. Rea, *T.A. Crerar: A Political Life* (Montreal and Kingston: McGill-Queen's University Press, 1997).

A few non-politicians who surfaced in the 1935 election have also received academic attention, in Claude Bissell, *The Young Vincent Massey* (Toronto: University of Toronto Press, 1981), and R. Douglas Francis, *Frank H. Underhill: Intellectual Provocateur* (Toronto: University of Toronto Press, 1986), and in the more recent Kenneth Dewar, *Frank Underhill and the Politics of Ideas* (Montreal and Kingston: McGill-Queen's University Press, 2015). The influential newspaper editor John Dafoe has also been scrutinized twice, in Ramsay Cook, *The Politics of John W. Dafoe and the Free Press* (Toronto: University of Toronto Press, 1963), and Murray Donnelly, *Dafoe of the Free Press* (Toronto: Macmillan, 1968).

Provincial politicians have been equally well served by biographers, although here, again, the election of 1935 is rarely the focus of much attention. Going from west to east, Robin Fisher's *Duff Pattullo of British Columbia* (Toronto: University of Toronto Press, 1991), and Norman Ward and David Smith's, *Jimmy Gardiner: Relentless Liberal* (Toronto: University of Toronto

Press, 1990), are thorough political biographies. For Manitoba, there is John Kendle, who produced the standard biography in *John Bracken: A Political Biography* (Toronto: University of Toronto Press, 1979). One of the best – and the most exhaustive – biography of a provincial premier is John T. Saywell's *"Just Call Me Mitch": The Life and Times of Mitchell F. Hepburn* (Toronto: University of Toronto Press, 1991), although some interesting material can still be found in the older Neil McKenty, *Mitch Hepburn* (Toronto: McClelland and Stewart, 1967). For Quebec, there are numerous works on Maurice Duplessis, few of which even discuss the 1935 federal election campaign. More valuable is Bernard L. Vigod's *Quebec before Duplessis: The Political Career of Louis-Alexandre Taschereau* (Montreal and Kingston: McGill-Queen's University Press, 1986).

The three new parties, whose appearance played such an important role in the election of 1935, have been fairly well served by historians. The rise of the Social Credit Party in Alberta has received the most academic attention, with the standard works dating back to the 1950s, including John A. Irving, *The Social Credit Movement in Alberta* (Toronto: University of Toronto Press, 1959), and C.B. Macpherson, *Democracy in Alberta: Social Credit and the Party System* (Toronto: University of Toronto Press, 1953). To these books must be added the relatively more recent Alvin Finkel, *The Social Credit Phenomenon in Alberta* (Toronto: University of Toronto Press, 1989). Walter D. Young produced the standard account of the Co-operative Commonwealth Federation in *The Anatomy of a Party: The National CCF, 1932–61* (Toronto: University of Toronto Press, 1969), and a briefer introduction in *Democracy and Discontent: Progressivism, Socialism and Social Credit in the Canadian West* (Toronto: McGraw-Hill Ryerson, 1969). A more recent book that focuses more on the working-class roots of the CCF is James Naylor, *The Fate of Labour Socialism: The Co-operative Commonwealth Federation and the Dream of a Working-Class Future* (Toronto: University of Toronto Press, 2016). The Reconstruction Party has never received the same amount of attention, perhaps because of its short life, other than in two articles (and in the other works mentioned above) by J.R.H. Wilbur: "H.H. Stevens and R.B. Bennett, 1930–34," *Canadian Historical Review* 43, 1 (March 1962): 1–16, and "H.H. Stevens and the Reconstruction Party," *Canadian Historical Review* 45, 1 (March 1964): 1–28.

On the growing role of women in Canadian politics, if not specifically in the 1935 election, Joan Sangster has produced the most thoughtful and meticulous works, including *Dreams of Equality: Women on the Canadian Left,*

1920–1950 (Toronto: McClelland and Stewart, 1989), and "The Role of Women in the Early CCF," in *Beyond the Vote: Canadian Women and Politics,* edited by Linda Kealey and Joan Sangster (Toronto: University of Toronto Press, 1989), 118–38. Another valuable work from the same edited volume is Patricia A. Myers, "'A Noble Effort': The National Federation of Liberal Women of Canada, 1928–1973," 39–62. More generally, some aspects of the role of Canadian women in politics have been examined in the edited collection *Rethinking Canada: The Promise of Women's History,* edited by Veronica Strong-Boag and Anita Clair Fellman (Toronto: Copp Clark, 1986), and in Strong-Boag's *The New Day Recalled: Lives of Girls and Women in English Canada, 1919–1939* (Toronto: Penguin, 1988).

As for the ethnic minority communities, there has been little work focused on the 1935 election or even participation in Canadian politics more generally. A few useful exceptions can be found in Howard Palmer, *Ethnicity and Politics in Canada since Confederation* (Ottawa: Canadian Historical Association, 1991), and in two articles: Jack Jedwab, "Uniting Uptowners and Downtowners: The Jewish Electorate and Quebec Provincial Politics: 1927–1939," *Canadian Ethnic Studies* 18, 2 (1986): 7–19, and George Hoffman, "The New Party and the Old Issues: The Saskatchewan Farmer-Labour Party and the Ethnic Vote, 1934," *Canadian Ethnic Studies* 14, 2 (1982): 1–19. Otherwise, one should turn to valuable but less focused general overviews, including Peter D. Chimbos, *The Canadian Odyssey: The Greek Experience in Canada* (Toronto: McClelland and Stewart, 1980); O.W. Gerus and J.E. Rea, *The Ukrainians in Canada* (St. John, NB: Canadian Historical Association, 1985); and John E. Zucchi, *Italians in Toronto: Development of a National Identity, 1875–1935* (Kingston and Montreal: McGill-Queen's University Press, 1988).

Political organizing and the financing of the political parties has received considerable academic attention, but it is unevenly divided among the parties, with some attracting sustained focus while others have largely been ignored. Janine M. Brodie has provided a general overview with *Crisis, Challenge and Change: Party and Class in Canada Revisited* (Ottawa: Carleton University Press, 1988). The Liberal Party has been best served of all the parties thanks to Reg Whitaker, *The Government Party: Organizing and Financing the Liberal Party of Canada, 1930–58* (Toronto: University of Toronto Press, 1977), and more specifically for 1935 by J.L. Granatstein, "Financing the Liberal Party, 1935–1945," in *Policy by Other Means: Essays in Honour of C.P. Stacey,* edited by Michael Cross and Robert Bothwell (Toronto: Clarke, Irwin, 1972), 179–99. See also David E. Smith, *Prairie Liberalism: The Liberal Party in Saskatchewan,*

1905–71 (Toronto: University of Toronto Press, 1975). The best work on the Conservative Party in the 1930s is Larry A. Glassford's insightful and detailed examination of R.B. Bennett in *Reaction and Reform: The Politics of the Conservative Party under R.B. Bennett, 1927–1938* (Toronto: University of Toronto Press, 1992). The other parties have been less well served, outside the works already mentioned above.

Brief mention should also be made of the ongoing international events that served as a backdrop to the 1935 election campaign. Generally, the best survey of the era remains C.P. Stacey's *Canada and the Age of Conflict: A History of Canadian External Policies, Volume 2: 1921–1948: The Mackenzie King Era* (Toronto: University of Toronto Press, 1981), and this work can be supplemented with Norman Hillmer's impressive *O.D. Skelton: A Portrait of Canadian Ambition* (Toronto: University of Toronto Press, 2015). How the trade negotiations with the United States affected the 1935 campaign is detailed in Marc T. Boucher, "The Politics of Economic Depression: Canadian-American Relations in the Mid-1930s," *International Journal* 41, 1 (Winter 1985-86): 3–36, and a more general account of trade in the 1930s can be found in the early sections of Ian M. Drummond and Norman Hillmer, *Negotiating Freer Trade: The United Kingdom, the United States, Canada and the Trade Agreements of 1938* (Waterloo, ON: Wilfrid Laurier University Press, 1989). The Italian-Ethiopian crisis is covered in Stacey's book and in Robert Bothwell and John English, "'Dirty Work at the Cross-Roads': New Perspective on the Riddell Incident," *Historical Papers/Communications historiques* 7, 1 (1972): 263–85, and the Quebec connection is examined by John MacFarlane in *Ernest Lapointe and Quebec's Influence on Canadian Foreign Policy* (Toronto: University of Toronto Press, 1999).

Index

Note: Page numbers with (t) refer to tables; pages with (f) refer to illustrations.

Finnish Canadians, 119–20
First Nations, voting rights, 117–18
First World War. *See* war and peace
first-past-the-post electoral system, 195, 197
Flavelle, Joseph, 38, 40
French Canada
  comparison of 1930 and 1935 elections, 206
  demographics, 117
  See also Quebec
Friesen, Gerald, 12, 253

Gardiner, James G.
  about, 61, 220
  cabinet (1935–57), 207–8
  election (1935), 61, 132–33, 157, 161, 177, 207
  King's relationship, 61, 132–33, 157
  Saskatchewan premier (1926–29, 1934–35), 61, 132–33, 207
  suggestions for reading, 255–56
Gazette (Montreal), 78
gender. *See* women in politics
Gendron, Emma, 183
Gendron, Lucien, 102, 177
general elections. *See* elections
German Canadians, 117, 118
Glassford, Larry A., 188, 258
Globe, 150–51, 182, 252
Gouin, Paul, 64
Gray, James, 11–12
Great Depression. *See* Depression
Green, Howard, 190
Guthrie, Hugh, 23, 31, 77, 91, 102, 183, 220

Hanson, Richard B., 83, 156, 160, 220–21
health services
  CCF's national health insurance proposal, 49
Heaps, Abraham Albert (A.A.), 22, 49(f), 50, 118, 172, 184, 189, 221, 255
Hepburn, Mitch
  about, 62–64, 158(f), 209, 221
  election (1935), 68, 133, 157–58, 158(f), 159, 162
  King's relationship, 62–63, 133, 157–58, 204, 209–10, 221
  Ontario premier (1934–42), 62–64, 221
  suggestions for reading, 256
Herridge, Mildred (Bennett's sister), 153(f)
Herridge, William (Bennett's brother-in-law), 72, 77, 129, 210, 221, 771
Howe, Clarence Decatur (C.D.), 162–64, 205–6, 221, 255
Howson, W.R., 95–96
Hull, Cordell, 203(f)
Hutchison, Bruce, 43, 154, 197, 221, 254

ideology. *See* political spectrum
immigration and immigrants
  anti-Asian racism, 33, 82, 113–14, 117–18, 211
  immigration laws, 5, 82, 117
  political participation, 117–20
  statistics, 117

Printed and bound in Canada by Friesens
Set in Zurich Condensed and Minion by Artegraphica Design Co.
Copy editor: Francis Chow
Proofreader: Kristy Lynn Hankewitz
Indexer: Judy Dunlop
Cartographer: Eric Leinberger
Cover designer: Will Brown